T0336415

THE PRIVATE EQUITY TOOLKIT

Founded in 1807, John Wiley & Sons is the oldest independent publishing company in the United States. With offices in North America, Europe, Australia and Asia, Wiley is globally committed to developing and marketing print and electronic products and services for our customers' professional and personal knowledge and understanding.

The Wiley Finance series contains books written specifically for finance and investment professionals as well as sophisticated individual investors and their financial advisors. Book topics range from portfolio management to e-commerce, risk management, financial engineering, valuation and financial instrument analysis, as well as much more.

For a list of available titles, visit our Web site at www.WileyFinance.com.

THE PRIVATE EQUITY TOOLKIT

A STEP-BY-STEP GUIDE TO GETTING DEALS DONE FROM SOURCING TO EXIT

TAMARA SAKOVSKA

WILEY

Copyright © 2022 by Tamara Sakovska. All rights reserved.

Published by John Wiley & Sons, Inc., Hoboken, New Jersey.

Published simultaneously in Canada.

No part of this publication may be reproduced, stored in a retrieval system, or transmitted in any form or by any means, electronic, mechanical, photocopying, recording, scanning, or otherwise, except as permitted under Section 107 or 108 of the 1976 United States Copyright Act, without either the prior written permission of the Publisher, or authorization through payment of the appropriate per-copy fee to the Copyright Clearance Center, Inc., 222 Rosewood Drive, Danvers, MA 01923, (978) 750-8400, fax (978) 750-4470, or on the web at **www.copyright.com**. Requests to the Publisher for permission should be addressed to the Permissions Department, John Wiley & Sons, Inc., 111 River Street, Hoboken, NJ 07030, (201) 748-6011, fax (201) 748-6008, or online at **http://www.wiley.com/go/ permission**.

Limit of Liability/Disclaimer of Warranty: While the publisher and author have used their best efforts in preparing this book, they make no representations or warranties with respect to the accuracy or completeness of the contents of this book and specifically disclaim any implied warranties of merchantability or fitness for a particular purpose. No warranty may be created or extended by sales representatives or written sales materials. The advice and strategies contained herein may not be suitable for your situation. You should consult with a professional where appropriate. Further, readers should be aware that websites listed in this work may have changed or disappeared between when this work was written and when it is read. Neither the publisher nor authors shall be liable for any loss of profit or any other commercial damages, including but not limited to special, incidental, consequential, or other damages.

For general information on our other products and services or for technical support, please contact our Customer Care Department within the United States at (800) 762-2974, outside the United States at (317) 572-3993 or fax (317) 572-4002.

Wiley also publishes its books in a variety of electronic formats. Some content that appears in print may not be available in electronic formats. For more information about Wiley products, visit our web site at www.wiley.com.

Library of Congress Cataloging-in-Publication Data is Available:

ISBN 9781119697107 (hardback)
ISBN 9781119697121 (ePDF)
ISBN 9781119697114 (ePub)

Cover Design: Wiley
Cover Image: © Hare Krishna/Shutterstock

SKY10034028_041822

To my family

Contents

Preface

The Private Equity Toolkit aims to be a book like no other in its field. It is the industry's first practical reference guide to cover all critical aspects of private equity deal execution, from sourcing to exit. As an experienced deal practitioner, I focus on the technical fundamentals and practical judgment skills required by investment professionals throughout the entire lifecycle of a private equity transaction.

This book will introduce you to a number of my proprietary frameworks, checklists and cheat sheets that will enable you to develop your own personalized blueprint for originating, evaluating, executing and monetizing private equity investments. With *The Private Equity Toolkit* by your side, you will be able to dive straight into actionable advice to address your most pressing needs, including:

1. Building a solid deal origination capability through thematic and opportunistic deal sourcing (Chapters 1, 2 and 3);
2. Identifying the best deal opportunities for your investment mandate and saving time by eliminating the rest (Chapters 4 and 5);
3. Evaluating the quality of the top management team you are seeking to back in your private equity investment (Chapter 6);

4. Analyzing the business plan of an investment target, identifying the main drivers of value creation and developing your own investment base case (Chapter 7);

5. Performing company valuation and robust deal structuring, for both majority and minority investments (Chapters 8 and 9);

6. Pursuing best-in-class deal execution through rigorous due diligence and thoughtful negotiation of the main transaction agreements (Chapters 10 and 11);

7. Adding value to your portfolio business by establishing effective governance processes and implementing an ambitious yet realistic Value Creation Plan (Chapter 12); and

8. Monetizing your investments through conventional routes, or alternative exit strategies (Chapter 13).

Private equity is one of the most fascinating fields in contemporary finance. Private equity professionals get to explore promising investment themes, meet accomplished entrepreneurs, walk the factory floors of real businesses, determine the value of illiquid assets and engineer the main transaction terms, with heated deal negotiations often extending into the late hours of the night. Since private equity is an interdisciplinary field, successful investors need to master a wide range of skills. Thorough technical knowledge of accounting and finance does not suffice on its own and needs to be combined with solid commercial judgment and exceptional relationship-building skills. Those private equity professionals who want to succeed are expected to originate attractive investment opportunities, generate differentiated deal insights, form productive working relationships with management teams, add value on portfolio company boards and achieve profitable investment exits.

How do they acquire these skills at present? Mostly, on the job. Apart from the book that you are about to read, there appears to be no universal reference guide that one can turn to in order to get a systematic overview of the practical aspects of private equity deal execution, from sourcing to exit. When investment professionals start their careers at a private equity fund, they learn how to do their job from senior colleagues by following a "master—apprentice" training model. However, senior private equity professionals generally have little time to dedicate to coaching new hires because they themselves are spread very thinly, often consumed by live deals or portfolio company crises that always take priority. Another obstacle that young investment professionals face is a lack of opportunity to acquire more advanced and specialized skills—for instance, those relating to creating effective reporting guidelines for an investment target post-acquisition, managing an investment in distress or preparing a portfolio business for exit—as these situations arise less frequently within the lifecycle of a typical private equity investment. Given these challenges, it takes multiple years for anyone to become truly skilled across all the main aspects of the private equity profession.

My experience was no different when I started my own private equity career a few decades ago. There was no practical handbook that could walk me through the key principles of private equity investing. I had to learn on the job and am grateful to all my senior colleagues who generously shared their knowledge with me. During my formative years as an investment professional, I thought it might be a good idea to start collecting various strategies and checklists that I came across on various transactions in order to create a single sourcebook to support me in my day-to-day work. Over the years, I incorporated a number of additional useful concepts that I discovered by reading books written by experts operating in adjacent business fields, such as mergers and acquisitions, value investing, equity research, behavioral finance, strategy, sales and marketing, business operations, restructuring, organizational behavior and corporate governance.

It took me a number of years to test the multifarious concepts in my "home-made" private equity primer on real-life transactions and transform them into a series of simple, actionable frameworks to underpin key decision-making principles that—in my opinion—apply best to each phase of a private equity investment, from sourcing to exit. This extensive compilation of ideas and multidisciplinary best practices formed the basis of my personal toolkit that I could turn to every time I needed inspiration or wanted to expand my professional repertoire. These proven techniques, together with the key lessons I learned during my own investment career, represent the core of *The Private Equity Toolkit*.

Remarkably, to this day, there is still no single finance book that can adequately fulfill the role of a practical "how-to" guide for the private equity industry. Even though there have been many useful private equity titles published in the last 10 years, you will quickly see that they are either academic textbooks that focus on theoretical principles, or private equity "war stories" that highlight prominent transactions in the industry. So far, not many private equity deal practitioners have taken the time to step out of the deal frenzy and write a practical reference guide capturing the industry's best practices across the private equity deal lifecycle. *The Private Equity Toolkit* intends to fill this gap and become the industry's missing manual.

The incessant growth of the private equity industry has created increased demand from curious professionals—such as yourself—who seek to embark on an investment career and look to acquire practical knowledge of the main skills required by the private equity profession. *The Private Equity Toolkit* will serve as a helpful guide for business school students, investment banking and consulting practitioners exploring a private equity career, as well as private equity professionals who are just starting their journey. Even though I assume that you possess a basic background in corporate finance and accounting, I made a deliberate effort to make this book as accessible as possible to a wide audience of readers by presenting the content in plain English, skipping graphs and equations and suggesting additional resources as I step through the chapters. While *The Private Equity Toolkit* primarily reflects my own subjective investment experience and utilizes stacks of personal notes, it is not entirely devoid of academic rigor. In fact, in preparing this book, I have performed extensive research of each topic across both the relevant academic literature and scholarly research in order to capture the most prominent findings and incorporate what I considered to be pragmatic, actionable advice.

Still not convinced? The chapter-by-chapter outline at the end of this section provides more insight into how you might be able to enhance your existing knowledge and optimize your own approach to private equity deal execution, from sourcing to exit. Use *The Private Equity Toolkit* as a reference guide and feel free to jump directly to the most relevant chapter whenever you require targeted support during a particular phase of a private equity investment. Once you've taken a look at the overall book structure, let's delve into the critical components of every deal that will make up your own private equity toolkit.

Disclaimer

While this book discusses at length my own approach to making decisions at every phase of the private equity transaction lifecycle, I am not offering any investment, legal or tax advice.

How to Get in Touch

If you have comments or suggestions, why not share them with me so that I can incorporate your thoughts in the next edition of this book? I welcome your contributions and feedback. Thank you! Please email me at: petoolkit@lavragroup.com

Chapter 1: First Thoughts on Deal Sourcing

Key Topics:
- Why deal sourcing remains an obscure field
- Six action steps to take today to enhance your deal origination prowess
- Proven deal sourcing strategies and the search for the mythical proprietary deal
- How to assess your current deal sourcing capabilities
- Key trends to look for now to spot future private equity deals ahead of others

Chapter 2: Thematic Deal Sourcing

Key Topics:
- Take the mystique out of thematic deal sourcing with the ICEBERG Roadmap™
- An effective way of breaking down your deal search into simple, executable steps
- How you can systematically generate promising investment themes
- Best practices for mapping out an industry, finding deals and meeting sector experts
- A time-tested strategy for approaching companies directly
- How to make the most out of your first meeting with a deal target

Chapter 3: Opportunistic Deal Sourcing

Key Topics:
- Develop an edge in opportunistic deal sourcing with the DATABASE Roadmap™

- No luck required: why having a clear focus pays off in an opportunistic deal search
- Actions you can take now to get the most out of your professional network
- How active brand management can help your fund stay top of mind
- Creative ways to supplement your opportunistic deal ideas
- How to manage your deal origination workflows effectively and effortlessly
- Does a dedicated business development function work for everyone?

Chapter 4: Deal Selection: Eliminating the Wrong Deal

Key Topics:
- Why killing deals is as important as doing deals
- How skilled investors overcome biases and minimize investment errors
- Why the best investment of your career might be a deal you never pursue
- Nine deal breakers you need to check for before proceeding on any deal

Chapter 5: Deal Selection: Identifying the Right Deal

Key Topics:
- Save time and effort: why it makes sense to evaluate the transaction dynamic first
- If you choose to remember one thing about deal selection, make it the business model

- The four most common sources of competitive advantage for any business
- Forget the detail: just a few key financial metrics that matter for deal selection
- How clever structuring can help you overcome valuation concerns

Chapter 6: Assessing the Top Management Team

Key Topics:
- Why motivating superb managers is the key ingredient in private equity's secret sauce
- Why the best CEOs are not the charismatic and articulate leaders we see in movies
- What makes the job of a private equity CEO among the most demanding in the world
- Nine key qualities to look out for when assessing CEOs for private equity businesses
- How you can apply the latest best practices in your assessment of management teams

Chapter 7: Analyzing the Business Plan

Key Topics:
- Why skilled investors explore business fundamentals before diving into the numbers
- Key problem areas to spot immediately in every business plan you review
- How to poke holes in overoptimistic projections and make your investment case add up

- Ten cold, hard questions that every solid business plan needs to address
- My trusted business plan tool: *Master List of Most Common Drivers of Value Creation*

Chapter 8: Valuation

Key Topics:
- Enterprise value, headline price and cash consideration: why they are each different
- How experienced investors use flawed valuation methods and still get to the right answer
- Seven valuation metrics and six valuation methods I like (and hate) to use
- Two valuation approaches for those times when you find "difficult to value" companies
- You've done the valuation: How much will you pay to win the deal?

Chapter 9: Deal Structuring

Key Topics:
- Capital structure considerations: what type of leverage to use and when it is too much
- Management Incentive Plans: target A, reward A and achieve A
- Enhance your deal through earn-outs, earn-ins, escrows and vendor loan notes
- Minority deals: negotiate robust exit rights or be held hostage by majority owners
- Advanced deal structuring techniques for minority investments

Chapter 10: Deal Execution: Transaction Process and Due Diligence

Key Topics:
- What to expect in a typical private equity transaction process
- Don't "boil the ocean": ten principles of a well-managed due diligence effort
- Who does what and why you need it: an anatomy of the key due diligence workstreams

Chapter 11: Deal Execution: Legal Documentation

Key Topics:
- Why you don't need to be a lawyer to provide valuable input in legal negotiations
- How to translate due diligence findings into legal clauses in the deal documentation
- My cheat sheet summary of common issues in the key transaction agreements

Chapter 12: Adding Value Through Active Ownership

Key Topics:
- Develop your own success formula with a Value Creation Plan
- Four value-accretive actions for every portfolio company to consider
- Create powerful performance improvement momentum with a 100-Day Plan

- Governance and reporting: strategic priorities of a well-run private equity board
- When things go wrong: spot the first signs of company distress and take radical action

Chapter 13: Exit Strategies and Deal Monetization

Key Topics:
- How to exit a minority investment (effortlessly)
- Exiting a majority transaction: Should you time the market?
- Conventional exit routes: an IPO, strategic sale or sponsor-to-sponsor buyout
- Can't exit your investment? Alternative deal monetization strategies to the rescue
- The finishing touch: exit preparation roadmap for every portfolio company

Acknowledgments

I owe a debt of gratitude to my family, who supported me throughout my book-writing journey and helped bring this project to fruition. A warm thank-you to my wonderful husband Frederik, who was the first reader of every chapter in the book (not always entirely by choice). I would also like to acknowledge the invaluable support of my children, August and Daria. Thank you for coming with me to my office during numerous weekends and inspiring me to persevere during challenging times. I also would like to thank my sister Julia, my parents and grandparents for instilling me with a strong work ethic and teaching me the importance of critical thinking.

I am fortunate to have an extraordinary group of friends, many of whom encouraged me to write this book and provided constructive comments on my manuscript: thank you, Stefan Loesch, Oksana Denysenko, Helena Clavel-Flores, Irina Grigorenko, Vittoria Stefanello, Leopoldo Carbone, Julia Shur and Oksana Tiedt. In addition, I am grateful to Lee Barbour for delivering first-class editing support, and to Emma Stefanello and Michael Majdalani for providing excellent research assistance.

I would like to express my gratitude to Eli Talmor, Dirk Donath, Giampiero Mazza, Joshua Rosenbaum, Joshua Pearl, Alex Emery and Ted Berk. Each of these highly accomplished individuals were kind enough to read my book and provide me with their personal endorsement.

A special thanks to everyone in the Wiley team who assisted me in making this book a reality: my acquisitions editor, Bill Falloon, my assistant acquisitions editor, Samantha Enders, my managing editor, Purvi Patel, and my Editorial Assistant, Samantha Wu.

Finally, I would like to say thank you to a long list of brilliant work colleagues who taught me everything I know about private equity and dedicated their time to developing my investment acumen early in my career. I can't name you all, but you probably remember the long hours we worked together and know who you are, folks. Thank you!

About the Author

Tamara Sakovska is a private equity investor, board director and the founder of Lavra Group. She has over two decades of finance and investment experience gained at Goldman Sachs, Harbour-Vest Partners, Warburg Pincus, Permira, Eton Park and Global Family Partners.

Tamara's investment experience includes originating, leading and executing leveraged buyouts, minority and control growth equity transactions as well as private investments in publicly listed companies. She has also invested in private equity funds-of-funds and structured strategic co-investment partnerships with institutional investors, corporations and ultra-high-net-worth family groups. During her investment career, she has gained in-depth, global transaction experience across 14 countries in the technology, telecommunications, energy, natural resources, real estate and consumer sectors, among others.

Tamara is a tenured board member with a strong track record of managing complex strategic and corporate governance issues in both publicly listed and private companies. She has extensive corporate governance expertise, holds a Diploma with Distinction in Company Direction, is a Chartered Director and a Fellow of the Institute of Directors (UK). In 2018, Tamara received the Director of the Year Award in the Chartered Director category. She currently serves as an Independent Director and

Chair of the Nominating Committee on the boards of two public companies listed on the London Stock Exchange and the Nasdaq, respectively.

Tamara holds an MBA with Distinction from London Business School (UK) and a BA with Honors and Distinction in Economics and Art History from Stanford University (USA), where she graduated Phi Beta Kappa and received the Anna Laura Myers Prize in Economics.

1

First Thoughts on Deal Sourcing

Key Topics in Chapter 1:

- Why deal sourcing remains an obscure field
- Six action steps to take today to enhance your deal origination prowess
- Proven deal sourcing strategies and the search for the mythical proprietary deal
- How to assess your current deal sourcing capabilities
- Key trends to look for now to spot future private equity deals ahead of others

---

Introduction to Deal Sourcing

Private equity begins with finding a suitable investment opportunity. Preferably, a great one. The first three chapters of this book discuss exactly that—the process of finding a private equity deal that represents a perfect fit for your investment mandate.

In my personal experience, I have found this to be a tedious and frustrating process. Why? The private equity industry has been operating for nearly half a century, yet there is no one source that educates others in a granular and systematic way about how to build a solid private equity origination capability. Therefore, I set out to put my own detailed thoughts and experience in writing in order to share my perspective with others about this complicated process. My aim is to be as thorough as possible so that, after reading these first three chapters, you will walk away with a couple of solid and useful frameworks that will positively transform your deal sourcing outcomes.

Let's begin.

Why is understanding deal sourcing important? There are two primary reasons. First, creating and sustaining a flow of high-quality deal ideas is one of the core competencies of a successful private equity professional. This competency resonates very closely with the perceived brand of every private equity fund and, eventually, with your personal brand. Every limited partner ("LP") investing in private equity funds is looking to identify a team of rainmakers who can demonstrate that they are capable of developing differentiated investment themes, finding sustainable sources of deal flow and closing successful transactions. As you get more experienced in private equity, the people you report to will increasingly expect you to originate your own deals proactively.

The second reason is that deal sourcing—while being critical to investment success—remains remarkably obscure. There is extremely little written specifically about private equity deal sourcing and how to master it. The books on private equity that I have researched seem to include only a high-level discussion of this topic. If you are interested in private equity, chances are you regularly come across articles in the trade press discussing the challenges of finding a good deal. If you have attended private equity conferences, as I have, then you've also heard a good number of deal origination war stories. However, I wasn't able to find a single resource that sets out a detailed private equity deal origination framework in one place. Hence, I believe I can make a contribution to this area with my deal sourcing guide.

In my research, I was able to identify only one study, conducted by Teten and Farmer (2010), analyzing deal sourcing strategies across the private equity industry and outlining a number of actionable steps aimed at improving the deal origination process. Unfortunately, I could not use the valuable lessons of this study in my own career because this research was published many years after I had been tasked with originating my own private equity transactions. In the study, the authors reaffirm the importance of deal sourcing in private equity: it turns out that late-stage venture capital and growth equity investors with proactive origination programs are almost all top-quartile performers across stage, vintage and sector. This makes sense. You can now understand why LPs might be very interested in examining your firm's deal sourcing process in agonizing detail.

When I started my first private equity job at a firm focused on large leveraged buyouts ("LBOs"), I found the process of deal origination and initial review fairly exciting. It was great to think through numerous business models and admire new ideas. However, it was also extremely exasperating. I was a member of the consumer team and it was not unusual for us to analyze over 100 large buyouts a year, bring 10–12 deals to the investment committee and work on three or four full deal execution processes in order to close just one transaction that year.

Yes, you read that correctly: the goal of my team was to review over 100 potential deals in order to close *one* deal per year. If you are lucky enough to complete one transaction a year, you are right on track! Sometimes, even this modest goal was out of reach. For example, when a target company was sold through a highly competitive auction process, our team would often not be chosen as the preferred (or highest) bidder. This means that there were years when we, as a sector team, would close no deals at all. Yes, we would still review over 100 potential deals that year and close zero. Talk about a low-energy Christmas party.

This is a rather frustrating, yet typical, fact in private equity: a lot of work goes into deal sourcing yet there is no guarantee of a successful outcome. Sometimes several years will pass from your first meeting with the management of a potential investment target to the time they are ready to consider a transaction. Sometimes the company will even go through multiple rounds of ownership until the management team is prepared to meet with you again. Sometimes the company shareholders are finally ready to accept a private equity investment, just not one from your firm! However, the stars do align at some point and, with perseverance, you can manage to get a private equity transaction to a final close.

What influences the successful outcome of sourcing and closing a private equity transaction? If you had asked me this at the beginning of my private equity career, I would have said that there was a fair degree of randomness and luck in this process. It is about being connected and about maximizing your options by doing 1,000 things to cover more ground. And being in the right place at the right time. And balancing cold-blooded investment analysis with the animal spirits of a competitive auction. Back then, I would have said serendipity deserves its fair share of credit, too.

Would I give the same answer now? Actually, I would not. I no longer think of sourcing and closing transactions as a game of chance. While the rules of probability do apply to finding good deals, I think there are steps that you can take to skew the odds in your favor. Sometimes significantly. Depending on what your competitors are doing in your sector or country of focus, you can definitely enhance your deal origination prowess by a considerable margin. I have certainly seen this in my own efforts of sourcing private equity transactions.

First, let's take a look at a broad overview of these action points and then I'll delve into each one in more detail.

- *Commit.* Make deal origination an institutional priority and aim to create a sustainable long-term competitive advantage both for yourself as an investment professional and your firm through sourcing high-quality investments. This means dedicating time to deal sourcing throughout the year even when it seems like there is no time for it.
- *Organize chaos.* Deal sourcing is tricky because it is an informal process that involves many variables. Decision-makers change their minds. Companies get taken over by strategic investors and cease to be private equity targets overnight. What can you do when things seem out of your control? Attack the mercurial nature of deal sourcing by turning your reactive activities into a number of intentional and predictable routines. Systematize your efforts and turn them into a framework. Focus on perfecting your deal sourcing process and do not pay excessive attention to interim outcomes. A better process will eventually lead to superior results.
- *Conduct deep industry research.* Create a unique information advantage for yourself and your team by developing expertise in a couple of industry subsectors. Make sure you build a detailed knowledge base in these subsectors, generate your own insights and initiate a flow of proprietary deal ideas. How do you do that? I have spent many late nights leading various industry "deep dives" and have developed my own framework for tackling this exercise. I will share these tactics with you later in the book.

- *Prepare your firm to move quickly.* Institutional agility can be a remarkable advantage, especially in a highly competitive deal environment. It is important to provide regular updates to your firm, especially your investment committee and key decision makers, on the main investment themes that you are working on. The goal is to get as much support as possible and ensure that everyone is aware of the detailed knowledge your team has acquired through deep research. One of the best ways to do this is for your team to develop and share their proprietary analysis of a sector with the rest of the firm. That way, once you identify a suitable deal in this industry, your investment committee should already be warmed up. They will trust your team to come up with a differentiated "deal angle," giving you the ability to move forward with confidence and progress the deal ahead of your competition.

- *Develop an efficient deal sourcing process.* Take a step back and identify the areas of your deal sourcing process where most of your time is wasted. Does it feel like you are busy creating too many options by doing 1,000 things? Are you attending too many meetings with intermediaries who miss the point of your mandate and bring deals that make no sense? Is your deal sourcing network fully optimized? Are your meeting notes well-organized, searchable, synchronized and easy to access, both in the office and remotely?

Once you have had an opportunity to reflect, try to come up with ways to streamline your deal sourcing process. Aim for the end result to resemble a clock with a precise Swiss movement. Instead of doing 1,000 things to cover more ground, reduce your efforts to the 10 most value-added activities and repeat them with precision 100 times. These numbers are arbitrary, but you get the point: abandon deal sourcing tasks that yield no result, focus on the most productive activities and pursue them in a disciplined manner. This process should free up some of your time and enhance the quality of deals under your review, both of which will boost the probability of a successful outcome.

- *Persist, smile, repeat.* Now that you have created a proactive deal sourcing work plan, make sure there are dedicated slots reserved in your calendar to keep the process moving. Deal sourcing should be relentless and tick away with the dependability of a clock. Do not be tempted to drop out of the deal origination process, even during busy times. You can simply do less deal sourcing work during busy weeks. The only way to beat your competition is to work smarter. Take the time to put necessary reminders in your system for any follow-ups and be disciplined about following through completely. Do your best to maintain a positive spirit when deals disappoint. Take a deep breath, smile, move on and start again. Deal sourcing is simply a fixed number of efforts, persistent and repetitive, that eventually result in a big payoff.

Originating new deal ideas can sometimes feel like a mammoth task, but taking small steps can make it much more manageable. Just a few hours a week of proactive and intentional deal sourcing work can make a big difference and help you stay ahead of your competition. As the old proverb goes, "Water dripping day by day wears the hardest rock away."

Deal Sourcing Strategies

What sourcing strategies are out there? Generally, people in our industry talk about two types of private equity deals: thematic and opportunistic. Thematic investments are potential transactions that you identify proactively through the rigorous and granular research of a particular industry subsector, emerging trend or a specific investment thesis. Thematic deal ideas sometimes do not have any obvious catalysts and can take a long time to become actionable. Opportunistic investments rely on a more passive effort on your part: they are inbound transactions that simply land on your desk. Opportunistic transactions are typically a lot more actionable: there is often a motivated seller who wants to get a deal done within a specific timeframe. The majority of opportunistic deals are introduced by sell-side intermediaries, professional connections and, less frequently, friends or acquaintances.

Based on what I have seen in the private equity market, most firms tend to pursue both types of deal sourcing approaches in order to develop a sustainable flow of new investment ideas. Thematic deal sourcing helps you narrow down your area of focus and build a knowledge base, which in turn increases the probability of finding an opportunistic deal in which your firm can position itself ahead of the competition as the most credible buyer.

The longer I worked on both thematic and opportunistic transactions, the more I thought about how to optimize the deal search process for both types of deals in order to create an effective routine. It took me many years, with many ups and downs, to outline a set of steps for myself that were easy to follow and gave me confidence that I was being thorough in my work and spending my time efficiently. The effort of documenting my deal sourcing approach ultimately morphed into a couple of fairly detailed frameworks which I will describe later in the book. What was I trying to achieve? I thought that the holy grail of my deal sourcing activity was to find a proprietary deal, either opportunistic or thematic.

Finding a proprietary transaction is a true obsession of the private equity industry. What makes a deal truly proprietary? When the transaction is not widely known in the market and your firm is the only party having discussions with the target company, then you are working on a proprietary deal. Sometimes the deal can be semi-proprietary: a few other market players might be aware of it and circle the same target. However, it is possible that your firm may be ahead in its learning curve and, therefore, manage to agree a period of exclusivity, during which you can evaluate and execute this investment. There may be cases when your firm succeeds in engaging in a truly proprietary dialogue with a great business found through months-long thematic research, only to be told by company owners that they will invite additional bidders. Why? Mostly because multiple bids typically make price discovery more accurate and give the owners an opportunity to maximize valuation. In this case, your proprietary idea will enter the open market and, I can tell you from my own experience, it is a rather painful feeling.

Why is it so hard to find proprietary deals? The private equity industry has matured over the years and there are literally hundreds of new funds entering the industry across the globe each year. As information barriers diminish, company owners are getting more sophisticated too, and are far more likely to hire a professional adviser than deal with just one private equity fund in a proprietary transaction. So, why do private equity investors continue to obsess over finding a proprietary deal? Well, everyone likes a competitive sport. Also, finding a proprietary deal is a great opportunity to showcase your professional finesse and highlight your fund's distinct advantage to your LPs. Your fund investors will feel like they have gained access to an exclusive deal club and, provided your fund's returns do not disappoint, will be keen to invest in your next fund when the time comes.

Theoretically speaking, finding a deal outside of a competitive auction should result in a lower entry valuation too. As the only bidder, your fund may avoid having to overpay in order to secure the deal. However, I am not so sure that the notion of a more reasonable entry valuation holds every time. I can think of a number of scenarios in which your fund may decide to pay a fairly high valuation in a proprietary situation. For example, your sector expertise may enable you to take an informed view of unique value creation levers that exist only in this company and not in other comparable businesses. You might decide to pay a premium because your fund may value transaction certainty and seek to benefit from lower execution costs. These are just some of the reasons that might explain a higher entry valuation in a proprietary transaction. Teten and Farmer (2010) remark in their study that sometimes private equity firms agree to pay a higher multiple of earnings for a proprietary deal because it enables them to pursue higher quality targets to begin with and also add more value after the deal closes.

In summary, proprietary deals have become exceedingly difficult to find—but they are not just a myth of the private equity industry. It makes more sense to think of them as an infrequent but completely plausible phenomenon, like a solar eclipse. As rare as they are, we can still expect to experience them once, and hopefully even multiple times during our careers.

Assessment of Your Current Deal Sourcing Capabilities

Let's take an honest look at where you are at the moment. Do you think your firm has strong deal sourcing capabilities? To distinguish good luck from a solid origination process, it might be helpful to think through and answer the following questions.

- Does your fund set tightly defined investment goals for the next 12–18 months? Does your firm have a well-articulated sourcing strategy?
- Does your firm pursue a research-driven thematic deal sourcing approach? Are there specific investment theses that you are developing in your area of focus?
- How many proprietary deals has your firm sourced and what origination strategies were most successful?

- Does your firm capture detailed data on the deal pipeline? Are you able to analyze past and current deal flow with basic pipeline key performance indicators ("KPIs")?

- Do you know what proportion of deals your firm has seen that are relevant to your area of focus? How many deals has your firm missed? Of those deals that were missed, how were they sourced? Do you have access to the same deal source?

- If your fund saw the deal and rejected it, is there anything in the investment thesis that you failed to detect that other firms were able to spot?

- Do you maintain a list of potential deal targets? Do you use a tech-enabled solution that allows you to keep track of them easily? Do you reach out to them consistently and follow up? Do you keep in touch with companies that currently appear to have no interest in selling?

- Do you record key takeaways from meetings and calls that various members of your team have had with a potential deal target over the years? Is this information stored centrally and easy to access?

- Does your firm have a good system of keeping track and systematizing firmwide relationships, such as with banks, consultants, industry experts and other professional intermediaries? Are you able to rank your relationships based on the value they provide to your firm?

These questions, no doubt, represent a degree of self-reflection and discipline that can seem hard to reach. If your firm does not follow most of these processes, do not worry. These procedures are fairly straightforward to establish and, once in place, they will produce substantial benefits. If your firm already operates in a fairly organized way, then you are already ahead of the game and any incremental deal sourcing efforts should result in an even greater tangible payoff.

Where Do Deals Come From?

Have you ever wondered how a deal actually originates? What factors propel private equity activity? And why do deals come in waves? The reason why I care about these questions is the following: if you understand what emerging trends are likely to spur private equity deal activity in the near future, you can focus your deal sourcing efforts on this arena and position yourself ahead of your competition. In other words, if you are more observant than others, you can try to figure out where deal activity might happen much earlier than anyone else.

One of the intriguing aspects of private equity deals is that they take place in both good and bad market conditions. Theoretically, most private equity deals should happen in a bear market. When the IPO window is closed, the public markets are pessimistic and banks are less willing to provide debt on attractive terms; thus the shareholders of target companies should view private equity as a more appealing financing option. This theoretical argument can be extended further: private equity funds themselves should be able to take contrarian views in a bear market and seek to invest heavily in a down cycle. This will allow them to pay relatively low entry valuations and generate attractive investment returns. Does this happen in reality? Not as often as it should.

My observation is that private equity activity as a whole ends up being quite pro-cyclical. Of course, there are disciplined private equity investors out there who abide by their strict valuation criteria and who avoid investing at the top of the cycle. However, most market participants are human and, therefore, are likely to succumb to hubris when they observe rapid economic expansion and rising stock markets. Valuations are high when the markets are optimistic; however, one can always justify paying a full price for a good business. A deal frenzy begins and eventually swallows the majority of market participants. This explains why deals come in waves.

Since little research exists that links emerging trends to the private equity activity, I found it useful to look at the field adjacent to our industry, namely that of mergers and acquisitions ("M&A"). There is an outstanding book by Bruner (2004) that, in addition to discussing nearly all key areas of applied mergers in impressive detail, addresses precisely this topic. Bruner (2004) looks at what drives the M&A deal activity and identifies areas of "economic turbulence." Some of these factors provide a good explanation of the private equity deal activity and are useful to keep in mind in your deal sourcing efforts. They are as follows:

- *Geopolitical change.* Political decisions can radically change the attractiveness of certain markets. Any shifts in policy that affect the prosperity of the economy, taxation, social environment and corporate governance will have profound implications for private equity transactions. For example, I owe thanks (and deals) to the following geopolitical developments that influenced my private equity career: the introduction of the single currency in the Eurozone, the inclusion of certain Central and Eastern European states to the European Union, the admission of China to the World Trade Organization as well as market deregulation reforms that followed the economic liberalization in India.
- *Secular trends.* Examples of secular trends include long-term shifts in the demographic makeup, the need of labor migrants to sustain economic expansion, vast differences in wealth distribution across generations, rising obesity rates and distinctive preferences of younger consumers, just to name a few. Any sustainable long-term macro shift could provide a fertile ground for investment.

- *Changes in regulation.* Deregulation is typically very beneficial for businesses, as their growth becomes less constrained and they can play by the rules of the market economy. Companies typically need to rationalize their operations in order to compete. On the other hand, when regulation tightens, businesses often have a need for fresh capital in order to comply with the changes that might be as extensive as having to adapt their entire business model. There are second-order effects too, such as the rise of new entrants providing tools and services that aid compliance in the new regulatory setting.
- *Technological change.* Do you remember how the world worked 10 years ago? Technological advances can be very disruptive for companies. Apart from requiring additional investments in infrastructure and personnel, technological shifts might compel companies to alter their strategic direction and invest in new capabilities in order to survive.
- *Innovation in financial markets.* Increasing market sophistication has a direct impact on the private equity industry. Examples of complex transactions that added fresh momentum to the sector include the advent of the LBO and securitization of leveraged loans. The introduction of certain structural features in private equity transactions such as a "sale and leaseback" has been replicated across numerous private equity–backed businesses that own hard assets.
- *Changes in capital market conditions.* Buoyant markets enhance deal activity. During record market highs, even businesses with no earnings, no revenues and, sometimes, no customers get bought and sold. When the markets are very liquid and are forgiving of corporate shortcomings, hubris takes over the world. As I mentioned earlier, private equity activity, at least theoretically, should abate. It does eventually but, as a rule, a little too late.

There are a couple of other deal factors not mentioned by Bruner (2004) that are important to include in this discussion:

- *Industry disruption.* Private equity firms are generally enthusiastic about backing industry disruptors. Traditional classroom education providers, retail banks and insurance companies are examples of industries being disintermediated by new entrants backed by private equity investors. However, it would be fair to mention that private equity funds sometimes fail to spot a terminal inflection point in the industry and let disruptors attack companies in their own portfolio. For example, some of the biggest losses in private equity occurred when the business models of music publishing and brick-and-mortar retail companies were completely dismantled by the online competition.

- *Sectors with substantial capital requirements.* Sometimes there are entire industries that announce large capital expenditures that will need to be incurred by companies operating in that sector. Examples of such capital investments include purchases of new spectrum in telecommunication auctions, the move to hybrid or electric engines in the automotive sector, the development of new techniques to extract fossil fuels and financing the gradual switch to alternative energy sources in power generation.

- *Applying successful business strategies to new industries.* Private equity excels at identifying proven business models that can be applied to new sectors. On-demand services, asset-light operations, outsourcing, "buy and build" strategies are just a few examples of what has been replicated across industries. Private equity investors look for appropriate business analogies and think: If restaurants operate as a chain, why don't nurseries or schools operate as a chain?

- *Replication of successful deal types in new geographical markets.* When private equity arrives in a new geography, especially in emerging markets, first deals tend to happen in telecommunications, breweries and branded consumer goods. Why? Because straightforward deals happen first. Private equity funds always seem to be keen to pursue proven investment theses in new countries where there are enough imperfections to warrant a high return.

Is this an exhaustive list? By all means, it is not. You can probably come up with additional factors driving private equity deal flow that are relevant to your industry or geography. It is always worthwhile to keep a close eye on any emerging trends in order to anticipate potential transactions and stay ahead of your competition. As soon as you identify the areas of so-called "economic turbulence" that seem relevant to your investment mandate, rush to your desk to research them so that you can spot future deal flow before anyone else.

2

Thematic Deal Sourcing

Key Topics in Chapter 2:

Take the mystique out of thematic deal sourcing with the ICE-BERG Roadmap™

- An effective way of breaking down your deal search into simple, executable steps
- How you can systematically generate promising investment themes
- Best practices for mapping out an industry, finding deals and meeting sector experts
- A time-tested strategy for approaching companies directly
- How to make the most out of your first meeting with a deal target

---

The Benefits of Thematic Deal Sourcing

Identifying, developing and monetizing an investment theme is a valuable skill. Thematic deal sourcing allows you to build an extensive knowledge base in a sector of your choice, develop differentiated insights and gain an information advantage over your competitors. Gaining deep industry knowledge helps to improve the quality of your investment decisions and provides you with a better understanding of deal targets operating in that industry. Your investment committee will have more confidence to move quickly in the competitive process if they know that you and your team have become experts on the subject, and your investment thesis is well thought out and credible because you have spent considerable time researching the industry.

Your industry expertise allows you to stand out from the crowd in a busy private equity marketplace. Deep sector research inevitably results in generating extensive (and potentially not widely known) information about key players in that market, and these companies might become interesting deal targets for proprietary transactions. Your sector knowledge will enable you to empathize with management teams on key industry issues and position yourself as a value-added partner of choice to them. Professional advisers working on deals in the sector that you know well will appreciate the fact that they do not have to spend time educating you about the industry and will be enthusiastic about engaging with you on potential transactions.

It sounds like there are only positives in a thematic deal sourcing process, right? Unfortunately, not. It is a time-consuming and resource-intensive task. It requires such an overwhelming effort on your part that it might be very tempting to return to your day-to-day reactive activities and abandon your goal of becoming an industry expert altogether. I have certainly experienced this feeling on more than one occasion, especially when working on sectors that I was less excited about. I felt like I certainly had enough to fill my days without taking a "deep dive" into a new sector.

What can make thematic deal sourcing less daunting? What I have found is that this task seems far less intimidating when thematic research is broken down into small, digestible pieces that form a checklist-like framework. It is much easier to check small items off your list than deal with one mammoth chore. Since I could not find such a detailed checklist aimed at a thematic private equity deal sourcing process anywhere, I put together this 7-step thematic deal sourcing framework myself. Here it goes.

Thematic Deal Sourcing: ICEBERG Roadmap™[1]

My framework is called the Thematic Deal Sourcing ICEBERG Roadmap™. Broadly speaking, the thematic deal sourcing process consists of the following steps:

I	C	E	B	E	R	G

1. **I**dentify a sector theme and build an investment thesis.
2. **C**onduct an in-depth analysis of the selected industry.
3. **E**laborate on your knowledge by mapping out key players operating in the industry.
4. **B**uild a network of experts and company executives to fill knowledge gaps.
5. **E**stablish a long list of potential deal targets and initiate coverage of these companies.
6. **R**ank the companies by attractiveness and approach two or three potential deal targets at a time.
7. **G**o visit companies to convert deal ideas into real transactions.

---

[1]ICEBERG Roadmap™ is a registered trademark of my company, Lavra Group Limited.

Let's go through these steps in greater detail so that you can understand how I developed this checklist and modify it as needed to create a framework that works for you.

1. Identify a sector theme and build an investment thesis

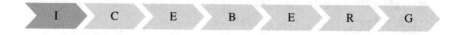

How do you come up with a good investment idea? It might seem easier said than done, but let us look in detail at some of the resources you can use to find a promising investment theme.

- *Knowledge you already have.* Is there an industry that your firm already knows well and in which your fund has already completed transactions? Provided that doing an additional deal in this sector is not going to produce an overly concentrated portfolio, consider capitalizing on the industry knowledge your fund has already acquired through owning this business.
- *Knowledge you can easily extend.* Are there any deals that your fund recently lost to your competition? Are there any valuable industry insights that your fund gained in these aborted deal processes? Are you able to take advantage of this knowledge, identify any second or third-order effects present in this sector's value chain and perhaps even seek to exploit the same investment thesis in a different geography?
- *Business press.* Ask yourself more broadly about what is going on in the world. Where are the pockets of "economic turbulence" I wrote about earlier? Have you recently seen any inspiring articles or interviews in the business press discussing emerging trends, interesting products, or fast-growing and under-capitalized industries?

- *Top-down sector analysis.* Choose a big sector to look at and go through its supply chain to identify interesting subsectors. Where is a good place to invest? Consider the example of aerospace and defense as a large industry. Instead of imagining large aircraft and helicopter manufacturers, think of this sector's smaller segments: Who produces passenger seats, lavatories, three-dimensional real-time maps and in-flight entertainment? What about runway lighting, airport equipment, avionics and aircraft simulators for pilot training?
- *Industry classification codes.* This strategy is for a slow and rainy day. It works well for obscure sectors, especially if you are not sure how to break down a big industry into smaller subsegments. You simply look for a publicly available source of standard industry classification codes and learn how that database breaks down a large industry of your choice into subsegments. For example, if you focus on the medical laboratory equipment sector and identify manufacturers of spectrofluorometers and turbidimeters through this analysis, then consider yourself to be on the right track.

2. Conduct an in-depth analysis of the selected industry

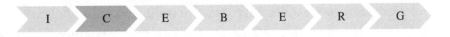

The objective of this step is to evaluate the attractiveness of the sector, learn about its structural features and identify profitability drivers. It is a dynamic exercise: even the most comprehensive attempt at answering all major questions about the industry will leave you with some information gaps. As you talk to sector experts and company executives, you will be able to fill these gaps and generate your own insights that will help you to come up with an actionable investment thesis.

I describe my own approach to industry analysis in broad terms below.

- *Sector scope.* I find that an appropriate sector definition is key before beginning this analysis. This should generally focus on a relevant geography and include all companies producing the same product or service, as well as those companies offering viable substitutes.
- *External environment.* What broad macro factors[2] are likely to have an influence on this industry? Take note of any political considerations, economic trends, cultural influences, legal or environmental concerns that are important to this sector.
- *Sector performance.* What is the total market size and historic growth rate? Is the industry new, mature or declining? What are the key drivers of projected growth? Is there a cycle and, if so, where are we now?
- *Demand factors.* What secular trends are influencing demand? Who buys the product and how are purchasing decisions made? Is this a discretionary spend? What are the key determinants of demand as well as its historic and projected growth rates?
- *Supply factors.* Understand sector capacity: historic, current and projected. What does the supply look like when broken down by product or service? Map out the industry's supply chain.
- *Competitive landscape.* What is the market structure: fragmented or fairly consolidated? What are the market shares

---

[2]For a comprehensive external environment analysis tool, please refer to Narayanan and Fahey (2001). Please refer to Chapter 2 References for a complete citation.

of top players? How attractive is the industry? To provide a comprehensive answer to this question, you may find it helpful to refer to the works of Porter (1985) and Grant (2002). In short, any industry analysis should aim to examine key sector forces[3] such as barriers to entry, the degree of rivalry among competitors, supplier power and buyer power as well as the prevalence of product substitutes and complements.

- *Pricing.* What grows faster: supply or demand? What side of the market has a greater influence on price? Are there any unusual factors influencing a free market price mechanism, like an ongoing price war, taxes, surcharges, government incentives or regulatory caps?

- *Typical cost structure.* What is the ratio between fixed and variable costs? What are the historic and projected trends in the major cost categories? Are companies able to pass cost increases to buyers?

- *Industry operating metrics.* What are the relevant aggregate sector statistics? What are the typical operating ratios at the company level? Is it a capital-intensive sector? Does the industry earn its cost of capital?

- *Sector risks and threats.* What are key risks faced by the sector, such as regulatory, economic, political? Is there a threat of industry disruption, product obsolescence or technological change?

- *Key takeaways and next steps.* Summarize the key insights relevant to your investment thesis to be confirmed in subsequent meetings with industry experts and companies. What are the recent sector developments or major sector news that you need to keep in mind? What are the gaps in the market data you have been able to gather?

---

[3]Porter (1985) provides a thorough analysis of all original elements of the industry structure ("Porter's Five Forces"), while Grant (2002) offers an extended framework to suit more contemporary sectors. Please refer to Chapter 2 References for complete citations.

These questions constitute the bulk of your research work and once you have gone through each one you will have learned a lot about the industry. Have you discovered any negative features of the sector, such as overcapacity, product commoditization, wild fluctuations in demand or major structural shifts? If, from the sources that you have reviewed so far, you come to a view that the industry is weak and not structurally suitable for private equity transactions, consider stopping your research at this stage. Making a private equity investment in a challenging sector is very risky and can make your life miserable down the road. Even teaming up with the world's most capable management team will hardly be enough to withstand the forces of abysmal industry fundamentals and it is best to stop work in order to avoid a potentially loss-making investment.

What sources can you utilize for your industry research, especially if you are on a limited budget? If there are publicly listed companies operating in the sector, I always find it useful to read reports prepared by equity research analysts that cover these companies. Typically, company initiation research reports tend to be quite comprehensive and feature a detailed industry section. It is also worth keeping an eye out for any up-to-date comments on the industry provided in the investor relations sections of websites of publicly listed companies as well as in their annual reports. Regulatory bodies, industry associations and trade journals may also publish extensive information about the sector.

Make sure to check out sources such as current news and in-depth articles about the industry as well. Is there valuable information you can gather from reputable industry blogs or relevant online business communities? If you have a budget for this project, you might decide to purchase extensive industry reports from specialized market research firms or hire strategy consultants to perform a tailored industry analysis for your fund. In case the sector becomes of significant strategic importance to your organization and there are imperative issues that you need to investigate, consider conducting a private survey[4] that addresses your specific research questions.

3. Elaborate on your knowledge by mapping out key players operating in the industry

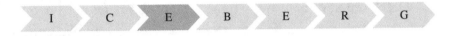

This step enables you to understand the market structure, evaluate what competitive forces are at play and benchmark the companies against each other as well as against best-in-class peers. You may also be able to discover valuable second-order effects from this exercise, such as identifying suppliers or customers of the industry that may be interesting deal targets in their own right. In every industry analysis, I find that some companies can be difficult to research because they may represent smaller subsidiaries of big publicly listed enterprises or may already be owned by private equity or big strategic conglomerates. Private companies, as a rule, do not disclose many details of their operations. Ideally, you should aim to gather enough data to cover the following areas:

- *Company overview.* This section should include a business overview, description of products or services, market share, strategic positioning, high-level financials, ownership details and any recent company news.

---

[4]For ideas about how to get started on a private survey, you may find it helpful to read Chapter 13 of Valentine (2011). Please refer to Chapter 2 References for a complete citation.

- *Benchmarking.* What are the key operating statistics for each company? How do they compare to direct competitors and global best-in-class peers? Are you able to assess the key success factors for companies operating in this industry? Are there companies that you have identified in the sector that went out of business recently? Are you able to understand why?

There are several ways I typically go about gathering the necessary information. To the extent that there are public companies in this universe, locating recent equity research reports can help you gain insight into the company itself, as well as its peer group and global competitors. Public equity research reports also help you to get up to speed on what operating metrics are used in the sector.

Other useful sources for mapping out who is active in the sector are participant lists of relevant trade fairs and industry award ceremonies, membership directories of leading industry associations as well as speakers and sponsors at industry conferences. Another option is to conduct a search through a paid-for company intelligence database that allows you to narrow down potential targets by industry classification, geography, company description, shareholder details and keywords. While potentially expensive, these databases provide comprehensive information on both public and private companies that includes key financials and recent developments, such as ownership changes.

4. Build a network of experts and company executives to fill knowledge gaps

I · C · E · B · E · R · G

We are more than halfway through the Thematic Deal Sourcing ICEBERG Roadmap™! Now that you have done a good amount of thorough sector research, you should have a good sense of the areas where there are gaps in your knowledge and who can help you at this stage. Apart from striving to perfect your understanding of the industry, you should begin to think about building productive relationships with people who might assist you with transactions down the road. Who can help you generate actionable deal ideas, introduce you to companies or even serve as a Chairman or a Chief Executive Officer ("CEO") in a target company?

There are numerous resources at your disposal:

- *The existing network of your firm.* If you are working on an industry already known to your firm (i.e. someone worked on a similar investment in a different geography), it is a good idea to connect with your colleagues and understand the sources of insight that they found valuable. What existing network does your firm already have and who can help you with introductions?
- *Your personal network.* Next, explore your own network, including any second or third-degree connections that you have: Can you detect any actionable links to the industry that you are researching?
- *Reaching out to industry experts on your own.* Through your sector research, you might have already identified prominent figures in the sector. Who is regularly talking to the press about key sector issues? Who are keynote speakers at industry events? Who is on the board of the industry association? Are there any retired executives currently working in an advisory capacity? Are there influential industry bloggers?
- *Networking at industry events.* Make an effort to go to industry conferences and trade fairs to meet people working in the

sector. Are there industry experts or company executives that you might be interested in meeting?

- *Expert networks and headhunters.* This strategy will require a budget from your fund; however, it will allow you to conduct a bespoke and precise search. You will be able to identify a number of industry experts, current or retired company executives as well as any other participants of the industry's value chain, such as customers, suppliers or regulators.

- *Other intermediaries.* Experienced accountants, lawyers, consultants and bankers generally have sector expertise and sometimes develop truly deep and unique insights into the industry, albeit shaped by the perspective of their profession. If they already work with your firm on other transactions, they should be willing to engage in a thoughtful dialogue with you and potentially introduce you to more people in the industry.

This brings us to a sensitive and a potentially awkward subject. As you are working on enhancing your connectivity in the sector, it is very important to keep in mind what may motivate the people you meet to spend their time with you. Sometimes your relationship will be very clear as some industry participants will work with you only on a retained basis and get an hourly or daily rate for their services. At other times, however, some experts may be talking to you as a gesture of goodwill. Why? Some of them might simply want recognition as a sector authority and an industry spokesperson. Others might be genuinely interested in your work and will, from an investor's point of view, find your insights educational. Finally, there will be some people who will hope to monetize their relationship with your fund in the future, either as retained advisers or members of an executive management team in a target company.

I was advised by my senior colleagues early in my career to approach industry and deal networking with caution and develop relationships as a two-way street. Even though I might be dealing with senior industry executives who know a lot more about the sector than I, I may still be able to provide them with something valuable—such as an important introduction, access to my network or our firm's take on the industry, provided that our insights are non-confidential. Sharing articles, exchanging views, organizing industry dinners or thematic away days at my firm have proven to be productive ways to keep in touch and ensure that my network remained active.

However, my colleagues maintained that I stay cautious throughout all of this. Why? Because it is important that my intentions remained completely transparent to the people assisting our fund. I needed to discern genuine goodwill from an expectation of immediate or future fees, especially those that had not been agreed upon or earned. In my personal experience (and in that of my peers), the only way to avoid a misunderstanding of this nature was to have an upfront conversation about how our fund worked with outside parties and enter into any written agreements fairly early in the project.

Finally, it is important to recognize that apart from getting truly valuable insights, your new network might provide you with information that is biased, speculative or outdated. Some industry participants may offer a perspective that is too narrow and rigid, driven by their subjective experience in the sector. Others may be so focused on their own visibility in the industry, talking to the press and other matters of personal prestige that they might lose sight of the fact that their sector views have long since become stale. For this reason, I recommend that you establish the credibility of your new contacts early on and verify some of their views with a couple of alternative sources of information. This is a good way to ensure that people entering your network are knowledgeable, thoughtful and can serve as trustworthy sources in your quest to develop proprietary insights into an industry.

5. Establish a long list of potential deal targets and initiate coverage of these companies

The real action starts now! It is time to revisit the market map of the key players in the industry you created in step three. What companies on this list could be viable deal targets? Are you aware of any deal catalysts that could facilitate a private equity transaction? As I mentioned before, some companies will be on your list for benchmarking purposes only because they may be too large, publicly listed or already subject to recent private equity activity. Your objective at this stage is to review the market map thoughtfully and create a list of possible deal targets, some of which might consider a private equity investment in fairly short order and some of which will need to be converted into transactions over a period of time. It is a great idea to keep this inventory of deal ideas confidential and not mention any of the companies to anyone outside your firm in order to avoid leaking your proprietary ideas to the competition.

Now is a good time to become more familiar with the companies on your list. The only problem is that they don't yet know that you are looking at them, so you will have to initiate an in-depth coverage of these companies from your desk. Set up alerts that capture valuable information, such as financial reporting, regulatory filings, public statements, press releases, interviews and comments in business and trade journals. Analyze the presence of these companies on the internet and on social media platforms, especially if they operate in a consumer-facing sector. There are data analytics tools that can help you monitor and systematize vast amounts of data, such as the number of posts, quality ratings and customer reviews. If you need help in this domain, there are specialized firms who can provide social media monitoring and who will alert you of any meaningful spikes in traffic.

What are you looking for exactly? You need to stay abreast of any latest corporate developments and watch out for what Teten and Farmer (2010) aptly define as "deal signals." These are trigger events that might make the company more receptive to accepting an investment from a private equity firm. They include any signs of instability affecting the corporation in the following areas:

- *Shareholders:* parent company in distress, fighting off a take-over approach, private equity owner seeking an exit, large enterprises selling non-core divisions and any subsequent events following "death, disease, divorce," especially in family-owned businesses.
- *Leadership:* changes in strategic direction, succession battles, resignations and new appointments in the top management team or at board level.
- *Company performance:* rapid growth that cannot be sustained with internal cash generation, production bottlenecks, large capital expenditure needs, persistent underperformance, excessive leverage or limited access to debt sources, or inability to exploit growth opportunities without additional capital.
- *Industry developments and pronounced structural shifts:* industry consolidation or disruption, increasing rivalry among key competitors, new sources of pressure from customers or suppliers and any significant macro shifts creating the pockets of "economic turbulence" discussed earlier.

6. Rank the companies by attractiveness and approach two or three potential deal targets at a time

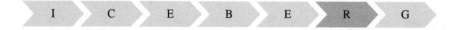

The time has come to start reaching out to the most promising prospects. By now you have hopefully spent enough time on desktop research of the companies on your deal target list and learned many noteworthy up-to-date facts about them. What's the best way to begin outreach? First of all, you will need to rank all companies in your deal inventory list: your top targets will be those businesses that feature the most obvious deal catalysts and represent the best fit with your investment thesis. Next, you will need to choose two or three top targets for your initial outreach. Why so few? Because reaching out to companies in a thoughtful and professional manner is time-consuming: you will need to craft a compelling initial message for each target and ensure that you follow up in an organized way. My advice is to start slow and add more deal targets only when you have fully exhausted the first few so that you are working on no more than two or three leads at any given time.

How do you contact companies? If there is no obvious way in through your firm's existing network and no possibility of a warm introduction by one of the industry experts you know, then the only way to make contact is through a cold call. Most private equity professionals feel nervous even thinking about cold calling, let alone going through with it. Unless you did door-to-door sales during your school years, you might have the same reaction to cold calling too. After all, most of us have developed a stigma toward irritating spammers and telemarketers, and none of us are in any rush to join their ranks.

As humans, we also suffer from fear of rejection: when you make your first contact with managers of a company you know only through desktop research, there is a considerable chance that they will decline your request for a meeting. If they are inundated with cold calls, they might even make you feel bad about yourself for trying to solicit their attention. What then? It is good to remember that cold calling is an effective, time-tested strategy and that some private equity firms really excel at it. There are a few funds, such as TA Associates and Summit Partners, who manage to differentiate themselves in the crowded private equity middle market by pursuing prolific cold calling programs that involve making unsolicited calls to literally thousands of companies every year.[5]

It is certainly possible to make cold calling a success and design a more palatable process for everyone involved, even if you are the type of a person who cringes at the thought of cold calling. Below are my suggested steps to maximize a positive outcome from an unsolicited approach:

- *Prepare a compelling message.* Review your research about the company and take note of any unique challenges that it is facing. If the owners of the company were to accept your investment, what do you think they might be using the capital for? What need do they have at an enterprise level that your fund can resolve? Once you have had an opportunity to reflect, prepare a creative and persuasive pitch that is specific to this business.

---

[5]Kevin Landry, the CEO of TA Associates, gave an interview in 2013 that appeared in the *Private Debt Investor*'s article titled "Cold Call Captain." He explained his firm's cold calling philosophy and provided a couple of interesting facts: at that time, his firm worked through a database of 280,000 companies and his team made unsolicited calls to over 8,000 businesses a year.

- *Do not call on the phone, write a letter.* To maximize the success of your first contact with the company, you need to choose an approach that will make you stand out. In my view, there is no better way to do so than by sending a well-written letter that introduces your fund, demonstrates your thorough knowledge of the business, showcases your industry expertise and outlines the strategic rationale of working with your fund. The person reading the letter should immediately understand how partnering with your fund can help the company resolve its pressing needs and bring clear strategic benefits.
- *Approach a decision maker at the company.* Make sure that you are addressing a person in a decision-making capacity, such as a shareholder, chairman or the CEO. If your deal target is a division of a large enterprise, then you need to approach the most senior person in the corporate development department.
- *Get the letter signed by a decision maker from your fund.* You only get one chance to make the right first impression. The person reading your letter should feel that your approach is credible and made by a senior person with professional gravitas and decision-making capability. If your position lacks seniority, it is a good idea to get a senior partner from your fund to co-sign the letter as well.
- *Outline next steps.* You need to suggest a process that will follow your approach. It might be a good idea to mention at the end of the letter that your fund would appreciate an introductory meeting and that you will follow up with a phone call in one week's time.
- *Attack from several angles.* To make sure that your approach is successful in reaching the right person and is differentiated from those made by other parties, send your letter by registered mail or by courier. Follow up a few days later by sending your letter again via email. One week later, call the company to follow up and hopefully set up a meeting.

This detailed plan should help you stand out from other funds making unsolicited approaches that are too generic and not as well thought out as yours. In an ideal scenario, you will succeed in setting up a meeting with the company. However, in the majority of cases, things will not go exactly as you expect. The company might decline to meet or inform you that it is not for sale. Other targets will be open to a potential investment, but the timing may not match yours. Plan to approach several companies before the stars align and allow you to progress to the next step.

You should expect that maintaining contact with the prospective companies will take significant time and effort. One of the worst things you can do at this stage is fail to follow up with a potential deal target because you are distracted or busy. It is important to stay organized and take notes of the multiple touchpoints you have had with each company by phone and email. If one of your deal targets is not prepared to start a dialogue with you due to a timing issue, schedule a reminder in your calendar to get back in contact with them in due course. Make sure both parties understand what next steps are discussed, follow up as agreed and never lose a promising deal prospect.

7. Go visit companies to convert deal ideas into real transactions

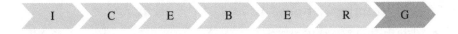

I   C   E   B   E   R   G

Now it is time to hit the road and meet companies in real life. This is the last step of the framework; however, you may find yourself having to repeat it over and over again, sometimes over a long period of time. The objective of this step is to make a strong connection with your deal target, learn more about its business and create actionable next steps that ultimately lead to a transaction. Since you have been evaluating the company only from the outside so far, it is difficult to predict where there might be vulnerabilities or mutual deal breakers. I recommend treading carefully: listen, observe, turn up your charisma to the max and be prepared to embrace your inner diplomat. It is worth keeping in mind that some of the company employees you will meet might feel anxious and uneasy about your visit, especially if they have limited experience dealing with investors. Be prepared to put them at ease.

Is there a wrong way to conduct your first meeting with the company? Yes, absolutely. In my experience, this happens when investors do not listen patiently enough to the company and prioritize their own needs over those of the deal target. For example, sometimes you just have to let the CEO veer off-topic for a period of time to avoid alienating him. Also, you have to suppress your inner desire to jump straight into clinical detail, even if you suspect potential deal breakers in these areas. As a rule, exploring recent strategic failures, asking pointed questions about the financials, or requesting a detailed data set are not appropriate actions at this stage. Stay away from sensitive topics and proprietary information, especially if you have not yet signed a confidentiality agreement. In summary, the first meeting with the company should not feel like an interrogation. It should feel like a friendly conversation between two likeminded parties forming a productive long-term partnership.

Is there a good template to follow for your first meeting with the company? Yes, absolutely. However, you need to go beyond private equity and look further afield into other areas where professional success stems from total mastery of communication and people skills. I personally found it useful to look into the field of sales. Yes, you read it right, sales. Many private equity investors are hesitant to admit that they are salespeople of their capital and value-added involvement in portfolio companies. They have to court companies, sometimes for years, to close a deal. That's not too dissimilar to what people do in sales, right? This is the logic that compelled me to investigate the techniques used by sales professionals and tone them down a few notches to make them appropriate for the more introspective field of private equity. Holmes (2007) provided a useful outline of key sales skills in his popular sales and marketing book. Let's take a look at these skills applied to the situation of a private equity investor meeting a promising deal target for the first time:

- *Create rapport.* Think about good ways to break the ice. A good starting point might be to mention topical industry news or congratulate the company on reaching a recent milestone. Focus on demonstrating empathy, having a sense of humor and, if appropriate, mirroring the attitude and tone of the people you are meeting.
- *Establish need.* What is the company's current positioning and what is its vision for the future? What are the most pressing needs and problems of the business? How can your capital help?
- *Build value.* This is an opportunity to introduce your fund, demonstrate your industry expertise and share your proprietary insights acquired through deep research. You need to come across as an empathetic and knowledgeable partner.
- *Create desire.* This is a good time to mention your fund's other relevant successful investments and explain how you were able to create tangible benefits for your portfolio companies. Provide enough detail about the issues faced by other businesses and describe how your fund was able to resolve them. Draw any meaningful parallels between your past investments and current situation.

- *Overcome objections.* Acknowledge any concerns that the company might have about accepting a private equity investment from your fund. Listen attentively and try your best to understand the company's perspective. Then isolate each objection and try to deal with one concern at a time. You might need to follow up with additional information after the meeting to strengthen your position.
- *Close.* One of the best possible outcomes of this meeting will be agreeing with the company on a set of actionable next steps. Hopefully, you managed to establish a strong bond with the management team and prepare a fertile ground for any subsequent follow-ups.

What happens next? There are three possible scenarios. The first one is that the initial meeting equipped you with enough disappointing information about the business to enable you to conclude that you are not interested in moving forward. In this case, it is best to thank the management team for their time, provide them with your honest feedback about why the company does not quite fit your mandate at present and discuss what business adjustments would be required for this decision to change in the future. The second scenario is that you like the business but you sense that the company will not be ready to accept a private equity investment for a considerable time. In this case, you need to make sure that you communicate your continued interest and schedule a follow-up meeting at some point in the future. I believe that keeping in touch with the company will allow you to build a good relationship with the management team over time and enable you to create enough neural pathways in their minds that might ultimately pave the way to a transaction with your fund.

The third and best scenario is that you like the business, and the company owners are ready to consider a potential investment from your fund. It means that the thematic sourcing approached worked and you are ready to start work on a new transaction, possibly even a proprietary one. Now is a good time to sign a confidentiality agreement and request enough information regarding company operations, business strategy, growth opportunities and financial performance to properly evaluate this investment opportunity.

Well, you have made it to the end of the ICEBERG Roadmap™. I know: it is a long and arduous journey to read through these 7 steps in detail. However, I believe that this framework (or your own adapted version thereof) will improve your deal sourcing approach and ability to deliver deals. Hopefully, proprietary ones.

3

Opportunistic Deal Sourcing

Key Topics in Chapter 3:

- Develop an edge in opportunistic deal sourcing with the DATA-BASE Roadmap™
- No luck required: why having a clear focus pays off in an opportunistic deal search
- Actions you can take now to get the most out of your professional network
- How active brand management can help your fund stay top of mind
- Creative ways to supplement your opportunistic deal ideas
- How to manage your deal origination workflows effectively and effortlessly
- Does a dedicated business development function work for everyone?

Developing an Edge in Opportunistic Deal Sourcing

Do you know what sourcing strategy is used by private equity professionals most often? I believe an overwhelming majority of all private equity transactions executed each year around the world are opportunistic. No matter what geography you look into, you are likely to observe a similar theme: private equity funds are expected to network with intermediaries, analyze pitchbooks and investment memoranda, attend company meetings and write numerous offer letters—all in hopes of executing a good deal. Some funds might develop a "deal angle," and some funds might not even do that—private equity professionals are under immense pressure to stay open-minded in an opportunistic environment.

Many funds choose to maximize their options by increasing the total number of investment opportunities they review every year. There is nothing wrong with this approach, provided you have enough time and bandwidth. Think about what takes up your resources: an average deal professional with a couple of years of private equity experience might amass over 1,000 industry-related connections. A good investment banker active in private equity transactions for at least a decade will probably have enough contacts to fill a large cruise ship. The people you meet professionally often seek to be in touch, send investment ideas, request meetings and, through various means, gently bombard you with vast amounts of information, only a small proportion of which might be relevant to your fund. Generally speaking, everyone in the private equity industry is reasonably well-connected, keen to get deals done and competing in a market with diminishing knowledge barriers. This makes the job of a private equity investor very difficult because the market is definitely overcrowded and information is overabundant.

How can you possibly gain an edge over your competition in this environment? How can you make sure that your opportunistic deal search is not just busy work, but a productive process with a good chance of uncovering a gem of an investment? Having spent considerable time thinking about it, I have settled on the two key factors that matter most. First, staying top of mind with your most relevant contacts, and second, getting the most out of your time by reviewing only relevant deals.

If you experience severe time constraints and are not able to dedicate resources at present to developing a systematic approach for finding opportunistic deals, you will vastly improve the quality of your opportunistic deal search by focusing on just these two areas. Spending time on relevant deals with relevant people should function as a powerful antidote to the intrinsic randomness of opportunistic transactions. Focus on these two things and see what happens. My guess is that you will cut through the noise in order to isolate only those deals that represent the best fit with your investment mandate.

And yet it is hard to see what can surpass a systematic deal sourcing approach if you are looking to build value for your franchise in the long term. Once you set the objective of generating a sustainable flow of high-quality opportunistic ideas, you have to invest some initial time and resources in order to lay a solid foundation.

DATABASE Roadmap™[1] for Opportunistic Deal Sourcing

So, how do you go about laying this foundation?

It depends on your starting point and your ambition. You are most likely to stick to the process that works for you in

---

[1] DATABASE Roadmap™ is a registered trademark of my company, Lavra Group Limited.

your specific circumstances and feels relatively effortless once it is set up. If you are looking for a general guide, consider the detailed framework below that I developed for an opportunistic deal search. I put this checklist together because I dislike chaos and frequently try to create order out of disarray. Below is my tried and tested recipe for taming the unpredictable force of opportunistic deal sourcing and improving deal search outcomes.

Opportunistic Deal Sourcing: DATABASE Roadmap™

Similar to the Thematic Deal Sourcing ICEBERG Roadmap™, this framework also has an acrostic name to help remember each step better: it is called an Opportunistic Deal Sourcing DATABASE Roadmap™. The steps are as follows:

D   A   T   A   B   A   S   E

1. **D**evelop a clear point of view about the kind of deals your fund wants to target.
2. **A**rticulate a concise and memorable message about your mandate.
3. **T**eam up with intermediaries who consistently add value.
4. **A**dd new relevant connections to your network.
5. **B**uild a strong brand.
6. **A**pply creative thinking to supplement your opportunistic deal flow.
7. **S**et-up a dedicated tech-enabled platform to manage your deal origination workflows.
8. **E**stablish a business development team fully devoted to deal sourcing.

This is not a prescriptive list. My objective is to provide you with just enough inspiration to create your own framework that incorporates your investment mandate and the inner workings of your firm. Let's start by going through each step in greater depth.

1. Develop a clear point of view about what kind of deals your fund wants to target

D   A   T   A   B   A   S   E

Opportunistic deal sourcing features an interesting paradox: in order to find more high-quality deals, you need to focus on fewer segments of the market. Cast your net wide, and you risk sinking in deal entropy of random sectors, business models, endless meetings and follow-ups.

When I started working in private equity, most large firms had a broad mandate that could roughly be described as follows: "We are sector agnostic investors looking to back market-leading companies with recurring revenue streams and sustainable margins led by experienced management teams with a proven track record. We like investing in companies with strong brands and solid customer relationships." Clearly, this acquisition strategy is too broad and would no longer be successful in today's significantly more competitive market.

It is far more effective to narrow your scope and cherry-pick the kind of deals your fund wants to do. What are some of the specific investment themes you have been developing? Is there a differentiated type of deal that your fund excels in? Do you have a good track record in a particular sector?

Ideally, you will focus on just a few investment niches where your firm has a strong competitive advantage, such as unique knowledge gained through existing investments, deep industry expertise or access to sector experts. If you work in a sector team, you might consider exploring specific subsectors within your industry. Once you have a clear point of view about what kind of deals you are targeting, stick to your investment focus and decline everything else coming your way.

By the way, I can tell you from my experience, this is a hard thing to do in practice. If you are intellectually curious or generally suffer from FOMO ("Fear of Missing Out"), it will take some effort to stay disciplined and not veer off your chosen focus.

2. Articulate a concise and memorable message about your mandate

Once you determine what type of deals you are targeting, your next challenge is to create a well-crafted message to share with a wide audience. You should try to convey two things: first, your specific investment focus, and second, why your firm is the best partner for this type of investment. Here is an example of a more pointed description of what a generalist private equity fund might target: "We are looking to invest \$50–100 million in businesses operating in the education, healthcare services or specialty chemicals sectors. Our firm has particular expertise in 'buy and build' strategies and taking portfolio companies to international markets." The mandate described here is brief yet quite distinct: it is limited to three specific industry categories and provides information about target deal size and potential value-add from the private equity fund.

If you are a member of a sector team, there is a good chance that you are covering a very large industry, like business services, technology, financial services or consumer. It might be more helpful to carefully think through and communicate to your network the investment niches within your broad sector that you are working on. For instance, rather than discussing your interest in transactions happening, say, in the consumer sector more generally, specify subsegments of interest, such as holiday parks, organic frozen food producers or manufacturers of ethical skincare products. Finally, aim to include specific and memorable details in your message about your fund's credentials in order to stand out.

3. Team up with intermediaries who consistently add value

Your next objective is to inform your existing network about what types of deals you are looking for and to stay top of mind with the people who might help you source opportunistic transactions.

Your fund has a whole ecosystem of advisers, such as bankers, consultants, industry experts or company executives. Not all of them are always helpful, however. Start by assessing your fund's existing network. Who are the top 10% of intermediaries close to your organization who consistently add value, either by introducing relevant transactions, providing differentiated insights, or keeping you up-to-date with industry developments? You might know the answer off the top of your head. Alternatively, your fund might operate a formal tracking system that allows you to evaluate the strengths and contributions of major service providers on a firmwide basis.

If this is not the case and you are interested in compiling a list of the most effective advisers, you can easily do it yourself by reviewing your pipeline in the last 24–36 months to see who made a material contribution to deal sourcing, industry analysis and transaction execution. Whatever method you choose, the final list should contain a manageable number of parties.

The next logical step is to reach out to all advisers on your list and schedule an update call or a meeting with them in the next few weeks. You can talk them through your current investment focus, provide examples of deals that might interest you and remind them of your fund's credentials in the industry sector that you are pursuing.

I typically follow-up with an email too, the point of which is not so much to thank them for their time (I do that too, in case you're wondering), but to provide them with three or four bullet points of information about the deals my team is targeting in the medium term. Effectively, this is an opportunity to broadcast the well-thought-out message you crafted in a previous step to a motivated audience. This summary can also double up as a useful reference for your contacts later, either to remind them what was discussed or even to forward it around to their colleagues and industry contacts. This approach will require an upfront investment of your own time, so it makes sense to contain it to a finite number of parties. I have found that this effort really helps to activate your firm's most valuable connections, leverage others to advocate for your mandate and create a virtuous cycle of new deal ideas, all of which are likely to have far more relevance than a random inbound transaction landing on your desk.

4. Add new relevant connections to your network

D   A   T   A   B   A   S   E

They say that success is not about what you know, but whom you know. But maybe it's actually about whom you do not know—at least not yet. Building a search network entails adding new connections that are relevant to your goal. According to Bruner (2004), networks reduce the cost of deal search and afford economies of scale and scope in your search efforts. Furthermore, networks provide a mechanism that helps you spread your message faster, as knowledge inevitably travels from one node to another in a well-functioning network. The nodes in our case are people who may have access to valuable information and potential deals. Metcalfe's Law,[2] which states that the value of a network is proportional to the number of working nodes in it, applies well in this instance. Based on this rationale, it makes sense for deal professionals to increase the number of working nodes by enhancing the diversity and breadth of their networks. Bruner (2004) asserts that professional connectivity is a form of social capital that should be cultivated as carefully as talent, financial capital, or physical property.

It sounds very convincing. But what are the concrete steps? You can start with these:

- *Analyze your firm's existing connections.* You have now had an opportunity to assess your firm's network and develop a list

---

[2]Robert Metcalfe, the inventor of Ethernet protocol for computer networks, stated that the usefulness of a telecommunications network is proportional to the square of the number of connected users of the system.

of the top 10% most valuable connections. What can you say about the rest of the network? Among the remaining 90%, are there parties who perhaps do not work closely with your fund at present, but potentially could provide you with access to markets that are relevant for your deal search? It makes sense to get closer to these intermediaries and educate them about your current investment focus.

- *Identify who you would like to meet and begin outreach.* Think about the gaps in your firm's network. What are the areas where you should aim to enhance your connectivity? Who can help you find relevant new opportunistic investments, given your current investment focus? Create a list of people and companies that you would like to meet. Determine how many degrees of separation are between you and work on gaining proximity to them. If you are looking for specific ideas for your outreach, it might be helpful to refer to my suggestions in Step 4 of the Thematic Deal Sourcing ICE-BERG Roadmap™.

- *Activate your "weak ties."* Chances are your best friend is unlikely to be able to introduce you to a good investment opportunity. That's because both of you probably operate in very similar environments and have an overlapping group of acquaintances, so you already know and experience a lot of what your friend does. However, more distant acquaintances are likely to operate in a completely different environment, have access to a totally new opportunity set and, therefore, present a valuable source of information.

It is especially worth mentioning the value of "weak ties" within your educational network, i.e. the people who went to the same university as you. Fuchs et al. (2017) conducted research investigating the role of educational networks in private equity by analyzing a data set of over 3,000 buy-out investments that were made in the United States and

Western Europe between 1984 and 2010. The conclusion is very interesting: not only do educational ties exist in 15% of buyout deals in this data set, but they also seem to improve the odds of a fund winning a deal by 79%.[3] Educational networks appear to serve as a productive source of deal origination and may provide easier deal access and a degree of exclusivity for funds sharing an educational connection with a target company.

- *Join new and relevant professional interest groups.* Given that you have a clear idea of what types of deals you are looking for, consider joining communities that will enrich and strengthen your ability to find them. Aim to broaden your social contacts by becoming a member of relevant trade associations, curated industry networks and online platforms, where you can connect with relevant people or get more insights into your target market. Use every opportunity to broadcast a clear message to your network about what deals you are looking for and then rely on Metcalfe's Law to work its magic.

5. Build a strong brand

D   A   T   A   B   A   S   E

We see brands everywhere. Does a private equity fund need active brand management? If the goal is to be top of mind, then most definitely yes. If your fund has a superb investment track

---

[3]The effect is strong for acquisitions of private companies but not for public-to-private transactions. This appears to make sense because private companies generally have more control over the choice of their acquirer.

record, your firm will be top of mind without any marketing efforts on your part. LPs will be lining up to make an investment in your latest fund, sellers of businesses will approach your fund directly, and there will be no shortage of qualified job applicants. People want to associate themselves with top firms in order to maximize the likelihood of their own success.

What if your fund's track record is broadly comparable to that of many other firms? Or, what if you work for a new fund? Then, a serious marketing endeavor might be in order. After all, your brand needs to be recognized and respected by those people most likely to help you with opportunistic deal search. Brand sets expectations, and it is important to differentiate and strengthen your company's external image. How do you do that? My guess is that it will be hard to execute in-house without hiring a brand agency with experience in financial services.

It's difficult to find research on trends in private equity branding. The only brand study I could find that is specifically related to the private equity industry is a survey published in 2017 by a financial marketing firm, BackBay Communications. It has useful insights about brand management, rebranding activities and effective marketing communication in the private equity industry. This study inspired me to look around and think about how the private equity firms that I know well stay top of mind in their markets. Here is a list of my observations:

- *Corporate website.* Private equity funds use every opportunity to communicate their history, investment approach and differentiated value-add on their website. It becomes increasingly more common to include fairly rich and highly specific content with insights about particular sectors, interviews with investment professionals and investment case studies about closed transactions.

- *Social media.* Even the most conservative funds with a global footprint, such as KKR and Carlyle, use social media to promote their brand through news updates, podcasts, blogs and video recordings.[4] It is easy to keep up to date with the latest investments, exits and fund closings.
- *Thought leadership.* Many private equity firms seek to showcase their expertise by distributing internally generated research, such as specialist whitepapers, in-depth commentary on financing trends, or deal flow analyses. This is an additional outlet for raising awareness, staying top of mind and connecting with the professional community.

6. Apply creative thinking to supplement your opportunistic deal flow

D A T A B A S E

We have already discussed a number of important ways for you to leverage the resources you can access. Now it's time to get creative in your search for opportunistic deals. Thinking outside the box can generate imaginative strategies to enhance your deal flow. Here are a few ideas to help you get started:

- *Second-order insights from your portfolio companies.* Your fund's existing portfolio represents not only a valuable asset base but also a prolific source of new deal ideas. As a private equity owner, your fund has unique access to first-hand intelligence about industries and operating models of your portfolio

---

[4]True as of March 2019.

companies. You can exploit this privileged knowledge by examining each portfolio company's strategic positioning and determining potential winners in its value profit chain. For example, do any of your portfolio companies' customers or suppliers look attractive as potential standalone investments? What other second-order insights can you derive from information about your portfolio companies?

- *Second-order insights from recent private equity activity.* Learn from your business environment as much as possible and generate your own insights from other people's deals. Look for notable transactions done by your direct competition. Can you apply the same investment thesis to a different sector or a new geography? Can you replicate any transactional breakthroughs, such as an innovative deal structure or a new financing instrument, to generate new investment opportunities in your market?

- *Second-order effects of M&A transactions.* Keep track of the M&A activity that is relevant to your market, including mega-deals involving large diversified conglomerates. Following the initial deal euphoria, the merged entity will take some time to satisfy any antitrust conditions, generate synergies and fulfill, or fail to fulfill, the strategic rationale of the business combination. Watch out for any disposals that might come out of the merged business and could be of interest to your fund as potential investments.

- *Deal renaissance.* This is a fancy expression for revisiting "dead" deals. Are you aware of any recent failed initial public offerings, broken auctions or unsuccessful private placements? Are you reviewing your own deal pipeline regularly to go over any old deals that your fund declined in the last 36 months because the companies were too small or too weak as investment targets? Focus on the most interesting companies on this list and try to think hard about potential ways to improve the investment thesis and turn these companies into compelling deal targets. For example, is it possible to manage investment risks by changing the structure of a transaction? Can you find an experienced manager who can lead and deliver an operational improvement plan at a target company? You might find that some dead deals are not as lifeless as they seem and are worth reviving.

- *Backing talent in your executive network.* Keep in touch with all impressive industry experts, operating executives and CEOs whom you admire for their vision, managerial skills, leadership and insight. There are numerous ways to stay top of mind in the absence of a live transaction, such as exchanging views on a particular sector, organizing thematic events or getting together informally. Make sure the executives in your network are aware of your investment focus and your enthusiasm about working with them on a transaction. You never know, one of them might call you up with a deal idea some day.

- *Discovering unconventional partners.* Are there any family offices, pension funds, sovereign wealth funds, multilateral institutions, fundless sponsors or other investment groups active in your private equity ecosystem? Spend time getting to know these investors and offering your knowledge, network and capital in exchange for access to their deal flow. While it is a less common strategy, consider forming a strategic joint venture with a corporation, either on a particular investment or a thematic strategy. Also, to the extent national or local governments own a stake in an attractive business in the market that you know well, position your fund as a value-added partner with strong functional expertise and explore potential options of working together.

- *Embracing distress.* Does the investment mandate allow your fund to be a white knight who can help out a company during troubled times? If so, you may find it useful to build connections with bank work-out departments, bankruptcy lawyers, restructuring teams at accounting firms and executors of estate assets. Set up alerts to inform you of all business news in your area of focus relating to companies that are reviewing strategic options, appointing administrators, negotiating to restructure or dealing with shareholders in financial trouble.

7. Set-up a dedicated digital platform to manage your deal origination workflows

We are fortunate to live during times of easy access to technology. When I started my career in finance, my colleagues and I thought our internal processes were quite high-tech: any paper documents were scanned immediately and virtually all of our workflows were backed up electronically. However, we operated a number of completely autonomous systems consisting of numerous spreadsheets, email messages, calendar entries and contact databases. While each team member was handling vast amounts of data, there was no easy way to connect various knowledge silos in order to inform our firmwide strategy. Integrating data was time-consuming and required cumbersome manual effort. These work processes were not considered unusual at the time, with most other funds facing the same challenges.

Luckily, legacy systems are being gradually replaced by powerful digital platforms that connect information from various sources quickly and seamlessly. Your fund is most likely already employing an integrated technology-enabled solution that allows you to optimize your workflows and access crucial information quickly. If this is not the case, you might want to raise this issue at your organization as a matter of priority: digital platforms provide significant operational efficiency and require relatively little human or financial capital. Learn to use and understand in detail the functionality of the technology platform that your firm has so that you can manage all your deal origination workflows digitally in order to enhance your productivity. What goals should you seek to accomplish? In my experience I have found several areas where digital tools can provide a competitive advantage:

- *Deal pipeline analytics.* Capturing historical and current deal flow allows you to analyze transactions by deal origination source, calculate conversion ratios and benchmark the number of deals you see against transactions done in the broader market over a period of time. You can also garner strategic insights from analyzing what areas of your activity create the most value over time. How many companies did you screen and how many deals were selected for further due diligence? How many deals got executed and closed? What were the common traits of successful transactions? Who are the intermediaries who consistently make a positive contribution to your deal origination process?
- *Transaction tracking.* Once you begin developing a deal lead or work on a live transaction, it is helpful to have one easily accessible place that keeps track of the current deal status and next steps. All your electronic notes can be tagged appropriately to make them searchable. You may decide to add any relevant documents, emails, meeting notes and latest updates on the transaction to ensure that your entire deal team has access to the same up-to-date information.

- *Relationship management.* This is a good place to keep your network of contacts and track your conversations, emails and meeting notes with them. You can leverage your relationships better if you log a history of your most valuable contacts, from how you met to their current industry position and previous roles. Record their contributions to your firm and set up future reminders alerting you to follow up with them at an appropriate time to keep your network active.
- *Knowledge repository.* This is very much an optional feature. To the extent your fund does not operate a firmwide information hub where teams can exchange insights or share industry reports, it might be appropriate to create a dedicated place for this kind of activity to live on the same platform. Integrating various knowledge silos across the entire organization, or at least across your team, provides you with a distinctive information advantage that will help you stand out from your competition.

8. Establish a business development team fully devoted to deal sourcing

Is your team busy around the clock with live deal executions? Do you feel like you are dropping in and out of the private equity marketplace and sometimes unable to follow up on some of the potential transactions that require an effort of being developed and nurtured? Do you operate in a market that is fiercely competitive, with numerous buyers vying for the same investment opportunities? If any of the above applies to your fund, there might be impending limits to your organization's ability to expand and accelerate its deal sourcing capabilities. It would definitely benefit you to consider establishing a dedicated business development function fully devoted to deal sourcing.

How to go about doing so is largely dependent on your fund's mandate and operating style. Let's review some options that exist in the private equity industry.

Firms operating in the growth equity sector and lower mid-market typically have to contact and follow up with several hundred potential deal targets every year in order to convert just a few of them into executed transactions. Given the sheer scale of the required deal sourcing effort, establishing a dedicated business development team is probably the best way to allocate organizational resources. Illustrative of this approach are the previously discussed business models of TA Associates and Summit Partners, which employ junior professionals to pursue high-volume cold calling programs. Another example is that of a growth equity firm, The Riverside Company, that has a dedicated deal origination team of nearly 20 professionals covering the firm's global investment mandate from offices on various continents. One point of differentiation, however, is that the majority of deal originators at Riverside are seasoned finance professionals. They possess the business experience and internal influence to enable a prompt and thorough transaction review before it is passed to the execution team.

Business development teams can be quite effective in large generalist funds, especially those operating in developed markets. From what I have seen in the private equity markets, once the investment team at a typical fund exceeds about 30 people, there is a tendency toward greater specialization, both by sector and by functional expertise. There are several solutions that a generalist fund might employ at this stage to enhance its deal origination capabilities.

One possibility is hiring young, bright and dynamic origination professionals who will be tasked with thinking creatively about unexploited investment niches, identifying new deal targets and ensuring timely deal follow-up. Another approach would be to designate a senior partner who will champion the deal origination strategy for the fund and make it an institutional priority across the firm.

The involvement of an experienced partner with authority and gravitas can be an effective mechanism for motivating the entire investment team to engage in deal sourcing. Greater emphasis on deal origination efforts will encourage the investment team to bring to completion the mundane yet unavoidable parts of the successful sourcing process, such as deal tracking and scheduled follow-up meetings with deal targets, even during the busiest times for the firm.

There are instances, however, in which an internal business development function may not be an appropriate solution. Private equity funds that operate in emerging markets tend to focus on finding great businesses in a riskier geography: for this mandate, a sector-agnostic approach in which all deal professionals actively filter through investment ideas might make the most sense. Similarly, investment professionals at deep sector specialist funds with unique expertise might find it difficult to outsource deal origination in their specialized industry to an internal business development team and are most likely to resort to finding deals themselves or enlisting industry experts for help.

No matter what the circumstances of your fund may be, the point of this discussion is to encourage you to keep up to date with the fluid landscape of business development best practices in the private equity industry in order to stay ahead of your competition.

Good news! We have now reached the end of the DATA-BASE Roadmap™. You're probably wondering who on Earth has time to go through every step described in the framework? I get asked this question often and the honest answer is nobody. But if nobody really does the whole thing, what is the point of considering every step? Here is what I think. The goal you should set for yourself is to do more than your direct competitors and at all times aim to be a few steps ahead of them. The objective of your job is to find practical ways to attain a competitive advantage. It can mean different things in practice. If you, like most of us, operate in a fiercely competitive private equity market, your best bet is to learn what best practices look like and incorporate as many of them as possible in your day-to-day deal sourcing activities in order to derive maximum benefit from your opportunistic deal sourcing process.

4

Deal Selection— Eliminating the Wrong Deal

Key Topics in Chapter 4:

- Why killing deals is as important as doing deals
- How skilled investors overcome biases and minimize investment errors
- Why the best investment of your career might be a deal you never pursue
- Nine deal breakers you need to check for before proceeding on any deal

---

Introduction to the Deal Selection Process

The earlier chapters of the book presented my thoughts on thematic and opportunistic deal sourcing. I hope that, regardless of whether you learned anything new from the first three chapters, your own deal origination process is prolific, and going to work feels like drinking from the horn of plenty. I can, therefore, think of no better way to begin this chapter than to share my views on how to kill deals. That's right. Working on an abundance of investment opportunities is hardly sustainable: as soon as you become a successful deal originator, you develop a vital need for rapid deal elimination. You may remember my comment in Chapter 1 about having had to review over 100 deals every year with the hope of bringing only one to completion. As it turns out, my experience is not too different from that of others in the private equity industry.

Gompers et al. (2016) studied the investment process of 79 private equity investors with combined assets under management of over $750 billion. Among other things, the research examined the deal funnel experience of these private equity funds. The authors conclude that for every 100 opportunities considered, the average fund investor deeply investigates fewer than 24, signs an agreement with fewer than 14 and closes on only six. This suggests to me that private equity investors find themselves in the business of eliminating deals a lot more often than in the business of bringing them across the finish line.

How do you know, then, which deals to kill and which ones to progress? What represents a better investment: a company in an exciting fast-growing market but with a mediocre management team, or the one in a traditional mature industry but with an opportunity to back a stellar CEO? Private equity professionals are paid a lot of money for their work because, in truth, the answer to this question is complex.[1] Deals have many intricate characteristics that may not be readily comparable to one another. Here is a good analogy that I once heard at a dinner party: starting to evaluate private equity deals is similar to

---

[1] If in doubt, buy the cheaper business.

being a novice spectator in a pole vaulting competition. When you see the first athlete, you get excited and impressed by the skill. When you see the second athlete, you wonder—unless the height hasn't been cleared—if he or she is better than the first one. And so on. It takes a lot of practice to determine who, indeed, is the best. After seeing hundreds of pole vaulters, you probably know exactly who will make the Olympic team. Similar logic applies to deal selection: practice makes perfect and one needs to go through hundreds of potential deal ideas in order to identify the best investments for the Olympic team, which—in this instance—is your fund.

I always found it very difficult not to get overly excited about deals. This was especially true early on in my career. I was very fond of Monday morning meetings at my first full-time private equity job: as I was just at the beginning of my private equity journey, I found it fascinating to hear my more experienced colleagues present new investment ideas for our fund's deal pipeline. Every potential transaction had a number of merits: here is a cash-generative technology infrastructure business for sale and there is a hotel chain with a terrific brand name finally talking to financial investors. I was sitting very quietly at these Monday morning meetings yet inside I was completely consumed by an adrenaline rush. I felt flattered that our fund had so many wonderful deal opportunities to choose from and thought that our investment team needed to give all of these great ideas an appropriate degree of consideration. Wrong.

Emotions are the enemy of investing: they distort sensible business logic and impair sound decision-making. Instead of feeling flattered by our pipeline, I should have thought about whether each deal on the list was cheap enough to represent good value for our LPs. However, human judgment is often flawed and investors are prone to succumbing to all sorts of biases. They can fall in love with their own investment ideas (affect heuristic), weigh one specific piece of information in their analysis too heavily (anchoring), or specifically seek information to confirm their initial perception rather than challenge it (confirmation bias). These are just a few examples. Experts in behavioral decision research and authors of *Judgment in Managerial Decision Making*, Bazerman and Moore (2009), identified and explained many more cognitive biases that arise in a business context of any organization on a daily basis. I certainly wasn't alone in experiencing overtly human reactions to investing.

Stephen Schwarzman painted a vivid image in his memoir about how Blackstone lost its entire equity in Edgcomb Steel—which was the firm's third-ever investment—due to errors in human judgment and lack of a systematic investment process (Schwarzman, 2019). While, in Schwarzman's own words, the investment was "disastrous," it served as a positive catalyst for Blackstone to establish a solid quality control over the fund's investment decisions by removing emotions and making the investment process more inclusive, consistent and de-personalized. While having an irrational response to an investment proposition is very common for human beings, good investors are skilled in making their decision-making fairly dispassionate in order to minimize investment errors.

And that's exactly what Bazerman and Moore (2009) suggest for optimum decision-making: determine the most important principles that ought to guide your thought process and create an analytical procedure that you can systematically follow in order to de-bias your judgment. According to Kahneman (2015), a Nobel-prize winning behavioral scientist and author of *Thinking, Fast and Slow*, this will allow you to switch off your brain from an intuitive thinking (System 1)—often fast, effortless and emotional—to reflective thinking (System 2), which is slower, deliberate and logical. Ideally, unhurried, intentional and effortful thinking should be used for all important decisions, including investing.

In private equity deal selection, therefore, it makes sense to shut down System 1 brain altogether in order to avoid my mistake of generating a response driven by adrenaline and emotion. Instead, System 2 brain should conduct the majority of the deal selection process. This is done by developing a framework of clear investment criteria and then testing each investment opportunity against these principles with a cool head in a deliberate and disciplined manner. This process will enable investors to overcome biases, cut through the marketing glamour of pitchbooks[2] and create a mechanism for benchmarking deals one against another through a standardized process. The latter is especially useful for generating a record of your deal evaluation outcomes for each potential transaction and tracking how your investment judgment muscle strengthens over time.

A record of standardized deal evaluation can also come in handy for conducting a *postmortem* analysis: if you miss a good deal and your competitor ends up making money on the investment, your boss will probably ask you why you passed on that transaction. You may even get a call from an LP in your fund, if the deal you missed was particularly successful and made all the papers. Your best defense is your investment discipline. If you are organized enough with your deal evaluation records, you will easily be able to revisit your logic and thought process

---

[2]Interpreting investment banking language in investment pitchbooks is a skill of its own. Rick Rickertsen, a private equity deal practitioner and the author of *Buyout* (2001), compiled an amusing list of investment banking jargon most frequently encountered by private equity professionals in the context of deal marketing. My favorites include translating references to a "cyclical industry" as the business "posting a huge loss last year," "long selling cycle" as "yet to find a customer who likes the product" and "entrepreneurial CEO" as "totally uncontrollable, bordering on maniacal." Full list is available online on the author's website (http://www.buyoutbook.com/bb_excerpts3.html).

to determine whether there was an error of judgment on your part, or whether your competitor just got lucky. Hopefully, it is the latter.

A successful deal selection process enables investors not only to identify winners, but also to avoid losers. One of the wisest and most intimidating investment committee members at my first private equity fund used to say, "Sometimes the best deal in your private equity career is the one you never pursue." I agree. Frankly speaking, apart from completing successful private equity deals, I was also a part of deal teams that made loss-making investments. Most firms invest in 10–15 transactions in any one fund. Depending on the average deal size and overall portfolio return, just one unsuccessful investment is capable of detracting from the overall fund return at least a couple of valuable percentage points. In the absence of very high returns from other deals, just one investment loss can push your whole fund into a lower performance quartile.

And that's the deal that, in hindsight, you wish you had never completed. There are several high-profile transactions in the global private equity industry that gained notoriety for producing the biggest losses of all time. It is a blessing in disguise for those private equity executives who viciously competed for these transactions but—for one reason or another—couldn't complete them and inadvertently avoided disastrous investments. These transactions certainly represent a notable highlight in their career as the best deals they have missed.

Now that the need for an effective deal screening tool is beyond doubt, where should you start? There are a couple of deal selection processes already described in the private equity literature: if you have time, I recommend looking into Finkel and Greising (2010), Rickertsen and Gunther (2001), or Walton and Roberts (1992), who all share their useful templates for deal evaluation. My own approach to deal selection was heavily influenced by Bain Capital's then Head of Europe, Dwight Poler and Professor Eli Talmor, who co-taught my first private equity class at business school. These two prominent teachers succeeded in instilling a logical framework in my brain—one I can still visualize after many years—that allows an investor to evaluate and benchmark deals against one another.

As years went by, I managed to accumulate my own experience of evaluating private equity transactions. I found it easier and quicker to sift the deal pipeline in two stages. First, I screen for instant deal breakers (nine, to be precise) that would allow me to eliminate an investment opportunity on the spot. This saves me a lot of time, as I do not need to perform a detailed analysis on a transaction that I already know simply won't work. Second, I evaluate all those deals that do not have instant deal breakers by using a standardized approach and the same set of investment criteria (see Chapter 5). By using a systematic framework, I can wave goodbye to deal adrenaline, bring rationality back into my decision-making, suppress my inherent human biases and dispassionately determine what potential investments represent the best fit for the fund.

Eliminating the Wrong Deal Through Negative Screening

The rest of this chapter will focus on how to spot instant deal breakers and promptly eliminate potential losers from your deal pipeline. I call this process *negative screening* because I am looking for serious weaknesses in each transaction. If I find one, I can stop caring about any merits of the transaction. Going back to my earlier pole-vaulting analogy, these deals are akin to athletes who simply do not clear the bar and, therefore, are definitely not going to the Olympics.

In my experience, every potential transaction needs to be checked for the most common potential deal breakers that might arise in nine different areas. Let's go through them one by one.

- *Breach of an investment mandate.* It sounds rather obvious that every investment your fund pursues should fit its stated investment mandate. But sometimes there are shades of gray, and it is not quite that simple to achieve in practice. On more than one occasion, I found myself spending way too much time on a deal that represented a tilt—ever so slight—from my fund's investment objective. For example, sometimes I would consider younger companies seeking growth capital, even though my fund's mandate dictated to invest only in mature businesses that are suitable for an LBO. In almost every case, I fell under the spell of an exceptionally charismatic and driven owner/CEO, who was great at convincing my team that provided our fund invests now, in a mere 12 months his business would fit our investment criteria exactly. You might have guessed already that we ended up walking away from every single one of these opportunities, having wasted multiple days on doing unnecessary work.

    I suggest that you avoid repeating my mistakes. Be disciplined about sticking to your investment mandate exactly in terms of investment stage, deal structure, sector and geography. Check your fund's investment limits for every investment from every possible angle. Do you work for a technology fund that is unusually successful in investing in semiconductor companies? Make sure that a new semiconductor investment does not end up producing an overly concentrated portfolio for your fund or introduce a conflict of interest with the existing portfolio businesses. Are you investing in companies operating across Europe and wondering whether you can invest in a company with significant exposure to

Belarus? Apart from evaluating your fund's risk tolerance of conducting business in Belarus, check your fund's legal documentation to see how Europe is defined and what exclusions there may be in terms of making investments outside of that definition.

- *Challenging geography.* The point above brings us neatly to the wider considerations of country exposure. Every time you evaluate a new transaction, it pays to check all geographies relevant to this deal. For a typical investment, there are several geographical angles one might have to consider. What is the company's country of incorporation? Where does the business operate? What are the locations of its key customers and suppliers? Where does the company labor force work from? While some funds are specifically raised to invest in emerging and frontier markets, many other institutional investors will find it too risky to invest in countries known for their weak corporate governance practices, inadequate legal systems and underdeveloped capital markets. It also makes sense to check the business that you are analyzing for any possible connections to sanctioned states, such as Iran, Cuba or Venezuela.

  Over a decade ago, my team spent several weeks working on a potential investment in what seemed like a very solid commercial bank operating in a perfectly legitimate EU country. Can you think of the worst thing a commercial bank can do? One day, we stumbled upon the fact that the bank had recently closed its small office located in Nauru. This baffling past link of a credible financial organization to the tiny Micronesian island country—pleasantly sunny yet sanctioned at that time for its money laundering practices— led us to drop this deal instantly.

- *Industry concerns.* Some investments should be rejected on the basis of their sector alone. As a rule, the industry subsector in which you are making an investment should have good

prospects and stand on a solid footing for at least the next
10–15 years. Why? Apart from supporting your own investment thesis, there should be plenty of room for another
investor, who will be buying the company from you at exit,
to construct a viable investment thesis 5–7 years down the
line. Sir Ronald Cohen, the founder of Apax Partners, aptly
called this concept "the second bounce of the ball" and wrote
a book with the eponymous title. Also, avoid any sectors with
poor structural characteristics, no pricing power, few barriers
to entry or those that you suspect might be in permanent
decline. Finally, I suggest that you avoid any industry that
you believe is likely to remain small or serve a highly specific
niche of customers.

- *Small investment.* Be firm and say no to small deals. I am guilty
  of not following this rule for the bulk of my early career, so
  I hope you will hear me out. Avoid spending more than a
  few minutes of your time and getting entangled into transactions—no matter how attractive—that are simply not large
  enough for your fund. It took me a long time to figure out
  that making investments that are too small is a highly inefficient use of my fund's financial and human capital.

  Here is an example. As a young investor hungry to source
  an attractive transaction and make an impact on my fund, I
  once fell in love with what I thought was a small and beauti-
  ful casual dining business. The company was unusually resilient because it operated multi-brand restaurants that were
  situated in the locations with extremely high footfall, such
  as airports and train stations. Since its existing shareholders
  lacked capital, the company was constrained in its growth
  and further restaurant openings. Somehow the business was
  not on the radar of other investors and I managed to build a
  good relationship with the management team.

I thought that my idea of backing a highly accomplished incumbent management team in a $300 million buyout was a brilliant one. The slight problem, however, was that my firm had over $20 billion under management at that time and was looking to invest in transactions with an equity investment of $400 million or more. The transaction that I was analyzing required slightly above $100 million of equity. But surely it will produce a high return, and our equity at exit will be worth at least $300 million? I did not take into consideration the fact that deal execution and monitoring costs are likely to be unusually high. Even for a small deal such as this one, our firm would use our usual group of advisers: a large and expensive law firm and one of the big accounting firms, to name but a few. Furthermore, this $100 million equity deal would require the same time for monitoring and exit as a multi-billion-dollar buyout.

I do not know what possessed me to spend more than 6 weeks on this deal and why my boss did not stop me earlier, but there you go. I wasted quite a bit of time on a deal that was too small. Then I did it again and again on a few other transactions. I hope I have convinced you not to do the same.

- *Recent loss in the same sector.* Every fund, sooner or later, experiences an investment loss. Has your fund had that misfortune yet? Avoid championing deals that are from the same industry, or have broadly similar characteristics, to the bad investment. As they say, "Never let an old flame burn you twice." If you recently joined a private equity fund, you will be doing yourself a favor by getting educated about the investment errors and unsuccessful deals of the past decade. Even if you believe that your firm has fully digested the loss-making event and fully learned from its mistakes, stay away from similar deals. Your fund's investment committee will probably be highly allergic to spending any time on anything reminiscent of an earlier investment embarrassment. There are probably quite a few investment professionals who had to spend many exasperating hours on irksome conversations with LPs explaining what went wrong in a bad deal. Since nobody in the fund will be in any rush to relive this experience, it is probably a good decision to drop any deals that will bring back bad memories.

- *Insufficient stake.* It is paramount that the stake that you get as an investor in a company as a result of a private equity transaction matches your desired degree of control over your investment. It is best to avoid any deals where you will end up with a minority stake but hope to behave like a majority investor. Even if the people on the other side of the negotiating table say that they will welcome your input irrespective of the size of your stake and your voting rights, my experience suggests that once the deal closes, very few people will let you throw your weight around beyond your entitlement as written in the legal agreements.

In my working life, I experienced being a private equity investor with vastly different degrees of ownership. In the very beginning of my career, I worked on LBOs where, excluding the management incentive plan, my firm had a stake of 100%. In majority control transactions, investors feel like masters of their own destiny. As you may hear in the jargon of the private equity industry, controlling investors "drive the bus." They have the ability to remove management, change company strategy, initiate a radical restructuring, pursue a major acquisition, sell the business or do many other things, whatever the circumstances might dictate as being the best course of action in the eyes of the controlling shareholder.

I also experienced being on the opposite end of the spectrum, as a deep minority investor with a stake in the business of less than 10%. To continue the earlier analogy, minority investors are "passengers on the bus." There is not much they can do, other than ascertain at the outset that they are fully aligned with the controlling shareholder and trust the management team to achieve the company's objectives. As a deep minority investor, you have virtually no influence on the company. If the majority shareholder decides to make changes that you do not approve of, such as firing the CEO or pursuing a dubious capital-intensive initiative, deep minority investors—other than voicing their concern—have to keep calm and carry on.

Larger minority stakes, typically upwards of 25%, provide investors with more oversight, a seat on the company's board of directors and significant negative control rights. However, even in these circumstances, the majority shareholder has greater influence on the company and, therefore, on the success of your investment. Hence, if you are looking to avoid disappointing investment outcomes, it makes sense to think carefully upfront whether the stake offered in any private equity deal is commensurate with the degree of control over the company that you and your fund will be comfortable with during the life of the transaction.

- *Reputational risk.* Stay away from any investments that might tarnish your firm's image. No matter how compelling the deal is and how great the investment return might be, it is always helpful to keep in mind your personal reputation in the private equity industry and your firm's long-term success. It is genuinely good to think about what kind of professional conduct will make your mother proud. Is it an obvious point? Then why are there so many corporate scandals, in and outside of private equity, that we read about every day? It is my strong suggestion to decline right away any deals where reputational issues might be at stake. This advice covers a very broad spectrum of situations that might detract from your firm's image, such as investing in companies in controversial industries, investment theses that rely on polluting the environment or firing the majority of employees, business operations featuring related-party transactions and shareholders or management with poor business conduct. It is best to seek transactions that will enable you to bring about lasting positive change and result in a rewarding experience for all parties, including your mother—by making her proud.

- *Insufficient time for deal execution and due diligence.* We have all been there. There is a frantic phone call, typically from an agitated intermediary, informing you of a remarkable, "once-in-a-lifetime" investment opportunity in a great business. There is a slight problem, however. There are only three weeks left to execute this transaction, or else the deal is off. Then you typically hear a flattering remark. For example, you are told that you are the preferred party due to your firm's ability to move quickly and its unrivalled expertise in the sector where the company in question operates. Are you up for this challenge, or are you going to lose the best deal of this decade and let your LPs miss out on a good return?

  In my opinion, the best course of action in this situation is to walk away. Even if it means potentially letting the LPs down, as you will be doing them a favor by sticking to your ironclad investment discipline. Private equity investing is a complex field involving numerous analyses and elaborate processes that require time and attention to detail. I am happy to let my LPs miss a good deal, if my team and I won't be able to ensure a high-quality investment process, free of unnecessary adrenaline and hubris. I don't want to get caught up in the heat of a deal. While every private equity investor is different, I personally need at least 8 weeks to execute each investment opportunity[3] and be able to consider every aspect of the deal. It is my strong preference to have adequate time to be able to assemble an effective deal team, appoint suitable deal advisers and obtain thoughtful feedback from the investment committee. The gestation period of a deal could be potentially shortened to 6 very stressful weeks in exceptional circumstances. However, that's the absolute limit for me. I would struggle to convince myself and others to risk our LPs' capital for the sake of what is destined to be a "half-baked" transaction.

- *Too many things need to go right.* Have you ever come across a transaction in which the base case return relies on five different drivers, all of which need to materialize during your fund's ownership? For example, a company might need to integrate a recent acquisition, build an additional manufacturing facility, enter a new market, upgrade its IT platform and hire a new CEO to oversee all of these initiatives. Assuming that each task in isolation has a 75% probability of success, the overall chance that all five will go right is less than 25%. That's obviously an insufficient headroom for a base case return. On that basis, it is better to stick to deals where there are only 2–3 major yet realistic objectives that need to be achieved to produce a successful investment outcome.

This completes the list of the nine most common deal breakers that I encountered in private equity transactions. As soon as you identify one of them in your early analysis of a potential deal, don't hesitate to down your investment tools and move on.

---

[3]Throughout my career, I have been mostly focusing on deals with equity commitments of at least $100 million. I personally don't find that smaller transactions reduce the time required for thorough analysis and execution.

5

Deal Selection— Identifying the Right Deal

Key Topics in Chapter 5:

- Save time and effort: why it makes sense to evaluate the transaction dynamic first
- If you choose to remember one thing about deal selection, make it the business model
- The four most common sources of competitive advantage for any business
- Forget the detail: just a few key financial metrics that matter for deal selection
- How clever structuring can help you overcome valuation concerns

---

Positive Screening Framework

Chapter 4 discussed the most frequent deal breakers that stand between you and a potential private equity transaction. What happens to all those deals that pass the deal breakers test? As I mentioned in Chapter 4, we then sift through them again. As the founding partner of Hellman & Friedman, Warren Hellman, puts it, "All potential investments should be considered guilty until proven innocent" (Finkel and Greising, 2010). However, the critical difference in this part of the deal selection process is that we use *positive screening* and evaluate the merits of each transaction. If you permit me to go back to the pole-vaulting analogy one last time, this process is similar to assessing the strongest athletes—all of whom successfully cleared a challenging height—and selecting the best ones for the Olympic team.

The positive screening framework that I use looks at ten different aspects of the deal. They are:

1. Transaction dynamic
2. Market
3. Business model and competitive position
4. Management team
5. Financial performance
6. Environmental, social and governance considerations
7. Investment thesis and value creation measures
8. Valuation and structure
9. Exit and return
10. Risk and reward

I always use the same framework and never deviate from it. Why? Because it really helps me ensure a careful, systematic deal evaluation process for each potential investment. This approach enables me to think analytically about each transaction, turns off my System 1 thinking and puts my System 2 brain in charge of the deal selection process, just as Kahneman (2015) instructed us in his Nobel Prize–winning work. Let's begin stepping through each deal evaluation aspect.

- *Transaction dynamic.* To avoid wasting your time on a deal that you will not have the opportunity to execute, it is important to establish upfront the credibility of the sales process. Why is the vendor selling? What are the vendor's objectives? Do you think there are legitimate reasons, such as a family succession event or a corporate demerger, that drive the transition of ownership? Is the seller exiting completely and, more importantly, do you get the feeling that they are in a rush to quit the scene as soon as possible, even if incentivized to roll-over a small stake? What does the seller know about the business that you don't know? It is always worth investigating carefully what truly motivates the seller in a sales process.

  Further, does the company require new capital as a part of the transaction, for example, for building a new plant or deleveraging its balance sheet? How desperately does the business need this new capital? If the sales process is a competitive auction, who else is likely to bid and are there strategic buyers[1] present? Is it a "hot" business or sector, and as a result, do you think the entry price might be irrationally high? At certain points of time, there may be private equity bubbles forming, as funds attempt to stay on trend and chase

---

[1] Typically, private equity funds dislike competing with strategic buyers in competitive auctions and sometimes pull out of a sales process as soon as they learn that corporates may be present in an auction. It is widely expected that corporate buyers will have a better chance of winning the auction because of their ability to pay a higher price for the asset due to incorporating synergies in their valuation analysis and generally having a lower return hurdle compared to private equity buyers.

the same type of asset, sometimes at any price. At one point, it seemed that every private equity firm was scouring deals in high-end baby products, education or public sector outsourcing. When evaluating a transaction, it makes sense to ask yourself whether you *genuinely and rationally* believe that you are looking at a good deal, or whether you are about to fall victim of the madness of crowds.

- *Market.* Some companies find it easier than others to make money partly because they operate in an industry with more favorable trends and better structural economics. What does a good market look like, in the context of a private equity deal? Ideally, you will be looking at a sizeable and growing industry with good prospects for the next 10–15 years, supported by clear long-term secular growth trends. Total market size matters because companies in larger sectors can succeed without gaining a dominant market share. Rapidly growing industries allow its participants to ride a rising tide during a period of substantial growth, and are forgiving of possible management mistakes, product flops or business model deficiencies. By contrast, successful companies operating in stable or contracting markets have little margin for error, and call for a well-thought-out business model, deep managerial expertise and high-precision operations.

  Additionally, compelling markets feature significant entry barriers, operate at an attractive point in their value chain, have pricing power and do not suffer from an abnormally concentrated buyer or supplier base. Ideally, these markets should have resilient structural economics and should not be easily disrupted by a change in exogenous factors—be it a change in regulation, a shift in the commodity cycle, fast-paced sector innovation, unfavorable movement in foreign exchange or interest rates. As discussed in Chapter 2, sector red flags include overcapacity, product commoditization or obsoletion as well as any long-term structural shifts in the industry leading to its inevitable decline.

What about cyclicality? Are cyclical industries bad for private equity investment? If the type of private equity investment you are pursuing dictates you to put very high leverage in each transaction, then—for the sake of not losing your shirt—it is probably wise to stay away from companies operating in cyclical sectors. Also, severely cyclical industries with excessive and unpredictable demand fluctuations are unlikely to appeal to many private equity buyers. However, cyclicality is not such a rare or necessarily bad phenomenon in business in general—as long as you plan for it. There is plenty of money to be made if you manage to pay a reasonable price for a company operating in a cyclical sector. Simply ensure at the outset that the business has a defensible balance sheet with plenty of working capital, a feasible solution for reducing operating leverage and a robust plan for what to do in a down cycle (ideally, buy out distressed competitors). Provided that the company is capable of surviving the full cycle, you can sell a thriving business as soon as sentiment improves.

- *Business model and competitive position.* This is the most critical aspect of the transaction evaluation process. In other words, in the absence of a convincing business model, there is no deal. The academic study of 79 private equity investors conducted by Gompers et al. (2016) I referred to in Chapter 4 arrives at a similar conclusion: when asked to rank various factors in choosing private equity investments, most firms indicated that company's business model was the most important component.

Since a business model is an economic framework that enables the company to create value and generate profits, the easiest way to start your analysis is by understanding how the business makes money. Michael Shearn, a public equities investor and author of *The Investment Checklist*, evaluates a large number of potential investment targets in his daily work and at this stage of the analysis finds it useful to ask himself how he would evaluate the company's business if he were to become its CEO (Shearn, 2012). I think it is an effective approach for private equity investors too. What is the company's value proposition? What does the customer buy and why? What is distinct about the product: price, features, service, brand or perhaps its proprietary technology? What is the company's market share, relative cost and quality position vis-à-vis competition? What marketing strategies does it employ? Does it operate a suite of defensible distribution channels? Does the business have attractive economics? What is unique about the company today and does it have a durable competitive advantage? Would many customers miss the business if it stopped operating today?

The point above merits a more detailed discussion. Thanks to Warren Buffett, the company's competitive advantage is sometimes referred to as an economic moat.[2] Pat Dorsey, an asset manager and a former Morningstar research professional, is widely regarded as the "moat guru" because he was the first to develop and popularize a methodology for the assessment and quantification of companies' economic moats. In his analysis, he defines an economic moat as a structural characteristic that insulates the business from

---

[2] While there are numerous references to economic moats made by Warren Buffett throughout the years, my favorite quote comes from the article titled "Striking out at Wall Street" by Linda Grant that was published on June 12, 1994, in the *US News and World Report*. In this publication Warren Buffett states, "The most important thing to me is figuring out how big a moat there is around the business. What I love, of course, is a big castle and a big moat with piranhas and crocodiles."

competition and provides it with a significant runway to reinvest capital at higher incremental rates of return (Beyon-dProxy LLC, 2014).

In Dorsey's view, reinvestment runways maximize the value of competitive advantage and reduce the risk of value destruction. Examples of businesses with a durable competitive advantage or—in his language—with wide economic moats, include those that 1) own valuable intangible assets, such as brands, patents or licenses; 2) are tightly integrated with customer business processes and, therefore, cause high switching costs for their customers; 3) produce significant network effects by providing a product or service that increases in value as the number of users expands; or 4) have considerable cost advantages that create a cheaper way to deliver a product that can't be replicated easily (Dorsey Asset Management, 2017). Luxury brands, stock exchanges, payment processors and enterprise software businesses are examples of companies with wide economic moats. I believe that Dorsey's analysis provides a very helpful framework for assessing a competitive advantage of any business as well as the company's ability to sustain and monetize it.[3]

- *Management team.* Another factor that is going to carry a lot of weight in your analysis is the quality of the management team. Top managers will either make you money or lose you money; moreover, they are capable of making your experience throughout the life of the investment either rewarding or exceptionally miserable. Given that your choice of a management team is consequential to your investment return, I devote the whole of Chapter 5 solely to this topic. For the

---

[3]If you are interested in learning more about economic moats, Pat Dorsey openly shares his publications with the general public on the website of his asset management firm, Dorsey Asset Management.

purposes of your deal screening process, a fairly succinct analysis should be sufficient. In short, all you need to understand at this stage is whether or not the management team can execute on what needs to be done on this deal.

Start by looking at the past track record of the management team. Have they done something similar before, and if so, what evidence are they providing to convince you that they will be able to recreate their past success? Does the top team have a razor-sharp view of critical success factors in their industry (Mullins, 2003)? Does the management team have a good understanding of the day-to-day life in a private equity–backed business? Have they guided their businesses through tough times in the past? Are they prepared to risk their own capital and ensure that their incentives are fully aligned with those of your fund? Look at the organizational chart: who is staying and who is leaving? Are there any gaps in the required skillset that you will need to fill? You may come to a view that the entire group of incumbent managers needs to be replaced—in which case, before you complete this transaction, you need to secure an experienced and dependable management buy-in team with a proven track record.

- *Financial performance.* Amid everything else you need to consider, there are the historical and projected financials of the business. Even if the company is willing to share an abundance of financial information, there is little merit in spending too much time on the financial statements at this stage. You are likely to see an optimistic business plan and a set of "hockey-stick" projections, with the future being painted much rosier than the past. I urge you not to dwell on these projections too long. Why? After all, provided the deal makes sense and you go ahead, there will be a formal evaluation and financial due diligence workstream later on, during which you can go through every number with a fine-tooth comb. For the purposes of the deal selection process, I suggest that you avoid over-analyzing the financials at this time and, instead, focus on bare fundamentals.

When I screen deals, I typically seek to tease out only the most essential facts from the historic and projected financials: 1) sales numbers and sales growth (separating organic growth from total growth); 2) gross margin and EBITDA[4] in absolute terms and as a percentage of sales; 3) maintenance CAPEX[5] in absolute terms and as a percentage of EBITDA; 4) EBITDA minus maintenance CAPEX as a rough proxy for free cashflow generation;[6] and 5) net debt. How do these metrics benchmark against the sector average? If the company operates in a cyclical industry, it is informative to understand to what extent margins compress and expand over time, and evaluate the earnings potential of the business over the full cycle. As the final step, I look at the existing asset base of the business and its expansion CAPEX, both historic and projected. That's it. This should give me sufficient information to form an early view of the company's ability to generate and grow cashflow, support acquisition leverage and produce an attractive equity return.

- *Environmental, social and governance ("ESG") considerations.* Once you have had a chance to learn more and reflect on the company's market, business model, financials and management team, it might be a good time to scan the business for any ESG concerns. What is the company's record at present of

---

[4] Earnings before interest, tax, depreciation and amortization.
[5] Capital expenditure.
[6] I am typically content to ignore changes in working capital ("WC") at this stage of the analysis, unless the business model of the company is such that WC produces or consumes a substantial portion of the company's cash.

sustainable performance and making a positive contribution to its sector, the local community, and society at large? How does the business demonstrate its commitment to employees within the organization? What is the company's current impact on the environment?

It is imperative to consider these issues not only because you want your fund to minimize any ESG-related regulatory, financial or reputational risks down the road, but also because ESG levers can help maximize value creation (WWF and Doughty Hanson, 2011). You might be able to identify a number of opportunities for improvement in the ESG arena, for example, by switching to responsibly sourced raw materials or generating eco-efficiencies through a more conscientious manufacturing process. Note down any conclusions—positive or negative—you may have on this topic in order to incorporate them later into your valuation and value creation analyses.

- *Investment thesis and value creation measures.* If you like the transaction so far and want to pursue it, you need to spend some time articulating your investment thesis. Why do you think it is a good idea to invest in this business? What is the source of the market dislocation to make this investment opportunity attractive? Are you a logical owner of this business? Do you have deep industry expertise, existing portfolio companies or special relationships in the sector that might provide you with a distinct view on this company? Record any ideas you may have that will enable your fund to develop a unique investing angle and create a winning momentum in the deal process.

  What value creation drivers will you activate during your period of ownership? Let's consider some general examples of how value can be unlocked in a private equity–backed business. First, there might be an opportunity to grow revenues. This can be done organically by turbocharging sales volumes or employing more sophisticated pricing strategies. Another route is inorganic: possible options include "buy and build" or roll-out strategies, major strategic M&A deals or entry into new markets, domestic or international.

Second, there could be significant operational improvement potential, especially in undermanaged corporate carve-outs or family-controlled companies. These improvements can come from a variety of sources, such as supply chain optimization, better procurement, lean manufacturing, waste reduction, enhanced sales force effectiveness, IT systems upgrade, or—a private equity classic—overhead reduction.

Finally, there might be opportunities to generate alpha through financial levers—for example, via eliminating value-destructive CAPEX programs, pursuing working capital improvements, renegotiating key contracts or making fundamental changes to the asset side of the balance sheet, such as through disposals of unproductive assets or sale and leaseback structures.

- *Valuation and structure.* It is very likely that you already have some idea about the price that the vendor expects to get for this business. If this is not the case, it is worth asking bankers or other advisers intermediating the transaction for guidance on valuation. The next step would be to check how the market prices similar assets, both today and over the cycle. What valuation multiples are you currently observing for publicly listed comparable companies? How about valuation multiples paid for similar assets in other private equity and M&A transactions? Finally, how much can your fund afford to pay for the company? In other words, based on realistic growth and exit assumptions for the business, at what valuation range can you earn your target return? This high-level analysis should enable you to produce 3–4 valuation data points, which you can then triangulate[7] in order to determine the price[8] which you might be willing to pay for the business. Your objective is to find the right price to get the deal done and not overpay.

Remarkably, the same entry valuation can produce very different equity return outcomes, depending on the deal structure. First, you need to determine whether you will be using acquisition leverage for this deal. If so, what is the borrowing capacity of this business and what level of debt might be appropriate—without endangering the company's future? Can you obtain a vendor loan for all or part of debt financing? Second, think about minimizing the risk of principal loss of your investment through a contractually agreed preferred return and liquidation preference: basically, structure the majority of your investment as a shareholder loan or preference shares, rather than ordinary equity. Third, if the entry valuation seems full, consider including an earn-out mechanism that splits your payment into an upfront portion and a deferred portion that is contingent on the company's performance 6–18 months down the road, or on a specific value creation event, such as the renewal of a big contract or the receipt of a patent.

---

[7]Originally a term from trigonometry that describes how to determine the size of an angle by performing three separate measurements, the word *triangulate* firmly broke into financial jargon. While nobody in finance can give you a precise definition of this term, we typically think that we *triangulate* when the task at hand is to look at several data points, assign different weights to them and derive a single plausible answer. Synonyms for *triangulate* that are widely used, especially in reference to valuation, include *calibrate* or *assess*.

[8]Should your task of *triangulation* be unsuccessful (for example, because there is a shortage of information), sometimes at the early stage of the transaction you can avoid being too precise by communicating to the seller a valuation range instead of a single number.

- *Exit and return.* The more plentiful exit options there exist for a company, the more valuable it is. If the business appeals to many potential buyers, then it will be easier to create positive pricing pressure at the end of your fund's investment horizon. Before agreeing to buy an asset (and buying is easy), it makes sense to think through how you will be exiting this investment (selling is far more difficult than buying). In that way, private equity deals are sometimes likened to Hell: easy to get into but hard to get out of! On a serious note, typical exit options include an IPO, a sale to a financial buyer, or a trade sale. Which of these options represent realistic exit routes for the business that you are analyzing? Apart from examining the underlying company, it is worth checking that the structure of the deal equips you with adequate rights to sell your stake when the time comes. There are many potential pitfalls in holding indirect stakes[9] or deep minority stakes[10] that might make your investment structurally difficult to exit, regardless of how attractive the underlying asset might be. When you have your back against the wall and you have to exit your complicated holding, buyers are likely to offer you only cents on the dollar.

  Your exit assumptions will have a direct bearing on the projected investment return. There are five components that

---

[9] I had to decline a number of potentially attractive transactions that offered stakes in holding company vehicles rather than directly in the target businesses. If there is no clear path to get to direct ownership, I see no point in acquiring a structurally complex private investment that will be difficult to exit.

[10] Small minority stakes in private companies are notoriously difficult to sell: there are fewer buyers for this type of asset, and the timing and exit route are often outside of your control. Your contractual legal rights as a deep minority shareholder might be difficult and time-consuming to enforce, making these investments far more challenging and risky than they might appear.

determine equity return: 1) timing of exit; 2) exit multiple; 3) leverage paydown during your hold period and debt at exit; 4) earnings at exit; and 5) size and timing of any interim distributions to equity holders. For the purposes of deal screening, I believe that estimating a rough equity return and comparing it to your fund's minimum hurdle rate should suffice. I would typically ignore any interim dividends at this stage and focus on the other four components.

I recommend spending some time supporting your exit multiple assumption by looking at the cyclicality of multiples over the last 10 years, as this will greatly inform your choice of a realistic range of potential exit scenarios. You might have a good argument for assuming a degree of multiple expansion at exit. For example, if the business significantly increases in size through a classic roll-up strategy in a fragmented market—i.e. acquiring many smaller businesses at low multiples—the company's scale should command a higher multiple at exit once the acquisitions are integrated.

- *Risk and reward.* You must be excited about the deal now, if you have come this far in your screening. Before deciding to go ahead with the transaction, you need to assess all the risks that might affect your investment. To do this, imagine you are stepping into the shoes of the Grinch who is trying to steal Christmas (Seuss, 2017). Wear the black hat and turn negative for a little while. Let's start with big-picture risks: What industry shifts, technology threats and regulatory changes might cause your investment to decline in value? What company-specific risks might materialize? Potential examples include risks relating to business plan execution, competitive response, management and/or financial underperformance, company liability and employee retention, and many other transaction-specific risks that are difficult to enumerate.

Do you sense anything odd about the deal? What are the weakest aspects of the transaction? Once you understand what may potentially go wrong on a deal, check your projected investment return again to decide whether there is enough headroom for a potential hit to the company's expected performance. Overall, is your projected reward commensurate with all the risks you are taking? Does the risk-and-reward balance represent an appropriate investment profile for your fund's mandate? Ideally, the deal should not be priced to perfection and should allow some room for things not going perfectly to plan. Conversely, remember that investors get paid for taking risks and it is only normal to identify a reasonable number of risk factors on any private equity investment. Use your judgment to decide how much risk to take and how it should be priced to make you feel confident about the investment.

This brings us to the end of the positive screening analysis. You should feel better informed about the various aspects of the deal to understand the opportunity cost of pursuing it at the expense of other transactions. The deal should certainly not feel marginal, or just barely passable. A good deal grabs you by the throat. If you decide to progress it, think about next steps. What are the main three or four critical issues on this deal? Who is going to champion this transaction internally? Do you have the right resources and enough time to execute? And remember: sometimes the best deal of your career is the one that you never actually do.

6

Assessing the Top Management Team

Key Topics in Chapter 6:

- Why motivating superb managers is the key ingredient in private equity's secret sauce
- Why the best CEOs are not the charismatic and articulate leaders we see in movies
- What makes the job of a private equity CEO among the most demanding in the world
- Nine key qualities to look out for when assessing CEOs for private equity businesses
- How you can apply the latest best practices in your assessment of management teams

---

Management Practices in Private Equity

What is the best aspect of the job of a private equity investor? Do you think it is a transaction completion? Or a successful deal exit? Or the handsome paycheck that comes with it?

Different private equity investors will have their own opinion on the matter. As for me, I don't find anything more rewarding than meeting and interacting with management teams. I like spending time with accomplished entrepreneurs, diving into the history of their business and walking the factory floors— provided I am invited to take a closer look at their operations. I enjoy this part of the job a lot more than transaction closings and deal exits. Why? That's because I learned the hard way that deal closings and exits tend to happen only once every blue moon. My best estimate is that I am destined to close and exit only about 15 or 20 transactions in my entire career. Meeting management teams, by contrast, is a regular part of my routine. More generally, I would say that it is quite typical for any private equity deal executive to hold about 50 management team meetings a year.

What is so special about management teams? As I mentioned in Chapter 5, management teams are very important people in your life: they will either make you money, or lose you money. The leadership performance of a CEO in a private equity– backed business and the ability of the top management team to deliver on the value creation plan are often the most critical drivers of your investment outcome. Fortunately, most private equity investors recognize this direct correlation between the quality of a management team and the investment's success, and spend considerable time honing and perfecting their approach to assessing management talent. It is quite clear that there has been a perceptible shift in the private equity industry lately to make management assessments more systematic, rigorous and data-driven.

While the private equity industry receives its fair share of criticism, there is one aspect that it gets almost consistently right: private equity investors hire superb managers to run their portfolio companies. Private equity–owned companies are considered to have significantly better management practices compared to those found in companies under other types of ownership. This is not just my subjective opinion: it is backed by the extensive empirical evidence produced by academics from Stanford, Harvard and the London School of Economics. Bloom et al. (2015) studied over 15,000 companies around the world and concluded that private equity–backed companies are significantly better managed than family-run, founder-owned or government-owned businesses. This finding is very robust and seems to hold regardless of the company's size, industry or location, in developed and emerging markets. And why is that?

Private equity ownership is associated with superior monitoring and operational practices, more efficient people management and greater delegation of authority to executives in mission-critical roles (Yeboah et al., 2014). In a typical private equity–owned company, the management team works in a faster-paced and more results-oriented environment, compared to those found in other companies. Furthermore, the high levels of debt associated with private equity ownership compel the managers to be acutely aware of the importance of strict financial discipline. Baker and Smith (1998) provided a detailed account of the evolution of the first buyout deals completed by KKR and noted the impact of high leverage on managerial behavior. During the first three years under the private equity ownership, managers had to enable rapid paydown of senior debt as it was overlaid with stringent covenants. In the words of Baker and Smith (1998), the strict discipline of debt allowed for "no slack, no surprises, no deviance. If problems lurked, candor was crucial."

The private equity setting also provides a clear alignment of incentives. Baker and Smith (1998) quote the internal KKR document on the firm's 1982 vintage fund that describes the emerging nature of the relationship between managers and private equity investors: "Make management owners by making them invest a significant share of their personal wealth in the enterprises they manage, thus giving them stronger incentives to act in the best interests of all shareholders." This principle was revolutionary—especially considering that at that time typical public company CEOs held relatively modest amounts of stock of the companies they were running—yet completely paramount to KKR's vision of the new financial capitalism. According to KKR's fund documentation, it was not uncommon in some early buyouts for management to own as much as 25% of the equity—and that's some *skin in the game*.

Not much has changed since 1982. To this day, private equity investors require management teams to co-invest a meaningful proportion of their personal wealth in the deal and reward them generously for achieving specific, pre-agreed milestones. This approach enables private equity owners to align incentives carefully and avoid a common pitfall for many organizations described by Steven Kerr in his management classic "On the Folly of Rewarding A, while hoping for B" (Kerr, 1995). In private equity, investors hope for A, reward A and achieve A. They design incentives that explicitly motivate management to deliver A—and A only. If this does not seem to work, private equity owners will have no qualms about swiftly replacing the management team with another one capable of getting to A.

Indeed, private equity funds change management teams very frequently. In my own experience, the funds where I worked were likely to implement management changes in the vast proportion of all majority control transactions. In the context of the broader private equity industry, the same seems to hold true: Cornelli and Karakas (2013) find that CEOs are replaced immediately upon transition into private equity ownership in 52% of the 88 LBO transactions they examined in their research. Alix Partners (2017) provide an even more striking estimate in their annual private equity survey: 58% of CEOs are likely to be replaced in the first two years under private equity ownership, with 73% of CEOs being replaced sometime during the investment life cycle. The most frequent reasons for being terminated early include a lack of fit with the new strategic vision as well as insufficiently strong capabilities, motivation and knowledge needed to deliver tangible results in a fast-paced environment. In other words, private equity investors steer clear of CEOs who are unable to stomach the pace of change and, therefore, are likely to underperform.

What Makes a Great CEO

If so many CEOs in private equity–backed businesses eventually get fired, who is actually hired to replace them? To answer this question, it might be useful to explore what makes CEOs great in general. What will you tell me if I ask you to imagine and describe the traits a successful CEO? Bold. Charismatic. Extraverted. Well-educated. Excellent strategist. Brilliant communicator. Is this right?

Apparently, not really. According to the *CEO Genome Project*—the most extensive 10-year study on this subject that assessed more than 17,000 successful C-suite executives worldwide by the researchers from the University of Chicago, Copenhagen Business School, the technology giant SAS Inc. and the leadership advisory firm ghSmart—there is a fundamental disconnect between what boards and the public think makes an ideal CEO and what actually leads to high performance (Botelho et al., 2017). The attributes I described above are merely our own stereotypes that do not necessarily lead a C-suite executive to professional success. The results of the *CEO Genome Project* are surprising: in fact, the details were so fascinating that they formed a basis of a highly engaging *The New York Times* bestseller on executive leadership, *The CEO Next Door* (Botelho et al., 2018).

Over a third of the CEOs describe themselves as introverted. Only 7% of the CEOs in this study graduated from an Ivy League college and 8% did not even complete a college degree at all, or took a very long time to graduate. Furthermore, the participants in the study who speak in a clear and simple language were considered more successful than those with complex and cerebral vocabulary. Another interesting fact: 45% of executives assessed in the study had at least one major career blowup that ended a job or was extremely costly to the business. Yet more than 78% of them were able to handle their mistakes and ultimately succeeded in winning a CEO role (Botelho et al., 2018). The value of the research findings from the *CEO Genome Project* lies not only in shattering widely held misconceptions about high-performing C-suite executives, but also in enabling the researchers to identify four specific behaviors that transform CEOs into successful world-class leaders.

First, high-performing CEOs are decisive: they make decisions earlier and faster while handling ambiguity and dealing with incomplete information. They waste no time and recognize that a wrong decision is often better than no decision at all. Botelho et al. (2018) quote a former Greyhound CEO, Stephen Gorman, who led the bus operator through a turnaround: "A bad decision was better than a lack of direction. Most decisions can be undone, but you have to learn to move with the right amount of speed."

Second, successful CEOs relentlessly drive business results and align people around them to deliver on a value creation plan. These executives are acutely aware of the priorities of their key stakeholder groups and make sure to engage with them on a regular basis. CEOs with these traits do not aim to be liked and do not protect their teams from painful decisions. They do not shy away from conflicts, if that's what drives business results. Furthermore, while these leaders listen to their team members, they do not necessarily give them a vote. "Consensus is good, but it's too slow, and sometimes you end up with the lowest common denominator," says Christophe Weber, CEO of Takeda Pharmaceutical (Botelho et al., 2018).

The third behavior of high-performing CEOs is their ability to adapt in a rapidly changing business climate. Adaptable CEOs pick up on early signals: they sense change earlier than others and make strategic moves to address it. They understand that there are certain situations that are not in the playbook and where a playbook cannot exist. Successful CEOs recognize that they might make a mistake and experience a setback. However, they will be the first ones to admit what went wrong and offer to change their course to achieve a better result next time.

Finally, the fourth behavior of high-performing CEOs is reliability. According to Botelho et al. (2018), an astounding 94% of the strong C-suite executives received a very high score for consistently following through on their commitments. These CEOs have excellent organization and planning skills. While it may sound a little dull, they are big fans of management systems, data charts, performance metrics and clear accountability. They monitor what their teams deliver and make rapid corrections, if necessary.

What Makes a Great Private Equity CEO

As evidenced by the *CEO Genome Project*, it is not an easy job to be a high-performing CEO. But it gets even harder to be a high-performing CEO in a private-equity-owned company. In fact, once we go through what's required, you might agree with me that being a successful CEO in a private equity–backed business is one of the most demanding executive jobs in the world. Private equity investors are looking to partner with senior executives who can bring their best management skills onboard while being able to stomach the daily challenges that are highly specific to leading a private equity–owned company. Apart from decisiveness, the ability to drive business results, adaptability and reliability, there are additional characteristics that private equity investors want to see in their portfolio company CEOs. What are they?

Let's go through them. In my opinion, successful private equity CEOs need to demonstrate strengths in quite a few areas:

- *Relevant track record.* The management team needs to be well-positioned to deliver on a value creation plan specific to a given private equity investment. If you are not convinced that the managers can execute on what you are asking them to do, you won't be able to sleep at night after you make the investment. Start your relationship with the management team on the right foot by ensuring that you see eye-to-eye on the strategic blueprint for the company and agree a plan on how to get there. Identify key value creation levers upfront and map management skills and experience directly to concrete targets that will need to be achieved during the investment life cycle.

  You need to assess the track record of the management team carefully in order to convince yourself that they are very likely to succeed in business plan execution. Furthermore, you should consider their earlier career—especially the financial responsibilities, available resources and organizational structures of their previous roles. Then, look closely at what you are trying to accomplish during your investment life cycle. Are you looking to drive topline growth? Achieve product leadership? Optimize the value chain and reduce CAPEX? Pursue an aggressive roll-out strategy? Then you better look hard for specific experience in the management team's track record that provides solid evidence of achieving tangible results in that exact domain—and delivering consistently good results in both benign and adverse economic conditions.

- *Overcommunication and transparency with the private equity owners.* Management teams new to private equity are inevitably surprised—and often taken aback—by the frequency of communication with their new private equity owners (Damon, 2016). Yes, private equity investors are constantly in the picture and won't go away until after deal exit. Compared to the boards of publicly listed companies that hold four board meetings a year on average, private equity boards typically meet every month.

Moreover, it is common for the senior member of the private equity deal team to connect with the CEO about every week to discuss opportunities and challenges, as well as brainstorm possible solutions for complex problems. Private equity investors demand complete transparency from the management team and expect to be notified quickly about any issues. If there is a persistent problem that hurts financial performance, private equity backers will literally move into the company's office until this problem is fully resolved.

Some hands-on private equity firms are known for being particularly bad at empowering their portfolio company CEOs and for having a tendency to micromanage. Even though some CEOs report that they benefit from such a close collaboration with private equity funds because they value a fresh perspective, financially astute advice and 24/7 hand-holding support, the truth is that not everyone is suited to work under constant surveillance. Michael Lorelli, a former president of two Pepsi-Co divisions, who became a CEO in a private equity–backed business, comments: "If you're going to make me CEO and you hire me to do the shoveling, then get out of my way and let me finish shoveling" (Prince, 2018). This approach might work for some funds, but not for others. As a private equity investor, it is your job to make sure that the management teams you are about to back are acutely aware of the dramatic differences in interaction with shareholders in the private equity setting compared to what they may have experienced in the past.

It is not all negative, however. Some private equity CEOs do relish the private equity experience and enjoy the ride. One such example is that of Dave North, a CEO of the US claims management company, Sedgwick. Dave North is considered to be somewhat of a legend among private equity CEOs. At the time of writing, he has been running the business for 24 years and during that time he led the company through six different groups of owners, including more than 20 private equity groups[1] such as KKR, Hellman & Friedman and Carlyle. When asked by *The Financial Times* about his interaction with yet another group of new private equity owners, Dave North said: "Up until the time the deal is sold, we are dating. . . Then at close, you are married. As soon as you're married, you switch over to a degree of intimacy, of conversation, of candidness that is different to when you were dating" (Ralph, 2019). I could not have put this any better.

- *Ability to deliver in a fast-paced environment.* Private equity funds tend to move very quickly. Why is that? Their investment performance metrics include not only the money multiple on

---

[1] The reference to 20 private equity owners is not a typo. This unusually high number of private equity groups is explained by the fact that some transactions were consortium deals.

their investments, but also the IRR and hold period—both of which have a timing component. As a private equity investor operating a limited-life fund, you constantly race against the clock: every time you don't move fast enough, your hold period becomes longer and your IRR drops. That's the reason why you are likely to encounter a private equity investor who is frantically trying to deliver a decent investment return and is, therefore, reminiscent of the White Rabbit with his clock from *Alice's Adventures in Wonderland*: "Oh dear! Oh dear! I shall be too late" (Carroll and Haughton, 1998).

The portfolio company CEOs need to be able to move at the same pace as their private equity investors: there are high expectations about the speed with which the value creation plan, with all its planned cost cuts and revenue growth targets, will actually be delivered. Fred Gehring, Tommy Hilfiger's Chairman, led the buyout of the fashion brand alongside Apax Partners in 2006 in a complex public-to-private transaction that enabled the business to undergo a comprehensive reorganization. The deal envisioned a dramatic restructuring that sought to revive the company by shrinking the wholesale business, reducing the US headcount by 40% and focusing the brand on the profitable high-end fashion lines. Gehring commented that once some of the heavy lifting was completed post-transaction, he was somewhat surprised when his new owners started planning the roadshow for a new IPO just 18 months following the acquisition (Gehring, 2015).

Numerous analyses of managerial practices in private equity point out the same thing: urgency outranks empathy (Harvard Business Review, 2016). Regrettably, when the portfolio company leadership team needs to lay off employees, the private equity owners expect them to make tough personnel decisions quickly and decisively. There is no time to listen.

No time to empathize. If it's a value-accretive measure for the business, it needs to be done. Michael Lorelli describes his experience making job cuts as a private-equity-backed CEO: "You agonize because you have loyalty, personal feelings, you like the person. . . But when you're agonizing, 11 times out of 10, you look back and say, 'What took me so long?'" (Prince, 2018).

- *Operational agility.* The CEO who comes from a traditional corporate environment with significant support staff, plush offices and an unlimited travel budget will probably be the wrong fit for a lean, ownership-driven culture of a private equity portfolio company (Damon, 2016). As a private equity CEO, you need to be able to drive results with limited infrastructure. You are on your own: no corporate staff to write a strategic review or remind of you of important milestones in the business plan. Private equity investors prefer a portfolio company CEO who has a clear hands-on operating style, a process-oriented mindset and a low-key attitude to corporate perks. Someone who can shoulder many responsibilities, juggle priorities and stay calm under pressure. According to Michael Lorelli, the private equity CEO needs to behave in some ways like a COO, "particularly since the focus on EBITDA often doesn't afford the management layer of a COO at all" (Lorelli, 2014).

- *Thinking like an investor.* The most successful private equity CEOs understand that they will be expected to focus on a completely different set of financial metrics compared to those in their previous roles—and the change occurs the moment the business comes under the private equity ownership. What does "thinking like an investor" actually represent? It means throwing out of the window common financial measures that are used in a corporate environment: nobody cares anymore about net income, earnings growth, earnings per share and price-earnings ratio. Apart from ensuring a healthy EBITDA to maximize the value of the company at exit, private equity owners monitor relentlessly two other financial indicators: cash flow generation and capital allocation.

Cash flow generation dominates everything else, especially in the context of a leveraged investment. Management teams need to recognize that cash is king. If there is excess cash, you can repay debt faster. Or deploy it productively in other growth areas that will result in a revenue and EBITDA uplift. Effective capital allocation, on the other hand, ensures that every capital project the company pursues increases the value of the business. Are you running a consumer company and think you need a flagship store? Calculate your return on this investment and think again. Are your fixed assets deployed productively? Prove it or dispose of them. Fred Gehring noted that his business gained a lot of financial discipline under the private equity ownership. Until the Apax buyout of Tommy Hilfiger, he thought that the company had done a good job in cash management and capital investment: in retrospect, he says, "We were actually amateurs, and Apax taught us a lot" (Gehring, 2015).

Management Assessment

Combining my own experience interacting with management teams with empirical results from the latest research, I feel quite confident that I know what characteristics to look for in a portfolio company CEO. And now, so will you. Let's run through them again and rearrange them in the order of importance:

1. Relevant track record;
2. Ability to drive business results;

3. Decisiveness;
4. Operational agility;
5. Reliability;
6. Adaptability;
7. Ability to deliver in a fast-paced environment;
8. Overcommunication and transparency;
9. Thinking like an investor.

In my opinion, the first six characteristics represent a complete must, whereas the last three are malleable qualities that a successful and collaborative executive can develop over time. As you go through the management assessment process—frequently long and draining—you would want these qualities to come up all the time, at every stage of your appraisal. Eventually, you are looking for a consistent narrative to emerge—and it needs to be supported by tangible results and verifiable achievements.

A thorough management evaluation typically involves conducting fit interviews, performing competency appraisals and talking to referees. Psychometric evaluation, computerized executive intelligence assessment and timed general ability tests are also rapidly gaining popularity among private equity funds who look for solid portfolio company management talent. Frank Partnoy wrote an informative article in *The Atlantic* about the proliferation of "people analytics" among private equity funds (Partnoy, 2018). For example, Vista Equity Partners attributes a large part of its impressive investment track record to their ability to hire the best management talent, which they claim to be able to spot through a proprietary test that "assesses technical and social skills, and attempts to gauge analytical and leadership potential (Vardi, 2018)."

Personally, while I value a structured interview approach, I am not an enthusiastic supporter of benchmarking portfolio company CEO candidates through a computerized assessment.

First of all, I find it contradictory to the concept of a "growth mindset" that was formulated and popularized by Dr. Carol Dweck, a renowned Stanford psychologist (Dweck, 2007). I believe that when failures, setbacks and mistakes are combined with reflection, effort and hard work, a person can change and eventually conquer new heights, including in the world of executive leadership. Second, I am not sure how successful CEOs with a learning difficulty might cope with an assessment of this type. For example, Sir Richard Branson is known to speak publicly about his struggle with dyslexia and his difficulties processing information the way most other people do. Should we just exclude Sir Richard Branson from the list because the computer is likely to say no?

Furthermore, I find it hard to visualize how one even begins to introduce the concept of taking a "people and aptitude" test to a seasoned CEO. Imagine I meet Mr. Fred Gehring and Mr. Tommy Hilfiger—which I did in 2005—in the context of the public-to-private transaction of their business and I really like the investment thesis. And then imagine I say—which I didn't: "Mr. Gehring, before we back you in this transaction in your capacity as Executive Chairman, my firm wants you to walk into this testing facility so that we can measure your IQ and EQ in standardized conditions. Also, I see Mr. Tommy Hilfiger on your left. Let's test him too." Clearly, this feels wrong. Unfortunately, my fund ended up losing the Tommy Hilfiger transaction to Apax Partners anyway—and thankfully, due to reasons unrelated to the above.

Every time our fund needs to hire an external CEO for a portfolio company, or change the whole top management team, we appraise potential candidates for this mission. I typically approach management assessment in three stages that involve formal and informal interactions, systematic assessments and references. My typical approach can be described as follows:

- *In-house meetings and interviews.* I really enjoy this part of management assessment: it allows me and my team to spend a lot of time together with the management team that we know that we already like. First, we go over the private equity investment in question and spend considerable time discussing the industry, the company and the value creation plan. Even though it feels like an unstructured discussion, I run a mental scorecard in my head and note down my observations about the key qualities and behaviors that are important for this appointment. My team and I also meet each manager separately to learn more about their individual career path. How did they rise to the top? What is their track record—and, moreover, what are the hard facts they can provide to evidence their accomplishments? How do they make decisions? How do they allocate capital? How long have they worked together? I also try to figure out what motivates the management team and how the internal dynamics play out within the team.

- *Systematic assessment.* This workstream of the evaluation process is typically outsourced to high-caliber executive search or leadership consulting firms who utilize a systematic approach for evaluating senior leaders. For example, Spencer Stuart employs their proprietary six-module *Leader Capability Framework:* executives are taken through a number of questions that seek to determine their core strengths, such as delivering superior outcomes, leadership, relationship-building and influencing skills, strategic thinking, ability to drive change and build organizational capabilities (Spencer Stuart, 2017). Other firms typically have their own bespoke assessments that

---

[2]Refer to the research paper for a detailed list of individual characteristics assessed by ghSmart, the leadership advisory firm involved in the *CEO Genome Project.*

deliver a comparable end product (Kaplan et al., 2012).[2] What you are looking to get is not only the executive search firm's view of the CEO candidate's past achievements, current ability and future potential. You also want to gain an insight into how this person's strengths and weaknesses benchmark to those of other leaders who had been evaluated using the same capability framework. The results could be very informative.

- *References*. This is a critical part of the management evaluation process. The CEO candidate will provide you with a list of referees to call. These people—typically top managers and senior leaders themselves—expect you to get in touch and already have a script filled with glowing adjectives to tell you. They represent so-called "on the list" references.

I never knew how to deal with these pre-manufactured reference calls and get value from these heavily scripted conversations until I heard an advice from an accomplished fund-of-funds manager, Graham Duncan. He assesses managers every day as a part of his day job and personally makes hundreds of reference calls every year. According to Duncan, the best way for you to get value out of these calls is to have a fairly long and comprehensive discussion with each "on the list" referee, so that they eventually run out of their script. *Then* the discussion really begins (Ferriss, 2019). Duncan recommends asking questions that might spark an insightful exchange: for example, you can describe the job and ask the referee what criteria they would themselves use for this appointment.

Duncan also suggests reaching out to "off the list" referees. If the senior executive is well-known in the industry, many people who work in the sector would be able to offer their off-the-record views in a confidential manner. I typically write detailed notes when taking references, so that any findings from these conversations can be included in the management assessment file. At this stage of the process, you are likely to discover that your views about the management team begin to firm up, and you will know for sure your appetite for backing this team in the private equity transaction that your fund is pursuing. If you have done all this work and remain unconvinced, then I am afraid to say that the management team is simply not the right fit, and you are better off looking for someone more suitable who ticks all your boxes. And now—since you've read this chapter to the end—you know what these boxes are!

7

Analyzing the Business Plan

Key Topics in Chapter 7:

- Why skilled investors explore business fundamentals before diving into the numbers
- Key problem areas to spot immediately in every business plan you review
- How to poke holes in overoptimistic projections and make your investment case add up
- Ten cold, hard questions that every solid business plan needs to address
- My trusted business plan tool: Master List of Most Common Drivers of Value Creation

---

Introduction to Business Plan Analysis

I started my first full-time job in private equity on a lucky Monday: the 13th of September 2004. Unusually for mid-September in London, it was a warm and sunny day. I was a post-MBA graduate and joined one of the largest pan-European private equity funds focusing predominantly on mega-buyouts. I was thrilled with my first full-time private equity role and particularly excited to become a member of the firm's consumer team. To me, it seemed like the most interesting sector for private equity at that time: I simply could not wait to evaluate and invest in retailers, leisure groups, and consumer products companies. "Maybe I will even get to invest in luxury brands!" I thought to myself.[1] Several weeks later, on a gray and rainy day in London, I was tasked with analyzing my first business plan of a consumer company that had already passed my fund's initial deal screening process. I felt confident that I knew what to do: my first instinct was to dive into the numbers immediately. "I can do that! I just go through all the historical and projected financials with a fine-tooth comb to make sure that everything makes sense and adds up, right?" As I learned later, however, this is not the best approach at all.

Think about it: What is a business plan? As William A. Sahlman, one of the prominent Harvard Business School professors, puts it, a business plan is merely an act of imagination of the management team that you are backing (Sahlman, 1997). It is their dream that may or may not come true. To be able to put any number they present to you into perspective, you are

---

[1] I subsequently transitioned from being a consumer sector specialist to an industry-agnostic investor. Unfortunately, my dream never came true and I never got the chance to work on my fund's investments in luxury brands. My experience of investing across sectors leads me to believe that there isn't anything special about any one industry: in fact, all sectors are capable of being compelling for private equity investors, provided that entry valuations are attractive. My enthusiasm for consumer companies has somewhat cooled over time, as I think that consumer businesses are exposed to human irrationality and, therefore, are particularly complex to analyze and forecast over a long-term horizon.

required to do quite a bit of qualitative work upfront to perfect your understanding of the industry and the company's existing operations. Without this thorough preparation, it will be difficult to judge how far management teams stretch reality. And stretch it they will. Joseph L. Rice III, the founder of Clayton, Dubilier & Rice, urged investors to go beyond the numbers: "Spreadsheets and balance statements don't tell the whole story. It's important to understand the operating challenges—and opportunities—when considering an investment" (Finkel and Greising, 2010). So, where and how do you start?

Let's consider the basics: What does business plan analysis actually mean? I find that to answer this question, it might help to focus on the output that needs to be produced by you and your deal team to help move the transaction forward. Personally, at the end of this phase of work, I would like to get to a place where I am able to state the following, and do so with confidence:

1. I understand the point of this company, I buy into its strategic narrative and I am convinced that its business needs to exist, now and in the future;
2. I became somewhat of a desktop expert on the industry structure and competitive dynamics;
3. I can tell in my own words how the company makes money and understand the economics of its business model;
4. I know what operational improvements and growth initiatives will be pursued and accomplished during my investment horizon under the ownership of my fund;
5. I have a solid operating model and a set of financial projections that I am prepared to underwrite as my investment base case. Furthermore, I produced sensitivity analyses to cover upside and downside scenarios; and
6. I identified a list of key assumptions that need to be verified and validated during the due diligence process, assuming the deal goes ahead.

I think your approach to analyzing a business plan is likely to differ dramatically depending on the type of transaction you are pursuing. If you are considering investing as a deep minority investor, it is fair to assume that you will exert virtually no influence on the business. Hence, your work will be extremely similar to that of investors analyzing publicly listed stocks. If, by contrast, you are working on a transaction that will enable you to purchase a majority stake, you will be empowered to make significant changes to the business during the period of your ownership. In fact, if your private equity fund is particularly focused on operational improvements or turnarounds of troubled businesses, at exit the company might bear only a slight resemblance to the business you initially acquired.

In majority control transactions, the work on business plans varies considerably depending on whether you are backing an incumbent management team, or bringing a completely new set of managers who will take over at completion. In my personal experience, in those transactions where we backed an incumbent team, the company's existing business plan often represented more or less our fund's base investment case, with some unavoidable tweaking that we will discuss later on. This is not at all the case in deals where you work with a buy-in management team. For example, one of my first public-to-private transactions was a potential acquisition of a listed group of high-end hotels operating throughout the UK. Until our first bid letter, the company had no idea our fund was looking to acquire its business and take it private. We worked with a very experienced buy-in management team and spent countless hours in our conference rooms poring over the numbers and plotting this company's future: in our minds, we sold some hotels, rebranded some others, invested CAPEX and redeveloped a good chunk of the currently idle but valuable land. While the company's then-current operating and financial metrics were useful to us as a starting point, our business plan was strikingly different to what the company had planned for itself.

Typical Issues in Business Plans

Business plans, even those produced by the world's most capable management teams, often pose problems for investors. Why? I don't know for sure. It appears to me that entrepreneurs and managers seem to wear the same brand of rose-tinted glasses that make them overly upbeat about the future. I recognize that it takes incessant perseverance and an unsinkable mindset to be an accomplished entrepreneur and a successful manager. Perhaps only those who are eternal optimists by default have the stamina to overcome numerous obstacles and succeed in their entrepreneurial path. Investors, by contrast, are so afraid of losing money, that they typically approach business plans with caution and tend to discount almost every number presented to them. If only investors could take management projections at face value and underwrite them as an investment base case, their work would be cut in half! However, none of us are so lucky. The job of every private equity investor is to inject an adequate degree of sobriety through careful thought and dispassionate analysis into overly ambitious and thus unrealistic management business plans.

Guy Kawasaki, an investor and a businessman, wrote an emphatic paper for the *Harvard Business Review* about the top ten "lies" of entrepreneurs that he sees in almost every business plan. The two exaggerations that top Kawasaki's list are the inflated management projections and the unrealistic assumptions about the growth and size of the market (Kawasaki, 2001).

I agree. In my own transactions, I met only *one* CEO who we, as a deal team, thought was too conservative.[2] More typical of my experience was to encounter overly bullish management teams who present business plans that contain a whole laundry list of issues that immediately catch the attention of a thoughtful investor. What are these issues? I can give you my top five—not quite "lies" but clear problem areas.

- *Excessive optimism.* We touched on this earlier. In essence, you are very likely to see "hockey-stick" projections in almost every management business plan you encounter. Typically, somewhat outsized cheer in the numbers will be driven by an assumed market growth that perhaps is too rapid and not entirely warranted; by gaining market share that perhaps is too implausible to achieve; or by price increases that perhaps are too aggressive and can't be safely implemented without putting off a very significant number of the company's existing customers. Further, management business plans generally give very little thought to any potential deterioration in the macro-environment and downward shift in the economic cycle during the projected period. If the starting point of a deal coincides with a recession, then sure, management teams are ready to bank on any signs of the economic recovery and projected increases in consumer spending. However, they are typically less rigorous about thinking whether the economy might at some point during the next five years be going the

---

[2]Backing a conservative management team presents a problem to investors in its own right. Throughout the transaction process, my deal team and I were questioning whether or not this CEO was too cautious and, therefore, might not dare to go for some of the initiatives to generate enough upside for investors. This transaction was terminated at an advanced stage for a reason unrelated to management, so we never found out how this dilemma would have resolved itself.

other way, from good to bad. As a result, management business plans often do not incorporate the effects of any headwinds coming from external forces.

- *Unrealistic timeline.* Things tend to move too fast in most management plans: sales cycles, especially for new products, are very frequently underestimated and assumed to be too short. Product launches, brand extensions and new formats never fail. Roll-out strategies seem to materialize like clockwork and never encounter any obstacles. Geographic expansion happens overnight. Generally, it is very common for management teams to push the limits of their own bandwidth— within a very finite timeframe of a private equity deal—by hoping to deliver on too many initiatives, including those, such as M&A, that are firmly outside of their control. It is all too easy to add lines in a spreadsheet and plan too much; however, one needs to keep in mind how difficult operational execution to a high standard will be in reality.

- *Idealistic perception of the company's capabilities.* Sometimes business plans assume capabilities, resources, skills or talent that are simply not present in the company as of yet. This is frequently the case when the company plans to extend itself well beyond its core competencies and, therefore, might accidentally end up in a business line that may no longer represent its natural fit. For example, I have come across industrial businesses that expect to be transformed into sales organizations within a short timeframe. As you can imagine, it is hard for me to make the cognitive jump and understand how a company run by engineers, who are used to working slowly, steadily and precisely, will find itself on the cutting edge of sales and marketing. Even though such a vast cultural and operational change is likely to scare me away from the deal, let's assume that I accept that it can happen and agree to stick around. After all, it is perfectly fine for companies to change the strategic *status quo* from time to time, especially under private equity ownership.

Then, however, I need to see in the business plan how the company intends to pursue this transition, step by step. How many people will need to be hired to support the new capability of the business? How much will they cost? How long will it take for them to ramp up and what additional resources will they require? And what happens to the engineers: Who is staying and who is leaving? Finally, given the radical nature of this business change, I would like to see an adequate buffer both in terms of cost and time budgeted for achieving this transformation.

- *Missing costs and investments.* Another business plan classic is a complete omission of certain costs and investments. Is there a business restructuring planned that will generate considerable cost savings going forward? This restructuring will cost money. Does the company plan to deliver significant growth and synergies via M&A? Pursuing acquisition targets, incurring broken deal costs and achieving synergies costs money. Further, all business plans—even those that assume a fair degree of cost-cutting and operational improvement—should assume some cost inflation in order to keep up with economic reality.

  Another point relates to an IT upgrade of any sort. If you ever see a plan that assumes an improvement in organizational effectiveness through a digital overhaul or—perish the thought—a company-wide adoption of a new enterprise resource system (ERP), then you can safely double the expenditure and time that management allocated to completing these initiatives in their business plan. Large-scale IT overhauls rarely go completely to plan, so budgeting extra time and money is prudent. Missing investments might also include little or no research and development (R&D) spend allocated to continued product innovation and strengthening sector expertise. Another area to check is timely investment in replacement CAPEX that might need to be incurred in order to keep the company's physical assets in good shape, especially those coming toward the end of their useful life. In other words, all costs, investments and cash outlays should be accounted for, quantified and matched to verbal statements made in the management presentation.

- *Lack of competence in the areas of capital allocation and cash flow management.* Some business plans reveal the fact that management teams don't realize that their day-to-day *modus operandi* will be quite different under private equity ownership. Specifically, sometimes they don't appreciate the fact that they will need to act like owners and not like employees of the company. One quick glance—and the investors see that management, in the jargon of finance professionals, "leave a lot of money on the table." And sometimes they leave money on the table everywhere! While a lot of detailed work is done on the topline growth assumptions, revenue projections and perhaps even costs, investors immediately notice if the company's cash flow generation forecast is not sufficiently detailed. Sometimes management teams make "lazy" assumptions about the working capital requirement going forward, simply calculating it as the percentage of sales or linking it to some other generic number. They don't analyze returns on CAPEX and don't test previous CAPEX spend. Moreover, at times they assume that they will keep investing on autopilot in the assets that will not be productively deployed by the company, only because these assets already sit on the balance sheet!

When I spot any of the above issues, I know that the time has come for all of us to book a large conference room where the deal team can get together with management, so that all of us can roll up our sleeves. We will have to step through the business plan carefully so that we can collectively reverse-engineer and challenge all costs, cash outlays and CAPEX assumptions. We will focus on possible cost improvements throughout the supply chain, brainstorm about potential asset disposals, calculate the return impact from every dollar of CAPEX to be incurred, discuss the potential reduction of slow-moving product lines to achieve superior inventory management, plan to renegotiate payment terms with suppliers and look into all other possible working capital improvements. The whole management team will need to understand—and most teams get up to speed very quickly—how important it is to focus not only on the topline, but also on cash management, cash profit and cash generation.

Business Plan Analysis Framework

I am not an eternal optimist by nature. This probably explains why I am not an entrepreneur at present and will probably never become one. I am simply not one to come up with a strategic vision for others to buy into and support with their capital.

Luckily, this is not a mandatory skill in my profession. According to Andy Rachleff, Co-Founder of Benchmark Capital, investors are not at all required to have visions of their own: they simply need to recognize someone else with a great vision (Rose, 2020). However, once investors find a team they would like to back in a transaction, they will have no qualms about poking holes in the entrepreneurial team's vision in order to provide them with—sometimes much needed—relief from their own excessive optimism. Tempering someone else's dream probably does not sound like a pleasant process, does it? To me, it is just business. As they say, "Hate me now, thank me later."

When the business has a particularly tough quarter down the line, the management team will be very grateful to the private equity deal team for not having to deliver on overly ambitious targets and explain to the company's lenders why the "hockey-stick" numbers never materialized. It is my job as an investor to protect the management team from themselves and ensure that the "hockey-stick" numbers never represent our investment base case and never feature anywhere beyond the first management presentation.

Is there an elegant way to poke holes in the business plan and not offend the management team who put it together? After all, there is an inherent asymmetry that needs to be overcome, with courtesy, charm and diplomacy. Think about it: the management team are probably industry experts—and you probably aren't. They can run real business operations, add value on the factory floors and motivate thousands of workers—and you probably can't. Yet, you can be very helpful to an experienced management team by dispassionately dissecting the target business in a multitude of ways and enabling them to analyze this seemingly familiar company in a number of novel dimensions they had never thought about. Further, you can open up your professional network to them, provide access to additional institutional contacts and industry experts, if they so wish, and educate them about capital markets. Finally, you will be the driving force of incorporating capital allocation and cash flow management best practices of the private equity ownership model into their company's business that will hopefully help management reap some handsome rewards at exit!

Once all parties have agreed that the management plan needs tweaking, the best way to start work, in my view, is to break the company's business into small building blocks and empower the management team to help you and your deal team to understand it from the very basics. It is helpful to stay patient and switch on your reflective and unemotional System 2 brain (Kahneman, 2015) that we already discussed in Chapter 4, to avoid conten- tious situations. There will be inevitable differences of opinion that may lead to heated debates: I try not to let them get out of hand by appealing to independent facts, objective numbers and third-party estimates, wherever possible. In other words, I try hard sticking to my task of poking holes, but with the courtesy and diplomacy mentioned above.

To progress our discussion from this point onwards, I am going to make the assumption that we are considering a majority control transaction that will afford investors significant influence over the business and, therefore, command the necessary attention of the management team. If you mostly work on deep minority deals that do not usually provide you with the luxury of driv- ing operational changes, you might find it helpful to supplement your reading by books written specifically for professionals who are exactly in the same boat as you—namely, analysts focused on publicly listed equities. I consider the works of Shearn (2012), Cahill (2003) and Valentine (2011)[3] particularly useful and appli- cable for deep minority private equity transactions.

Personally, I analyze every company's business plan in a major- ity control private equity transaction by utilizing a framework that I put together for myself over the years. It is certainly detailed and—I admit it—at times tedious. I believe it will be of value to you.

In every business plan analysis, I seek detailed answers to the following 10 questions:

1. What does this company do? Does it need to exist? What customer needs does it serve?
2. What macro factors are likely to affect this business during my investment horizon?

---

[3]Please refer to Chapter 7 References for complete publishing information.

3. What do I need to know about the industry to put the company's business plan into context?
4. What are the key building blocks of this company's business model?
5. How is this company positioned at present compared to its competitors?
6. What does the company do well now and what does it do badly?
7. How has this business done historically?
8. What 5-year projections am I underwriting as an investment base case? What are the key sources of value creation during my investment horizon?
9. What are the risks? What is my downside investment case?
10. Does my investment case add up?

1. What does this company do? Does it need to exist? What customer need does it serve?

Considering how much work and company analysis happens at the initial deal screening phase I described in Chapters 4 and 5, you might genuinely wonder why I bother to ask myself these seemingly redundant questions at this stage again. Don't we already like the business? My logic is simple. The job of every investor is not only to evaluate a potential investment critically and dispassionately, but also to avoid possible errors of judgment. In my experience, it is best achieved if I provide myself with an opportunity to step back to basics and ask myself—sometimes repeatedly—straightforward questions about the fundamental merits of the business. That's how I gradually gain more conviction about the company and its prospects, or lose my conviction altogether. Therefore, I personally believe that it pays to ask yourself again precisely at this stage of your analysis: What does this company do *exactly* and where does it sit in the overall value chain? Does it have a solid and demonstrable customer benefit (Sahlman, 1997)? Does it operate in a marketplace with continued and sustainable interest in its products (Osterwalder and Pigneur, 2010)? Are the company's customers buying into its strategic narrative? Are they satisfied with the company's product or service? Does the company have a point today and, more importantly, in several years' time?

Some businesses are remarkably pointless. They appear to serve a customer need of some sort; however, as time goes by, it becomes apparent that the benefit that they bring to their customers gradually wanes and becomes entirely skippable. Take the example of Woolworths Group, a publicly listed UK retailer that operated about 800 stores before it stopped trading on the London Stock Exchange in 2008. The company's stores had been in business in the UK for over 100 years and offered a somewhat odd assortment of merchandise that consisted of children's clothes and toys, its own *WorthIt!* value range, alcohol, perfume, jewelry, electrical goods, CDs, DVDs and a truly enormous selection of *Pick' N' Mix* sweets. Quite a few people who grew up in the UK in the 1970s and 1980s regularly got together with their friends after school in order to spend their pocket money on the confectionery products at the Woolworths shops and, therefore, strongly associated the retailer with a fun and positive experience. Woolworths was endorsed by celebrities; the general public in the UK adored the store chain for its affordability and often affectionately referred to it as "Woolies."

When the company's stock price commenced its steady decline in the early 2000s, Woolworths caught the attention of a large number of private equity investors. Could this be a viable turnaround and an attractive public-to-private investment opportunity? Incidentally, when I was an investment executive in the consumer team at my private equity fund, I also got to sit in a number of meetings with investment bankers and strategy consultants discussing a potential take-private of Woolworths. We tried to understand the merits of its exceptionally well-recognized brand, get our heads around its customer offer and assess the value of its real estate portfolio. The sad truth emerged from these discussions: nobody needed Woolies. It did not need to exist. After more than 100 years of operating in the UK, the company no longer had a point. It failed to keep up with the rapid changes in the retail landscape of the early 2000s, could not compete online with new entrants in most of its product categories, had a jumbled and confused customer proposition and—other than nostalgia and sweet childhood memories for the middle-aged crowd—offered close to nothing. Even the new generation of children stopped visiting Woolworths to get their sweets: they were too consumed by computers and video-games at home.

As you probably know already, a company that does not have a point has almost no chance of survival. It struggles to become relevant to its customers again and inevitably goes out of business. Despite its respectable heritage and strong brand, Woolworths failed to attract serious private equity interest and never became a take-private target. At some point, the company's board rejected a modest takeover bid from Malcolm Walker, a well-known UK retail entrepreneur. The stock price of Woolworths continued its decline for several years after my fund looked at it and the company ultimately died a slow and painful death. And I received my first investment lesson of how not to mistake a fundamentally sound business experiencing a temporary performance blip with a pointless company in permanent decline.

2. What macro factors are likely to affect this business during my investment horizon?

This analysis is critical. Changes in macro factors, especially sudden ones, are capable of turning businesses upside down overnight. I already mentioned the importance of understanding the external environment for any business when I introduced you to the Thematic Deal Sourcing ICEBERG Roadmap™ in Chapter 2. To evaluate the macro aspects of a transaction, my deal team and I typically go through a simple checklist and ask ourselves, "If something goes awry in these areas during our fund's investment horizon, can the business land on its feet and still hit our investment base case?" Should your analysis lead you to believe that the investment case will be impacted by one or more events that you consider quite probable, I recommend including an adequate buffer in your investment base case upfront. Things we watch out for include the following:

a. Political factors and events;
b. Economic trends and key indicators affecting the company's industry;
c. Financial indicators, such as interest rates, foreign exchange rates and commodity prices;
d. Social, demographic and cultural trends;
e. Potential changes in the legal and regulatory environment;
f. Globalization or de-globalization: impact on the product, customers and the supply chain;
g. Environmental and sustainability concerns;
h. Disruptive technologies and projected changes in the rate of business innovation;
i. Digital trends, both in terms of customer preferences as well as the company's product or service value chain; and

j. Adequate business insurance to cover specific unforeseen events, such as natural disasters or litigation risks (for example, relating to product safety concerns).

Do you feel the urge to do more work on understanding the external environment in your transactions? If so, you may find it useful to take a look at the works of Narayanan and Fahey (2001) and Fleisher and Bensoussan (2007).[4]

3. What do I need to know about the industry to put the company's business plan into context?

Industry analysis is complex. Why? I believe it is the case because the work devoted to understanding a new sector can potentially be endless. To this day, any time I need to analyze an unfamiliar industry, I find it useful to grab my old editions of Porter (1985) and Grant (2002) from my bookshelf and place them on my desk. The sage advice laid out in these two books is a perennial source of my confidence and sanity when I am confronted with a company operating in a sector that I don't know well. Before plunging into an exhaustive industry analysis, I need to keep in mind that if a transaction goes ahead, the deal team will have to perform detailed commercial due diligence anyway and— should the transaction progress as expected—this will happen in just a few weeks. At that stage, most funds engage a professional strategy or management consulting firm to assist with finding and validating the answers to the most intricate questions relating to the company's sector and the business model. Therefore, I force myself to take a balanced view on how much industry

---

[4]Please refer to Chapter 7 References for complete publishing information.

work to do at the business plan stage: I aim to gain just enough knowledge to be able to claim "desktop expertise" but I resist going into complete overdrive. Why? I simply want to avoid wasting my time, as the transaction may be terminated for a number of reasons at any moment. Basically, it is my personal judgment call to decide when to stop sector work.

You are already familiar with my approach to industry analysis from earlier chapters.[5] While it might seem initially that industry considerations will be dramatically different for various sectors, there are five recurring aspects that are worth trying to get right every time for any industry.

- *Sector attractiveness.* If the companies in the industry display rational competitive behavior and generate high returns on invested capital (ROIC), it is generally good news. However, will the sector draw numerous new entrants who will be lured by these attractive economics? On the contrary, if the industry features relatively stiff competition already and sector ROIC is barely passable, it might be worth asking yourself why you are still looking at a deal in this industry. Are you sure that you are not about to invest in a bottomless pit? Common red flags include irrational competitive behavior, sector overcapacity, severe cyclicality, excessively high capital intensity, product commoditization and weak pricing power.
- *Market size.* Even though no sector or market can be sized with a high degree of precision, you will have to estimate it twice: at entry and at exit. Since you already know from Guy Kawasaki (2001) that eternal optimists from the management team are very likely to overestimate the size and growth of the market, it is your job to stay grounded. First of all,

---

[5]If you can't remember where you have seen it, please go back to Chapter 2.

consider what geographies are relevant and accessible to the company during your investment horizon. Second, it might make sense to spend some time understanding what assumptions the business plan is making about the market exactly. Is the company focusing on its *penetrated* market, *target* market, *available* market, *potential* market or *total* market?[6]

- *Industry cyclicality*. I personally believe that it is perfectly fine to invest in cyclical industries, provided that you are aware of the cycle, can quantify potential demand fluctuations and already have a plan of action during the downward swing. Make sure that you understand the drivers of cyclicality: Is the cycle driven by changes in consumer preferences, seasonality, commodity prices or capital investment? What is the current point in a cycle? What was sector performance like, from peak to trough, in prior cycles?

- *Demand factors*. Who buys the company's product or service? What functional needs are the customers trying to satisfy? What is important for them: price, brand, proprietary nature of the product, customer service, loyalty benefits? Is the purchase discretionary, high value, impulsive or planned? Is the purchase frequently repeated by the same customer? Do customers shop around for the product and switch frequently? Are there network effects that might be responsible for customer stickiness? What are the key determinants of changes in demand: secular trends, product penetration levels, swings in economic or income levels, or other external factors?

- *Product price formation*. Who sets the product market price? What are the relative sizes of customers and suppliers, and

---

[6]I learned these definitions of the various markets in my marketing class in business school. If you are looking for more detail, I believe that most introductory marketing textbooks might be a good source of further research on this topic.

who has greater pricing power? Is the product price volatile and can you spot any trends? It is worth watching out for anything unusual that is likely to distort the forces of a free-market price formation, such as regulatory caps, taxes or tariffs. If there is a price war, you should consider again whether or not this deal is worth your while. I personally wouldn't believe any optimistic projections of returning to price normalcy, as it is truly difficult to predict how long the irrational competitive behavior is likely to last: it might exceed my investment horizon!

4. What are the key building blocks of this company's business model?

This is a simple one. What's a good business meant to do? Apart from making its customers happy, a well-performing company also needs to generate an economic profit and an attractive cash return. If it does not make money now, an adept business model should enable a company to get there eventually. Osterwalder and Pigneur (2010) provide one of the best definitions of a business model that I have come across: "A business model describes the rationale of how an organization creates, delivers, and captures value." As a generalist investor, I have been tasked at various stages of my career to analyze a wide variety of businesses operating in completely distinct sectors, such as electricity generation, asset management, shipping, retail, natural resources and consumer goods. While abundant differences set these businesses apart, most companies, in my view, tend to follow the same basic anatomy consisting of just six building blocks. What are they?

- *Building Block 1.* A company produces *a good* or delivers *a service* to satisfy a customer need in one or more customer segments.
- *Building Block 2.* It employs a pricing mechanism to create *a value proposition* to attract a customer in its chosen market segment and generate revenue.
- *Building Block 3.* A company has *an asset base* that constitutes its resources and supports its capabilities, such as:
  a. Brand, reputation, license, patent or other type of intellectual property;
  b. Physical, human, technological and financial assets;
  c. Operating infrastructure to maintain its day-to-day processes; and
  d. Partnerships to support its strategy, gain market access or secure key parts of the supply chain.
- *Building Block 4.* A company incurs *costs* in order to produce goods or perform services. These costs include:
  a. Direct input costs of manufacturing a product or performing a service;
  b. Cost of identifying, acquiring, retaining and communicating with its customers through sales and marketing channels, as well as forming customer relationships;
  c. Logistical and fulfilment costs, so that the product or service can reach its customers; and
  d. Operating costs incurred to run the company's product implementation processes as well as general operations. These costs include both in-house and outsourced activities.
- *Building Block 5.* A company needs to invest *capital* in order to:
  a. Renew, replace and support its existing asset base;
  b. Innovate and establish new capabilities; and
  c. Expand into new markets or product segments.
- *Building Block 6.* Once the company is successful, it generates a sustainable and growing *economic profit* and generates an

attractive *cash return* on capital invested. A high-quality business with a wide economic moat—a concept that I already covered in Chapter 5—is capable of reinvesting its cash profits at high incremental rates of return enabling the company's *value* to accrue over time.

As I step through these building blocks in my analysis, I would like all of them to be visible and quantifiable in the company's business plan.

5.   How is this company positioned at present compared to its competitors?

Let's look at the company's competitive universe. Who is there and what are the competitors doing? Compare the target business you are evaluating to its peers across a number of dimensions.

- *Target market.* How is the market currently segmented and who is operating in each segment? Who captured the most attractive and profitable customer groups? Are the company's current customers the best ones for its products (Osterwalder and Pigneur, 2010)?
- *Revenue models.* What differences in revenue-generating approach can you see among the company's competitors? For example, some companies might be selling their products upfront, whereas others might employ a subscription approach, follow a "printer and cartridges" model, operate under a license or a franchise agreement. Are any of the companies particularly successful in producing network effects or imposing significant switching costs on its customer base?
- *Value proposition.* Think again about what the customers want to buy and what drives their purchasing decision: price, specific product features, customer experience, brand or

proprietary technology? Who in your competitive universe is offering the cheapest product or service? Who is charging a premium? Map out how the value proposition of your target company compares *vis-à-vis* competitive offerings.

- *Business systems and supply chain.* Step through the value chain of each key competitor to understand their approach to development and innovation, procurement, manufacturing, marketing, distribution and customer support. Do you notice any unusual power nodes, such as proprietary processes, unique distribution gateways, a patented technology, significant cost advantages due to scale, a secret recipe, special ingredients or raw materials (de Kuijper, 2009)? Note your observations, as any of the above competitive advantages can be deployed as harmful—and potentially lethal—competitive weapons against your target company.
- *Cost structure and profits.* How do margins compare among the companies in the same competitive universe? What activities are integrated and what is typically outsourced? What is considered best-in-class performance at the operating margin level? What can you say about the current profits generated by your target company compared to those of its competitors? How about the profit potential? Who is generating an attractive return, who is tolerating losses and how deep are their financial pockets?
- *Strategic objectives.* The information you gathered so far should equip you with a good understanding of the state of the industry and your target company's positioning against its peers at present. However, you need to spend some time researching and thinking about what may happen in the future—specifically, during your investment horizon. Can you read into the strategic plans of the key competitors of your target company? Since strategic change costs money, the companies have to inform investors of their plans: you

should be able to find some of this information by reading relevant press releases and strategic announcements or going over the CAPEX plan of each key competitor. Who is preparing to dominate the market and who, by contrast, is planning to remain in its niche? Who is aiming to be the fastest, cheapest and nimblest operator? Who is investing in brand-building? Who is pursuing activities that might produce future network effects or impose switching costs on their customer base going forward? Is anyone planning a serious sector disruption? What competitive strategies can harm your target business? Given what you learned about the competition, what competitive fights can your target company plausibly win (Christensen and Raynor, 2003)? Apart from the direct competitors operating in the market already, beware of other forces that might disturb the current equilibrium during your investment horizon, such as new entrants, product substitutes as well as disruptors appearing out of the blue.

6. What does the company do well and what does it do badly?

Since you are evaluating your target company for a potential private equity transaction, there is a very good chance that it has not yet fully maximized its potential. Therefore, the business is likely to have some attractive characteristics as well as considerable shortcomings. To evaluate what they are, I rely on a business model assessment tool of Osterwalder and Pigneur (2010). However, I modified it to a significant extent to suit the private equity mindset and the transaction process.

- *Customers.* Do the company's customers recognize its brand and buy into its strategic narrative? Is the current value proposition aligned with customers' needs? Does the company serve suitable customer groups and does it segment the market appropriately? How is the company doing in terms of its net promoter score (NPS) metrics? Is the customer base concentrated or diversified, by customer type and geography? Are the customers generally sticky, or do they churn frequently? Are there opportunities for cross-selling and satisfying more needs of the same customer base? How big is the proportion of unprofitable customers? How predictable are sales to existing customers? Is the company generally successful in acquiring new customers? What are the average customer acquisition costs? How do they compare across the industry and against the average customer's lifetime value? Does the company have good customer relationships?

- *Products.* Does the company have a product range that is appropriate for its customers and consistent with its market positioning? Are the products sold in a relatively saturated market? What is the quality of the company's products compared to similar competitive offerings? Are all product lines attractive? Are there synergies among the various product lines? Does the company depend excessively on a single product? Are there additional product features or add-on services that customers might be willing to pay for? Does the company focus on product innovation? How successful were its recent new product launches?

- *Price.* How does the company set prices? Does the current pricing mechanism capture the customers' full willingness to pay? Does the company have pricing power? Is there a record of successful price increases, at inflation or beyond, in the company's recent history? How predictable are the average selling prices of the company's key products?

- *Costs.* Is the cost structure consistent with the company's business model? Does it have high operating leverage? Does the company benefit from economies of scale? What is the dynamic in the company's main cost factors: raw materials, labor, marketing and distribution? Does the company require scarce inputs, such as unique materials or highly specialized skillsets in its labor force? Are the company's key cost items generally predictable? How cost-efficient is the business compared to best-in-class players and the industry average?

- *Capital, physical and human resources.* Does the company have a historical record of major investments? Does it have an appropriate fixed asset base, or does it need to acquire more equipment or build additional capacity for its manufacturing, warehousing or distribution activities? Can the company adequately predict its resource needs? Are all physical assets fully utilized? Does the company have adequate human resources, talent and skills to execute on its strategy?

- *Operations.* Does the company manage its supply chain well and does it have a demonstrable capability of matching demand with supply on an ongoing basis? Are its operations scalable? Is there a history of successful initiatives to enhance productivity? Has the company explored outsourcing agreements or strategic partnerships to make its operations more efficient? Are all high-touch points fully automated? Is the company's IT infrastructure up to date? Are the company's operations fully optimized compared to its best-in-class competitors? Do the company's general managers deliver high-quality operational execution?

7. How has this business done historically?

One of the greatest Roman philosophers, Seneca, wrote: "Life is divided into three parts: what was, what is and what shall be. Of these three periods, the present is short, the future is doubtful and the past alone is certain (Seneca, 2004)." The same can be said about any company's financials. Even though the past alone should not be used by an investor as a guide to the company's future, at least the past is certain and represents the financial performance that the company has "in the bag" already. Are all historical numbers equally dependable? Not necessarily. If they are audited, it is a plus. However, there is always a possibility of the company management engaging in aggressive accounting practices, creative profit manipulation or even outright fraud. For now, however, let's assume that the historic financial statements are truthful and leave all of our worries until the financial due diligence phase of the transaction.

The first step is to determine the relevant operating metrics for the company's industry. For example, you will need to know that subscription-based consumer businesses calculate average revenue per user ("ARPU"), hotels care about occupancy and average daily room rate ("ADR"), hospitals look at patient days, bed utilization ratios and average cost per treatment, while insurance companies live in the world of loss ratios, expense ratios and combined ratios. The quickest way to determine the right industry jargon and operating metrics is to look at the appropriate public comparable companies and take note how sell-side analysts break down the revenue and costs into the relevant components and operational metrics.

The second step is to calculate and analyze historical revenue growth, margins, profitability and capital efficiency ratios, return on investments and cash conversion. As an investor in a majority control transaction, I spend only a modest amount of time looking at the company's current leverage. I am typically curious to see how much risk the company is taking with its present capital structure and whether or not there is a worrying mismatch in the maturity and currency of the key debt instruments on its balance sheet. Since all of the company's debt will be refinanced anyway upon the private equity deal closing, I don't spend much time delving into the liquidity and solvency ratios based on the old capital structure. All I need to see is that the company can pay its bills and stay afloat until my transaction closes. I will also typically look at the cost of refinancing and the magnitude of the early redemption fees that will be incurred in connection with retiring the company's debt instruments before maturity. If I happen to work on a minority deal, then—more likely than not—I will be buying into the existing capital structure, as my fund's investment won't trigger a full refinancing of the company's balance sheet. In this instance, there is significant work required in dissecting the financial obligations currently present on the balance sheet, understanding covenants and key debt terms, and calculating liquidity and solvency ratios.

Here is an example of how I might structure an analysis of historical financials. I assume that you already know how to calculate key financial ratios: if you require a refresher, I recommend looking at the books on financial analysis written by Higgins (2009) and Walsh (2008).[7]

- *Revenue.* Is the revenue stable, growing, cyclical or perhaps even countercyclical? Does it follow a predictable pattern? Total revenue growth is hardly informative, so it always makes sense to separate organic growth from the impact of acquisitions or disposals. How do the growth metrics look when the revenue is broken down by geography, customer type,

---

[7]Please refer to Chapter 7 References for complete publishing information.

product or business line? Is growth driven by pricing or volume within each business line? Did the company manage to pass inflation to its customers in prior years, or does the product price fall in real terms year-on-year? If I have access to customer data, I find it useful to calculate the percentage of recurring sales, customer churn and retention rate.

If the company's revenue growth is particularly strong, I might start to worry that not all of this growth is profitable. I ask myself whether or not the company's current strategy can actually be sustainably funded in the future. Excessive growth depletes financial resources, so at some point the company will be able to fund it only through increasing leverage or issuing new equity. Moreover, too much growth and shrinking margins might inform me that the company has given up on regular price increases and is chasing volumes and market share instead.

- *Costs.* The first thing I do is look at the proportion of fixed and variable costs, as high operating leverage makes it tougher to predict the company's bottom-line profit. High operating leverage, combined with cyclicality of demand, will make certain sectors—such as airlines—almost untouchable by private equity investors. Further, high operating leverage goes hand-in-hand with considerable capital expenditure requirements and high cash outlays for inventory—both of which we will consider later. The most basic cost analysis will split out cost categories and represent them as a percentage of sales, so that I can compare them to the industry average, see the year-on-year trend and also judge inflationary pressures on the cost base. Do discretionary costs, such as R&D and marketing, recur on a consistent basis or do they zig-zag in order to artificially smooth earnings? Also, sometimes the financials are loaded with one-off exceptional items, which need to be either excluded from this analysis—provided that I accept that they are truly rare one-off items—or just re-labeled and included in the cost base, if I suspect that they are indeed recurring items. Benchmarking the company's cost structure to that of its competitors generally enables me to generate fruitful ideas about potential sources of upside, for example, via outsourcing opportunities or cost-cutting initiatives.

- *Margins.* The most important profitability metrics for private equity professionals are gross and EBITDA margins. Net profit margin is far less important, as it is affected by the company's capital structure and, therefore, is more difficult to analyze year-on-year in a business with changing leverage, which is a feature of most private equity deals. It is also harder to benchmark net profit margins across various comparable businesses, as the analysis makes sense only if you take the time to re-lever each business to an identical capital structure. Therefore, net profit margin is typically disregarded by private equity professionals altogether: we calculate it and quickly forget what it is, as—apart from capital structure—this metric is also affected by exceptional costs and numerous other accounting decisions that may not be comparable at all across companies operating in the same sector.

  Gross margin, on the other hand, is a source of valuable information. In fact, if gross margin is persistently low, some private equity professionals might walk away from the deal then and there, as there is a significant chance that the company might end up in a full-blown loss very quickly. When gross margin is broken down by product line, an investor instantly sees what business lines are lucrative and what products are marginal at best, and perhaps should be discontinued in the future. EBITDA margin is a private equity investor's best friend, especially when there is scope to grow it. Private equity professionals most frequently think of the entry and exit valuation as a multiple of EBITDA, and also examine EBITDA on a monthly basis during the monitoring stage of the transaction. Since EBITDA is calculated after central costs are taken into account, it serves as a reliable guide to the overall profitability of the business.

When I look at gross and EBITDA margins of a business, I try to understand how these metrics have fared year-on-year over the full business cycle, how they compare to the competitors' metrics, and whether or not there is a one-off effect—such as a cost hedge—that might be boosting margins temporarily. I find it useful to quantify what business lines are most profitable at the EBITDA level, and how a potential change in product mix or pricing structure might improve EBITDA margins going forward. As you already know, private equity investors seek to establish the level at which profit margins can be deemed sustainable and grow particularly concerned when margins significantly contract in the presence of rapid sales growth as, in this case, this kind of growth is most likely value-destructive.

- *Working capital.* This area of company's performance can be analyzed by using myriad ratios, such as working capital days, stock turnover ratios, average receivables period, cash conversion cycle and so on. Many financial analysis books, such as that of Walsh (2008), dedicate several chapters to the calculation and interpretation of working capital metrics. What ratios are most useful? Personally, I think all of them! My own approach is to use as many different working capital metrics as possible and here is why: First, working capital is an important measure of the company's immediate liquidity; if it fails to pay its current obligations to suppliers, the consequences might be grave, and can range from a temporary business interruption to a full-scale bankruptcy. Therefore, using as many different ratios as possible is a good way to become highly informed about how cash moves in and out of the company's tills and how inventory travels to and from the company's warehouses. Second, my personal experience leads me to believe that it takes a conscious effort on the part of the management team to optimize working capital. Therefore, unless working capital improvements have been fully exhausted in the past, you are very likely to identify potential sources of viable upside by employing a detailed and thorough analysis of historical working capital ratios. Every tiny penny that management can free up from working capital will improve the company's cash flow.

In my working capital analysis, what do I need to understand exactly? I start by assessing how quickly a business can turn its inventory to cash. Moreover, I am curious to see if working capital consumes the company's cash or—in case the business collects payments from its customers upfront and pays its suppliers much later—working capital is actually a source of cash. Investors typically like businesses with negative working capital, as the companies benefit from a cheap form of financing from their customers and suppliers. This is the case as long as the company's revenues continue to grow: should the trend go into reverse due to a sudden drop in customer demand, then the company might be confronted with a liquidity gap and will have to pay its suppliers straight out of its cash balance.

Insufficient working capital will preclude the company from taking advantage of business opportunities and might stress it to a degree that the business might fail to pay some of its bills. Too much working capital, on the other hand, might reduce the company's profitability if the business keeps sitting on idle funds that are not productively deployed in generating earnings for the company. A similar logic applies to the right levels of inventory on the balance sheet: low stock introduces a risk of inability to fulfil customer orders in a timely manner, whereas excessive stock means that the company has to finance surplus inventory, incur the cost of storing it somewhere safely and bear the risk of a possible stock deterioration.

In other words, no matter which way you look, there is frequently room for improvement in the working capital arrangements until management is able to strike a delicate balance. How do you know what to aim for? You can start by looking at the working capital trend analysis overtime and also consider industry averages. Higgins (2009) makes an amusing comment by stating that the sector average may not always be that helpful, as sometimes the whole industry doesn't know what it is doing. Therefore, it also makes sense to look for best practices in other sectors. For example, Dell went completely against convention widely accepted by the computing industry in the early 1990s by deciding to carry no inventory of finished goods on its balance sheet at all, and manufacture all personal computer equipment to specific customer orders instead. Rather than looking at its direct competitors, Dell considered an unrelated industry of tailor-made goods, be it garments or furniture. However, Dell wisely decided not to daze its customers with infinite choice, and push them to choose from just a couple of options in two or three key areas, so that the company could actually deliver a rapid turnaround time.

- *Cash conversion and returns.* Since I already know enough about the company's earnings and movements in working capital, it is a good time to examine historical CAPEX, so that I finally get to a full picture of historical cash generation achieved by the business. First of all, are the capital requirements for the company in line with its industry? Did the company regularly maintain and replace its fixed assets over the years? This analysis is critical, as the majority of private equity targets tend to under-invest in some aspects of their asset base. Unfortunately, some cash-constrained companies might choose to defer maintenance CAPEX, sometimes year after year, and their valuable property or equipment might be at risk of having to undergo expensive repairs or outright replacement in the near future.

Outside of maintenance, what can I say about historic CAPEX programs and the company's policy on acquisitions, disposals and other expansion projects? For specific capital initiatives, what was the payback period and time to break even? What cash return was achieved on cash capital invested? What do the historic expansion CAPEX programs tell me about the financial discipline of the management team? For any past M&A transactions, did the company manage to fulfil the strategic rationale of the deals, in terms of cost-cutting, increased market share or geographic expansion? Were these transactions done at attractive stand-alone valuations and what was the return on invested capital for each deal?

What can I say about the overall predictability of cash flow and main sources of cash generation (ideally, most cash should come from earnings, and not from squeezing working capital or historic CAPEX underinvestment)?

Finally, does the company have an adequate fixed asset base to take it into the future? When were its major assets, such as land and property, last valued? Consider potential sources of upside by calculating asset utilization ratios, as well as key asset and capital return metrics to be able to compare them to the sector average. How can the company's capital be utilized more efficiently?

- *Red flags for accounting due diligence.* In this section, I note any areas in the historical financials that I consider odd and that I would like professional accounting advisers to focus on during the financial due diligence. For example, could historical revenue have been manipulated, if I see a portion of sales to related parties, or if I suspect that some of the revenue is booked before sales take place? Does the company pay fair wages and appropriately classify its employees from a tax and benefits point of view? Are there contingent liabilities, unclear reserve estimates, questionable write-offs, complicated lease arrangements, existing social obligations, pension deficits or underpaid corporate taxes? Have I come across any recent changes in the accounting policy employed by the company? Have I encountered too many exceptional items during my analysis that might need to be verified during the accounting due diligence? Could some of the accounting decisions be deemed too aggressive, such as choosing to capitalize some expenses (especially in the areas of software development or IT, customer acquisition costs or license spend), that might overstate the company's EBITDA? Unfortunately, the potential issues I mention in this section are not that rare, and I have come across nearly all of them in my own transactions.

8. What 5-year projections am I underwriting as an investment base case? What are the key sources of value creation during my investment horizon?

Building an investment base case doesn't need to be a daunting task. I already have management projections, as well as the detailed analysis covering my business plan framework points 1–7 above, so I have plenty of information to get started.

Let's begin with something very simple and assume that my forecast period will be five years. This is what my deal teams typically have projected in our own transactions—apparently, with the rest of the private equity industry: 96% of the 79 private equity funds surveyed by Gompers et al. (2016) underwrite their base investment case to a 5-year horizon and believe that using a standard period allows investors to compare different deals on an equal footing. Then, let's consider what is likely to happen during the forecast period in terms of the relevant macro assumptions (point 2 of the framework). Further, where are we in the cycle at present and should cyclicality be explicitly modeled? Are there any reasons to believe that there are structural factors, such as impending excess capacity or reduced consumer spending, that might make the cycle more pronounced (point 3 of the framework)?

Next, let's focus on the strategic considerations for the target company once it goes under the private equity ownership. I would like to ensure that the company sticks to its core by continuing to resolve a specific customer need and offering a compelling value proposition (point 1 of the framework). However, it might need to improve its strategic positioning, for example, by focusing on more profitable target markets or by improving its revenue model. The company will operate in a competitive environment that we have already investigated in point 5 of the framework, so I should be able to narrow down my focus to about three key strategic objectives for the business to help me craft a strategic narrative. My aim is to ensure that the company retains and defends its competitive strengths while improving some of its fixable weaknesses—and we identified what they are in point 6 of the framework. Finally, the company will gain financial discipline under private equity ownership, and will seek to become more efficient in terms of its cost base, operational effectiveness and capital allocation. Does this strategic perspective match that laid out in the management plan? Probably not entirely: I am very likely to see that the management team is optimistically planning to deliver on 7–10 strategic initiatives over the same time period. I will need to agree with management what key activities will be pursued as a matter of priority and reflect only those in my base case appropriately. The rest is a source of potential upside, in case the management team is right and I am wrong.

What numbers do I need to change in the management projections? Apart from removing a good number of the far-reaching and more improbable initiatives we just discussed, I need to step through the business plan line by line and remove overoptimism driving the macroeconomic forecast as well as specific assumptions about prices, volumes and costs. In addition, I will need to tighten any projections affecting cash generation in order to ensure that they not only represent reality, but also encourage the company to embrace known best practices of prudent cash management. Next, I need to consider how the projections compare to what the company was able to achieve historically, so that—after criticizing "hockey-stick" business plans for much of this chapter—I don't end up with one myself! According to Gompers et al. (2016), 44 funds in their study reported that a typical private equity investment case penalizes management forecasts by roughly 20% in projected EBITDA terms. This seems like a fair estimate to me. However, I am not solving for this answer explicitly—I simply keep this metric in mind while diligently ploughing through the business plan line by line.

What are the key sources of value creation in the business during the projected investment horizon? At first sight, each private equity target is faced with a unique set of challenges, so operational improvement and profit growth can be achieved in a variety of ways. The longer I worked in private equity, however, the more I became convinced that potential sources of value creation under private equity ownership were quite predictable and, most importantly, finite. In fact, they can be boiled down to a list. When I cross-check each transaction against my *Master List of Most Common Drivers of Value Creation*, I generally can get a good idea of what might be relevant to assume in my investment base case. I think about value creation in the following sequence: 1) achieve operational and financial efficiency; 2) optimize existing customer proposition; and 3) pursue profitable growth via new products, new markets or new geographies. I endeavor for the business plan to assume relevant activities to be pursued roughly in the same order: focus on the low-hanging fruit first (#1 and #2), and then aim for the skies (#3). Shall we step through the master list? Here it is:

Master List of Most Common Drivers of Value Creation

- **#1. *Achieve operational and financial efficiency*.** Below is a list of the value-accretive activities that will have a fairly immediate positive impact on the company's bottom line and cash generation:

  a. *Better governance and reporting:* establish a transparent decision-making process across shareholders, management and the board of directors. Introduce strong governance discipline through a formal board cycle and regular reporting procedures. Ensure that all required financial statements embrace industry best practices, and are produced and audited on a timely basis;

  b. *Promotion of management accountability through incentives:* empower top and middle-management by assigning clear responsibility, promoting high-potential employees, attracting fresh talent and introducing incentives that reward success. Create management succession frameworks for key management roles, identify underperformers and confidently pursue management changes in important positions, if required;

c. *Reduction of operational complexity:* evaluate core operational and production processes, question existing conventions and redesign business processes, if necessary, to achieve industry best practice;

d. *Optimization of head office and central functions:* challenge the *status quo* in the overhead functions, eliminate redundant processes and reduce central costs wherever possible;

e. *Operational cost-cutting:* review, reverse-engineer and question all costs through the supply chain—from development and procurement all the way down to distribution channels and customer support—and rationalize the cost base through automation, use of IT, renegotiation of key contracts, forming partnerships, outsourcing or—if it makes more sense to cut out the middlemen—integrating outsourced processes;

f. *Reduction of waste and promotion of sustainable working practices:* reconfigure the company's operational or production processes to enable the company to target best practices in the area of ESG by aiming to improve workers' safety and well-being, improve resource efficiency as well as reduce waste and negative impact on the environment;

g. *Working capital efficiency:* optimize the working capital cycle by reducing slow-moving inventory lines and improved payment terms with customers and suppliers;

h. *Asset disposals:* explore alternative arrangements for financing fixed assets (e.g. through sale and lease-back or equipment financing) and dispose of underutilized capital assets, such as land, property, equipment or production facilities;

i. *Elimination of inefficient CAPEX spend:* introduce clear hurdle rates for all CAPEX projects and cut all "nice-to-have" expenditures; and

j. *Cash generation focus:* emphasize the importance of prudent cash management and cash profit maximization through regular measurement and reporting of cash profit-focused KPIs.

- *#2. Optimize existing customer value proposition.* The key objective of the activities below is to focus on the company's core competencies in order to maximize the sustainability and profitability of the current product portfolio.
  a. *Improvement of product perception in the market place:* strengthen brand recognition and focus on the clarity of the existing customer offer;
  b. *Revenue optimization:* evaluate the existing pricing mechanism, challenge the current product mix and optimize the revenue model on the basis of price versus volume to identify the levers of profitable growth. Analyze sales drivers and grow average transaction values through better merchandising, sales incentives, loyalty programs, ancillary services or product bundles. Enhance the features of the existing products to command higher prices and introduce greater price discrimination;
  c. *Reduction of customer churn through better service:* improve customers' experience by conducting up-to-date research of their needs and empowering them with better product and brand knowledge, improved "speed to market," convenience and superior after-sales support. Understand the reasons for customer churn and identify tools for greater customer retention. Reduce customer concentration and diversify revenue streams from the existing product portfolio;
  d. *Elimination of uneconomic product-related activities:* test the effectiveness and productivity of the sales team and make changes, if required. Quantify the ROI achieved by marketing campaigns and eliminate all ineffective spend. Cut unprofitable product lines from the current product portfolio, close loss-making locations and sell non-core company divisions.

- *#3. Pursue profitable growth.* Once the company's operations and the existing product offering are optimized, it is only natural for the business to seek additional growth strands for profitable expansion. These growth activities consist of the following:

    a. *Expansion of target markets:* evaluate the market opportunity and extend the current offering to additional target customer segments or new geographies;

    b. *Introduction of new products:* test and launch new products, services, locations or formats—however, continue to refine the offering through trials and detailed sales and ROI analyses. Invest in a swift roll-out of the winning ideas while not extending dangerously beyond core competencies;

    c. *Growth through acquisitions:* target profitable add-ons and value-accretive M&A while taking into account execution and integration risks. Pursue rapid shut-down of any growth initiatives that fail to succeed and provide poor cash return.

Beyond what's included on the master list above, I can't think of many other sources of value creation in a private equity transaction. Every time I work on a deal, I explicitly review this list to ensure that my deal team's investment case captures the key areas of profitability growth and operational improvement that might be relevant for the transaction under review. It is easy to plan too much, however, and—it goes without saying—no private equity deal should assume all possible value creation levers under the sun. Therefore, I pick and choose from the list above based on what realistically can be achieved during a 5-year investment horizon.

Specifically, I believe that every investment base case should most definitely assume nearly all activities aimed at reaching a high standard of operational and financial efficiency (#1) during the first 6–18 months of the private equity ownership. Further, the company should realistically focus during the first 24 months on addressing only two or three fixable weaknesses in its current customer proposition (#2), ideally geared at optimizing the revenue model and eliminating customer losses. Revenue growth is by far the most important source of value creation in private equity deals: the 74 funds that responded to a survey conducted by Gompers et al. (2016) reported increase in revenue as a key value driver in nearly 70% of all these funds' transactions. Finally, I personally am inclined to let the company spread its wings by expanding into new markets or pursuing add-ons (#3) only once #1 and #2 are achieved, which typically coincides with the beginning of year 3 onwards in most business plans. By then, the company will have already clarified its strategic priorities, optimized its product portfolio, stopped leaking cash and adopted a cash profit-focused mindset—all of which should reduce the likelihood of expensive mistakes that are associated with ambitious growth initiatives.

As a result, any 5-year investment base projections are derived from the management plan by making more realistic assumptions about the macroeconomic environment, understanding and modeling the cycle, reducing the number of the strategic initiatives during the investment horizon to a realistic target and quantifying the benefits arising from a select number of value creation activities. In my view, an investment base case can be deemed solid if the deal team believes that it can be achieved with a probability of 60–70%. All other assumptions in the management plan—should they even materialize—are a source of a potential upside.

9. What are the risks? What is my downside investment case?

Howard Marks, a prominent investor in distressed assets and founder of Oaktree Capital, provided a fitting comment about investment risk in his book: "Investing consists of exactly one thing: dealing with the future. And because none of us can know the future with certainty, risk is inescapable. Thus, dealing with risk is. . . *the essential.* . . element in investing" (Marks, 2011). How do we know exactly the risks in any given private equity investment? Well, we don't—at least not with any degree of precision. In Marks' view, prospective risk is "subjective, hidden and unquantifiable." Even though this comment sounds gloomy and offers little consolation, there are steps that investors can nonetheless take in order to recognize, model and possibly control certain risks when evaluating investments.

The first step is to remember that—unless you invest in a jar stuffed with cash—risks are always present and investors actually get paid for bearing a distribution of various investment outcomes. In private equity, investors choose to hire the best managers who—when faced with business challenges or a macroeconomic misfortune—might be capable of skewing the odds to a greater likelihood of investment success. The second step is to recognize key risk areas historically experienced by the business: while history may not repeat itself exactly, it will certainly inform the deal team of the historic impact of adverse events on the company's revenue and the bottom line. The third step is to review all assumptions in the business plan, top to bottom, and examine them carefully through a sensitivity analysis.

I personally start my downside analysis by evaluating the magnitude of the impact produced by changing one key assumption at a time. What if the macroeconomic environment is going to be far worse during my fund's investment horizon? What if the company won't be able to change its pricing model? What if the projected revenue growth is going to be far more modest than forecast and what happens if there is no revenue growth at all? What if the margins don't improve, stay at historic levels or decline? What if the company invests CAPEX that won't generate an acceptable return? You probably get the point: I aim to generate a range of possible outcomes through systematically testing each key assumption. I am trying to be realistic about what's probable and what can be characterized as a high- or medium-probability risk. I do not spend too much time focusing on a low-probability event, such as all of the company's facilities burning down to the ground. In my opinion, the single objective of a basic sensitivity analysis is to inform me about those assumptions that have the strongest impact on the projections.

I regard a downside case as an investment outcome that has a probability of 10–15% and takes a punitive view on several key assumptions made in the base investment case. In essence, I am choosing to combine 4–5 sensitivities into a single scenario in order to evaluate what happens to the company's performance over a 5-year period. However, I need to remember that various assumptions are linked to each other and might produce complementary effects: a more negative forecast about the economy or the cycle will affect the company's topline, and slower sales will reduce cash generation and increase working capital needs— all of which might in turn result in having limited financial resources for the planned CAPEX program. If the company does not invest, it probably can't grow as planned—and so on.

On the other hand, I might also identify several risk mitigants that might be available: for example, if CAPEX does not pay off, the business can turn off future expansion spend and wait for better times ahead, rather than keep destroying value year-on-year. In a similar vein, the company can choose to cancel expensive product launches, cut more fixed costs or temporarily reduce discretionary expenditures. In my view, a downside investment case is complete when it describes a plausibly negative economic scenario that imposes operational challenges on the business and features a coherent set of business plan assumptions that might realistically describe the company's reality when it faces adverse—but not quite cataclysmic[8]—circumstances.

10. Does my investment case add up?

As a last step of the business plan analysis framework, it is prudent to check whether or not the resultant investment base case and the downside case actually make sense. After so much work, it would be a pity if they didn't, right? First, I start with a set of fairly straightforward sanity checks. What market share is implied by the total revenue projection in year 5 of the investment case? How realistic is this market share projection in the context of the market growth trends as well as the company's capabilities? Provided that there are market share gains, who are the competitors who will lose out and how might they react? Are all management initiatives that are included in the plan backed up commensurately by the numbers in the base investment case? How much confidence do I have that all costs and cash outlays are adequately accounted for? If I step through the investment case projections of revenue, cost structure and profit margins in year 5, how do the operating ratios and year-on-year growth

---

[8]Modeling a cataclysmic scenario makes little sense, in my view, as the answer is quite clear: this investment will result in a loss. If the business repeatedly experienced cataclysms in the past, consider walking away from the deal.

metrics benchmark against those of best-in-class peers today? Is this operating performance plausible in the context of the target company? Finally, does the investment case exhibit any oversimplifications, like straight-line extrapolations or optimistic beliefs that "this time it's different"?

Second, I will seek to identify an experienced sector expert outside of the management team to opine on the projections in both the investment case and the downside case. If my fund does not have an operating partner with relevant industry expertise, I might have to resort to finding someone new, either through executive search firms or expert networks. In essence, I need a fresh perspective from someone with direct senior operating experience in the same industry who will offer an honest view on the financial forecasts, highlight operating challenges and critique the assumptions made by management and the deal team. I will note down carefully any impartial input provided by the industry expert that might lead us to further finesse the numbers and enable the deal team to finalize both the investment base case and the downside case with confidence. What happens then? We collectively exhale. Job's done. It is such a relief to end up in a place where the whole deal team has sufficient conviction to underwrite the deal on the basis of solid projections and all members are proud to put their names on the memo to the investment committee!

8

Valuation

Key Topics in Chapter 8:

- Enterprise value, headline price and cash consideration: why they are each different
- How experienced investors use flawed valuation methods and still get to the right answer
- Seven valuation metrics and six valuation methods I like (and hate) to use
- Two valuation approaches for those times when you find "difficult to value" companies
- You've done the valuation: How much will you pay to win the deal?

M uch has been written about valuation. There is an overwhelming number of valuation books and online resources already in existence—with many more in the pipeline. McKinsey alone recently contributed almost 900 pages on the topic of assessing corporate value by publishing an updated edition of its venerable valuation manual

(McKinsey, 2020).[1] As you can imagine, writing something distinctive on valuation is a tall order in this context: What can I say in this chapter in order to maximize its utility for the reader? Perhaps it is best if I refrain from rebroadcasting the concepts that are already well-covered by other finance writers. Instead, I will provide my subjective—and perhaps not entirely academically accurate—view on the valuation techniques that I believe to be suitable for a private equity setting. I will describe the valuation metrics that I use most frequently and the valuation methods I rely on. Finally, I will discuss the thought process that I employ to get from the company's valuation to deal pricing.

To stick to my goal of not wasting my publisher's ink on duplicating the material already presented elsewhere, I need to make the assumption that you are relatively well-versed in the topics of finance and valuation. If this is not the case, I recommend reading the highly accessible books on valuation by Aswath Damodaran, a Professor of Finance at the Stern School of Business at New York University. While it is hard to pinpoint the most useful title from Damodaran's entire bibliography, my personal favorite is his work about the techniques one can use to determine the value of any asset (Damodaran, 2012). Other helpful resources include the top-selling book by the investment banking practitioners Rosenbaum and Pearl (2009) as well as a fairly academic yet highly sought-after book on valuation by Arzac (2007).[2]

Not everyone is thrilled by the prospect of having to value private assets: by their nature, valuations are often subjective and highly imprecise. Bruner (2004) issues an explicit warning, "Virtually every number you use in valuation is *measured with error*, either because of flawed methods to describe the past or

---

[1]Please refer to Chapter 8 References for a complete citation.
[2]Please refer to Chapter 8 References for complete citations.

because of uncertainty about the future." Roberts (1992) offers his perspective on valuation in the context of a private equity transaction: "No single valuation can capture the true value of any firm. Rather, its value is a function of the individual's perception of opportunity and risk, the nature of financial resources available to the purchaser, the prospective operating strategy, the time horizon of the analysis, alternatives available given the time and money invested, and the potential methods of harvesting." This is well-said, even if a little disheartening.

There is a persistent debate in the academic and professional circles: Is valuation an art or science? Should we approach it with human imprecision or robust quantification tools? Fabozzi et al. (2018) published a paper that—apart from attempting to determine whether valuation is an art, science, or craft—characterized private equity as a tricky area of finance where valuation of the assets is impacted by information asymmetry, timing of the offer and behavioral characteristics of buyers and sellers. If this is the case, is private equity valuation an art, science or craft? Personally, I believe it is none of the three. I mainly regard valuation as a judgment call. Preferably, a wise one. Ideally, this judgment call is based on exhaustive information about the company and further calibrated by transaction experience, industry knowledge, market sentiment and sound logic.

Some businesses are harder to value than others. Plenty of tools exist that can help determine a valuation range for a profitable and cash-generative company, with a long and consistent track record, no accounting irregularities, featuring a clear strategy and an accomplished management team. This description, sadly, typically applies only to a small proportion of private equity targets. The majority of companies will be far more intricate and, therefore, more cumbersome to value. Consider, in particular, why a given company is regarded as an attractive private equity target to begin with: more likely than not, it is on the cusp of a significant transition. It might be in a decline or distress; it might require divestitures and a complete strategic overhaul; or—more optimistically—it might be hungry for a fresh investment to fund a new trajectory of growth. Whatever the future course, historic numbers in all of these scenarios become less relevant, and all key parameters driving the value will need to be reassessed.

Value, Price and Cash

When engaging in a valuation process for a private equity transaction, I personally differentiate among the following three concepts: 1) value of a business; 2) headline price that unlocks the deal; and 3) cash consideration paid by the investor. While related, these three concepts can sometimes equate to three completely different numbers in the same private equity transaction.

Value stems from a variety of sources. Ultimately, it is driven by the fundamental characteristics of the business and its future prospects, as measured by the company's earnings growth and cash flow generation potential. For each investment target, private equity investors might examine the following aspects:

a. Value in growth;
b. Value in existing operating cash flows;
c. Value in the existing asset base;
d. Value in a competitive advantage (such as brands, patents, customer switching costs, network effects or economies of scale);
e. Value in an operational improvement potential, including possible synergies;
f. Option value, such as platform value or access to a unique asset or an individual; and

g. Value in control and ability to make strategic, operational and financial decisions.

Some people like to bring up another measure: the intrinsic value of a company. While it is a neat theoretical construct, intrinsic value can't be reliably assessed and is completely unobservable. Since it is actually not known to the seller, to me or to my investment committee, it appears that there is not much to discuss. I will be frank: I choose to disregard the concept of an intrinsic value in a private equity context altogether.

The price of a transaction is a headline number that is agreed between a willing buyer and a seller. While directionally it corresponds to the valuation of an investment target, it is also influenced by the specific motives of a seller and a buyer, market sentiment, industry outlook, the negotiating skills of the people involved in a deal as well as the availability of alternative options for both parties. Further, the price might feature a discount or a premium to the value of the underlying business: for example, companies that dominate their sector may be priced above fair value because of having a larger market share and more diversified revenue streams; minority stakes might be sold at a discount to compensate investors for illiquidity and reduced governance rights; and companies acquired in a public-to-private transaction in most cases offer a generous premium to the stock market price in order to encourage the public shareholders to sell.

The headline price in turn may not at all be equivalent to the cash consideration that will ultimately come from the investor's pocket. Actual cash paid depends on the form of the purchase consideration agreed between a buyer and a seller, and may include cash, non-cash and deferred portions of the purchase price. In addition, the headline price might be propped by a variety of structuring mechanisms, such as earn-outs and ratchets, that will in effect split the purchase consideration into an upfront portion payable at closing and a performance-based element payable in the future, subject to specific performance targets being met. Lastly, the headline price in a transaction typically assumes an acquisition of a business that has no cash, zero borrowings and a normalized level of working capital. This convention requires investors to negotiate a variety of post-closing adjustments with the seller—and this may lead to further amendments to the headline price in order to get to the ultimate level of consideration paid by the investor.

I find it quite remarkable: what a business is worth, what you agree as a headline price and what your fund might end up paying are all three different figures!

Valuation Metrics

The bad news is that nearly all metrics can be misleading when considered in isolation. The good news that the very same metrics can be useful, despite their limitations, when combined into a single valuation exercise. What valuation metrics do I use most frequently? Before I answer this question, let me explain the objectives that I set myself every time I engage in the valuation of a private asset. Since valuation is highly subjective and inexact, I seek to examine in detail as many valuation metrics as possible: I tend to pay attention to both the outliers and the averages. Further, since market sentiment and timing have a pronounced effect on company valuations, I believe it makes sense to perform any analysis of multiples and other metrics over a full cycle, if possible, in order to assess whether the current market is "hot" and also estimate the likely valuation trajectory of the business during my investment horizon. In addition, each metric gains the greatest revelatory power when it is calculated on all possible bases: historic, forward, last-twelve-months ("LTM") and run-rate—not only on the basis of a single number that people working on a deal expect at the time of the upcoming reporting period.

Moreover, the financial information that I work with should be scrutinized and "sanitized" as much as possible to present a normalized state of the world: I aim to understand maintainable revenues and maintainable earnings of a company, so anything abnormal—such as windfall sales, extraordinary gains, one-off charges and other random or non-recurring items—should be excluded from the financials. It is also good practice to check if there is potential manipulation from the seller's side in advance of the transaction that attempts to make the company appear more attractive to prospective buyers. If I see expenditure on maintenance or repairs in a recent reporting period pointing sharply downwards, or certain discretionary costs—such as R&D or marketing—dialed down or suddenly turned off completely, there is a good chance that these figures need to be adjusted to normalized levels before any coherent analysis can take place.

In terms of valuation multiples and metrics, I consider the following seven.

- *EV/Sales (Enterprise Value to Sales).* This is a helpful metric to calculate for a company that has not yet reached a sustainable level of profitability because it is either growing rapidly or, rather less fortunately, is undergoing a turnaround. The sales multiple is also informative for companies where the cost structure—when expressed as a percentage of sales—might be changing or volatile, such as for cyclical businesses, new ventures or companies with very low or excessively high operating leverage. In all of these cases, earnings are likely to be either negative or not reliable. Since EV/Sales is a top-line metric, it is less influenced by the accounting policy compared to other multiples (although manipulation is still possible, especially for business models that feature long-term sales contracts). An EV/Sales multiple has a number of limitations: it gives credit to both profitable and unprofitable sales and ignores the fact that not all sales translate into free cash flow. In effect, it may compel the buyer to overpay for revenue growth, especially for those companies that chase market share at all costs. Finally, the EV/Sales multiple is really not that applicable for conducting any cross-industry benchmarking, especially for sectors with vastly different capital requirements, margins and growth expectations.

- *EV/EBITDA (Enterprise Value to Earnings Before Interest, Tax, Depreciation and Amortization).* This multiple is the industry standard in private equity: all parties working on a deal will look at this multiple as a measure of valuation both at entry and at exit. It is particularly informative when examined through the cycle and benchmarked against relevant comparable companies and transactions. It is mainly applicable for companies that operate in stable and mature sectors, where EBITDA can serve as an appropriate measure of earnings. When used in the context of a comparable analysis, EV/EBITDA multiples can be presented on a scatterplot against EBITDA growth: this could be a good way to get an impression of a valuation premium that might be expected for a target with a specific growth profile. Even though EV/EBITDA is a popular metric, EBITDA excludes depreciation, which is nonetheless a real cost of doing business. Further, EBITDA ignores the reinvestment needs of the company, so it is not an appropriate approximation of cash flow (which will need to include maintenance CAPEX and working capital required for the business so that it can operate under normal conditions). Special mention should be given here to another related multiple, EV/EBITDAR (Enterprise Value to Earnings Before Interest, Tax, Depreciation, Amortization and Rent). This may be a more appropriate multiple to use for valuing companies where rent expense is an integral part of business economics, such as restaurants, casinos, supermarkets and other retail operators.

- *EV/EBIT (Enterprise Value to Earnings Before Interest and Tax).* Similar to EV/EBITDA multiple in its spirit, EV/EBIT is used more frequently for companies with a high fixed asset base and significant invested capital. The multiple has similar limitations to those we already discussed for EV/EBITDA; however, there is an added complication: this multiple incorporates the impact arising from the company's choice of depreciation and amortization policies.

- *EV/OpFCF (Enterprise Value to Operating Free Cash Flow).* Possibly the holy grail of all multiples: this metric incorporates free cash flow, which is one of the best measures of value in the context of a private equity transaction. The calculation includes actual CAPEX, which makes this multiple truly powerful, especially in the context of a year-on-year comparison as capital intensity might be changing over time. One possible drawback of this multiple is the following: for businesses with varying capital requirements (for example, due to the occasional changes in technology), there might be meaningful swings in operating cash flows, which will make EV/OpFCF very volatile. However, it is always possible to make this multiple more useful by calculating a normalized level of operating free cash flow in the denominator.

- *Industry benchmarks.* A smart way to express the price of a company or its enterprise value might be through the lens of a sector ratio. Here are some examples: price per square foot (for real estate); price per subscriber or price per click (for internet-based businesses); and price per bed (for care homes and hospital). Virtually all industries have their own bespoke ratios and benchmarks: you can learn which ones to use by reviewing analyst research reports for any public company operating in the same industry.

- *P/BV (Price to Book Value).* I typically ignore book value figure in most transactions, unless the business operates in a sector where book value closely corresponds to the market value of the company's assets. For a regular operating business, book value may not be refreshed in the financial statements for quite some time, making it an irrelevant accounting entry. For a company that has been accumulating losses for a few years, it is not unusual for P/BV to hit negative territory— and there are plenty of such examples in the stock market. However, P/BV is absolutely key for valuing financials: this is everyone's go-to multiple for the evaluation of banks, insurance and consumer finance companies, as the ratio of price to book value clearly expresses the premium to asset value that the purchaser is expected to pay. To make the analysis even more informative, it might be interesting to examine the relationship between P/BV and return on equity on a scatterplot, both for the target business and its peers: what you will typically see is that companies that earn a higher return on equity command a higher price on a P/BV basis.

- *P/E (Price to Earnings).* The majority of private equity professionals treat P/E multiples with skepticism bordering on disdain. There is some logic to being dismissive: P/E multiples are hardly comparable for companies with different amounts of net debt, different depreciation and amortization policies and different tax structures. Net income, being the bottom-line figure, is influenced by myriad accounting decisions and potential manipulations. Static P/E multiples also provide no information about revenue growth, cash generation or returns that companies earn on their investments. While I recognize all of the problems detailed above, I nonetheless include P/E in my analysis. First of all, my view of valuation for a private deal in the US will most definitely be influenced by the forward P/E multiple at which a relevant stock market index, such as S&P 500, is trading at the time of the deal. Is it 15 times? Is it 30 times? Second, if I look at a foreign transaction, it definitely makes sense to check at what multiples the public markets are trading in that geography. I have seen this metric as low as 4× forward P/E in some markets during especially gloomy times.

That's what I like about P/E multiples: this information is instantly available and can readily inform me about the current behavior of market participants. When looking at P/E multiples across a comparable universe in connection with a particular transaction, I might go as far as re-levering all of them to the same capital structure; however—because I have a life to live—I probably won't make any adjustments to normalize depreciation, amortization and tax. Unfortunately, this approach will be very wrong if my comparison includes companies operating in different jurisdictions with dissimilar accounting rules—but *c'est la vie*. In summary, I am reluctant to discard the P/E approach: I believe it can help contextualize the current state of the market and provide another—imperfect yet colorful—stroke of paint to my valuation canvas.

Valuation Methods

We all appreciate that there are scores of valuation methods available for valuing a private equity target. My personal philosophy is fairly simple: use all possible methodologies, including the ones that might be somewhat deficient—as long as I understand the potential caveats. The more data points I can generate, the easier the valuation exercise becomes: after a while, I begin to get a sense of a value range that can plausibly reflect the company's worth.

A good starting point is to determine where the market is pricing similar companies and transactions.

- *Publicly listed comparable companies.* In a perfect world, the publicly listed universe used for this analysis should consist of companies that are similar and relevant to the investment target. It is best to keep the comparison to the same geography and the same industry, if possible, in order to minimize the potential impact of accounting differences, uneven capital requirements and dissimilar growth prospects. Once the comparable universe is identified, there is plenty that can be done. The most obvious advantage of this valuation approach lies in the large volume of publicly available data that can typically be sourced for listed businesses. One can add useful dimensions to the analysis by gradually introducing additional layers of complexity.

    For example, I might start by calculating static multiples, such as those we discussed above—EV/Sales, EV/EBITDA, EV/OpFCF and industry benchmarks—on a historic and forward basis. However, given that I am valuing a company that my fund will hold for 4–6 years, it also makes sense to consider cyclicality of the most relevant multiples over a longer time horizon, such as over 5, 7 or even 10 years. This analysis will immediately enable me to achieve two things. First, I will be able to develop an informed view on how sensible the entry valuation multiple for my transaction might appear in the context of historic values. Second, I can calibrate a range of plausible multiples that my investment might achieve at exit. It is probably an obvious statement, but I am going to make it anyway: if you invest in a business in buoyant times and pay a record-high multiple, it is prudent to assume a lower multiple at exit—and every thoughtful investment committee will undoubtedly ask you to do exactly that.

Any analysis of publicly listed comparable companies can add value in a number of additional ways: I can opt to look at means and averages, or choose to review specific outliers in greater depth. Virtually any multiple is capable of revealing more information when it is displayed on a scatterplot against the most relevant growth or earnings metrics: EV/Sales versus sales growth; EV/EBITDA versus EBITDA growth; P/BV versus return on equity; and so on. This approach of displaying information visually for the entire universe of comparable companies can help you determine the magnitude of the expected valuation premium.

- *Transaction multiples.* Given how quickly financial information goes stale, I personally choose to select a fairly short data set of no more than 10–15 comparable transactions that closed during a fairly recent period of, say, 2 to 3 years. Why do I consider only a few handfuls of transactions? Personally, I do not believe in means and averages for transaction multiples, and instead prefer to consider each comparable deal in isolation in order to assess its relevance for the investment that I am working on.

More generally, I have to admit that I take any information originating from the comparable transactions analysis with a gigantic grain of salt. Let me take a moment to explain my perspective. In the world of venture capital and accounting, the purchase price that was crystallized in a recent transaction is considered to be an indication of a fair value of a company. I tend to disagree: a transaction price *might* be an indication of fair value, but it can also be the product of a winner's curse and have little to do with fair value. And, in a hot market overflowing with hubris, it is more likely to be the latter. Therefore, I need to be quite clear about the fact that the transaction comp sheet is nothing other than a display of the latest deal activity that serves as a barometer of the current state of the markets.

If someone decides to pay a certain multiple for a company, it does not necessarily mean that I should follow suit and pay the same multiple for a comparable business. How do I know that this buyer is rational? In 2015, Microsoft wrote off 96% of the value of the handset business it has acquired from Nokia for $7.9 billion the previous year; in 2011, HP bought Autonomy and wrote down $8.8 billion of this acquisition a year later (Martin, 2016). Private equity, too, unfortunately amassed plenty of examples, such as the buyouts of Harrah's and TXU, where seemingly ingenious deals ultimately fell apart and resulted in large losses for their sponsors (Indap, 2017 and Levine, 2014). Undoubtedly, all of these deals were at one point listed on somebody's transaction comp sheets.

Given my intense skepticisms, you may wonder how I am actually using the information about the comparable transactions: Am I using it at all, for anything else other than rolling my eyes? Yes, I do use it. My approach is straightforward: I am trying to review the comp sheet carefully and identify only those deals that resonate especially well with the transaction that I am working on.

First of all, I pay more attention to the multiples paid by the financial buyers: strategics underwrite M&A deals to a lower return hurdle (most commonly, corporate finance and M&A arms of corporates get approval to execute any deal that generates a return in excess of their own cost of capital). Corporations also have the benefit of either real or perceived synergies and can sometimes get away more easily with embarrassing write-offs as the examples of Microsoft and HP above suggest.

Second, I tend to compare deals with similar governance packages available to the investor: a majority deal might include a control premium, whereas a minority deal is more likely to feature a discount to account for illiquidity and reduced governance rights. Finally, I try to abide by the same principles as those I already discussed in the section dedicated to the publicly listed comparables and focus on those transactions that take place in the same geography and in the same industry as my target business. You might have guessed already that based on this conservative approach, I am likely to end up at most with only 2 or 3 comparable deals from a transaction comp sheet of 10–15 entries. And that's fine by me. I would much rather study in detail these 2–3 most relevant deals, uncover valuable transactional nuggets and generate the most actionable read-across that can be applied to my transaction.

The two market-based valuation methods above equip me first-hand with the view of how the current sentiment might impact my assessment of value. What about other approaches?

- *Liquidation value.* Not the most cheerful of the valuation methods; however, it can help me establish a floor value of a business. The liquidation value approach gives no credit to the company on a going-concern basis and solely looks at the net amount realized if all company's assets were disposed of and liabilities settled. There is an implicit assumption that the liquidating business is under time pressure (as bankruptcy might be breathing down its neck), so the analysis typically assumes that the disposals take place relatively quickly. In this context, one should expect to apply considerable discounts to the carrying values of the receivables, inventory and hard assets.

Assuming an orderly disposal takes place, some assets might prove to be quite liquid and relatively easy to realize, such as warehouses full of grain or other generic commodities, attractive real estate, or hard assets—for example, aircraft, shipping vessels, or a fleet of trucks. The liquidation value for more complex assets—such as a specialized manufacturing facility—might be impossible to determine without the involvement of a professional appraiser who can provide guidance about typical recovery values achieved in similar liquidations. This valuation method might be mostly applicable to an investment scenario where the target company is in a distress or a decline. For a regular investment, this approach is too severe—as nobody will look to liquidate a business which is a going concern. However, I find that using this method nonetheless allows me to quantify the magnitude of the maximum downside by calculating the difference between the purchase price and the liquidation value. This metric can sometimes provide peace of mind in a transaction with an above-average risk profile.

- *Replacement value.* It makes sense, in my mind, to consider replacement value only in a transaction where the company acquired its tangible assets relatively recently: it is a way to estimate how much credit the company can get for significant investment CAPEX that was incurred to build something valuable. In all other cases, I struggle to see the merit of this valuation method. Suppose that I am evaluating an electricity generation business that happens to operate a gas-fired power plant that was constructed in the late 1970s: can anyone walk me through how to even begin to think about its replacement value? Surely, this plant is inefficient and less advanced compared to any other modern power plant alternatives—so, I would argue that this asset is simply not replaceable on an equivalent basis. However, I can see how the replacement value approach makes sense to apply to a business that just spent millions of CAPEX dollars on a state-of-the-art waste management facility, or to a broadband provider that recently invested in a comprehensive upgrade of its network to the latest standard of technology.

Are you getting lethargic from reading about the various valuation methods? Let me perk you up by throwing something in that might come across as a bit controversial.

- *DCF (Discounted Cash Flows).* The honest truth is that DCF is typically ignored by the majority of the private equity industry and is not considered to be a reliable valuation tool. Investment professionals dislike the fact that terminal value frequently accounts for the majority of the enterprise value derived from a DCF method and that minor changes in some numbers, such as projected growth rates or the weighted average cost of capital ("WACC") assumptions, may produce considerable differences in the valuation output. "Garbage in, garbage out," exclaim some sarcastically when asked about the usefulness of a basic DCF. Perhaps this perception among the private equity investment professionals explains why fewer than 20% of the 79 private equity funds surveyed by Gompers et al. (2016) admitted to using some form of the discounted cash flows approach for valuing investments.

  I am firmly in the minority on this one. I actually believe that DCF—when used thoughtfully—can be theoretically sound and provide another useful data point about the fundamental value of a company. Why don't I have a problem with terminal value? Well, that's because, in my mind, terminal value is equivalent to the concept of the exit value in any LBO model. Why don't I shy away from the DCF model's extreme sensitivity? That's because I actually like reflecting about the outliers and find that the DCF model is most informative when certain assumptions are sensitized.

I can assure you that any LBO model will be as sensitive to the changes in the projections of growth rates and margins.

Nonetheless, there is one aspect of the DCF that I find bothersome: there is a chasm between the theoretical rigor and lazy day-to-day practice. For reasons unbeknownst to me, most finance practitioners calculate WACC only once, typically in Year 1, and carry this constant assumption through the entire modeling period. This laid-back approach clearly ignores academic guidance and produces nothing more than "garbage in, garbage out" type of output in the context of private equity, where investments—in most cases—feature rapid debt paydown. If you have a private equity pitchbook handy prepared by *any* investment bank on *any* private equity target, take a moment to examine the DCF section: I suspect that in 9 out 10 cases, you will detect the use of a constant WACC.

This explicitly contradicts the academic approach that warns the users of DCF about the significant impact of leverage on the magnitude of the WACC and calls for re-calculating an appropriate WACC for each discount period. If you don't feel like restating WACC for each discount period, there is a handy subtype of the DCF method, adjusted present value ("APV"), that is specifically designed for valuing companies with a changing capital structure. APV has its pros and cons. Denis Gromb, one of my business school professors who currently serves as a Chair Professor of Finance at HEC Paris, used to say in our class, "The advantage of APV is that it is a transparent valuation tool. There is no contamination and it is easier to track down where value comes from. It has one major disadvantage: nobody uses it."

It is crucial, however, not to overstate my reliance on the DCF. It is indeed capable of providing the valuer with a false sense of precision. However, DCF and APV—when applied appropriately—are perfectly fine valuation tools to use alongside other valuation methods. The discounted cash flow approach is particularly applicable for infrastructure-type businesses or for asset-based companies with finite cash flows and limited terminal value, such as those engaged in shipping, satellites and drug royalties. Next time you come across a transaction involving a company with these characteristics, do something extraordinary: run an APV.

And now let's look at the bread-and-butter valuation approach used by nearly every private equity investor, where the valuer explicitly solves for the purchase price that will generate specific return targets, as measured by the gross equity IRR and the multiple on invested capital ("MOIC"). It is most frequently performed as a "back of the envelope" calculation at an early of stage of the deal, and then transferred into a more detailed returns model, such as an LBO, once the transaction progresses to the deal pricing phase.

- *Private equity method.* This approach is focused on deriving the enterprise value of the business by using a standard private equity logic: Assuming a reasonably achievable leverage multiple and my best estimate of the price that will enable me to win the deal, can I hit my required return of 2.5×–3× MOIC? The most appropriate operating model to use in this context is the base investment case I covered in Chapter 7: the projections describing this scenario will produce interim cash flows that, in a typical leveraged acquisition, will be directed to paying down debt. If you reflect on this valuation approach for a brief moment, you will notice that it amounts to nothing more than a stripped-down variant of the DCF model, where the cost of equity is the deal IRR and the terminal value is the exit value of the business.

There are two specific valuation examples that I believe I ought to mention because they frequently present a degree of difficulty: valuation of cyclical business and valuation of emerging market companies. Don't be scared of them! The very fact that challenging deals limit competition is the very reason to consider them. Would you like to find out about the specific approaches that work for me?

- *Valuation of cyclical businesses.* You may remember from previous chapters that my personal view is that cyclicality is not such a rare or frightening phenomenon in business. When saying this, I—obviously—don't encourage you to close your eyes, take the plunge, invest in a cyclical business and hope to generate handsome returns. Far from it: I encourage you to keep your eyes open and be completely aware of the cycle. It makes sense to try to explore the drivers of cyclicality in detail: Is the cycle driven by changes in consumer demand, commodity prices or capital investment? Moreover, having a solid plan that will keep the company afloat in a down cycle is an absolute requirement. Make sure you know cold to what extent margins compress and expand over time as a function of historic demand fluctuations. Can you evaluate the earnings potential of the business over the full cycle, from peak to trough?

  Once you possess enough information about the cycle itself, a good place to start a valuation exercise for a cyclical business is to obtain as much historical data as possible, so that you can derive long-term trend line in revenues, profits and cash flows. This will allow you to utilize a variety of conventional valuation metrics and methods. However, instead of grappling with volatile numbers, you can base them on normalized estimates around the trend line. When making an assumption about acquisition leverage, it is prudent to take into account the company's financial performance at the lowest point in a cycle to ensure solvency—in other words, it is wise to assume minimal leverage. The company needs plenty of liquidity and a defensible balance sheet going into a down cycle. Furthermore, the most attractive investment thesis for acquiring a cyclical business is to outsmart the others: negotiate a purchase price that takes into account historically low earnings and stockpile cash upfront in advance of a further downward swing. This strategy will enable the target business to buy out distressed competitors or lock into capital projects during a cyclical trough, when commodity prices and other capital inputs are cheaper. Provided that the company is brave enough to embrace this contrarian logic and capable of surviving the full cycle, it can emerge as a flourishing and desirable business at exit.

- *Valuation of emerging market companies.* How many times have you said no to an attractive deal simply because the target company is located in an emerging market? I have a lot of sympathy: less developed markets present a whole host of hazards, the biggest of which is unsystematic risk. It can manifest itself through unexpected government interventions, social unrest or the sudden inability to repatriate profits. Combined with sharp macroeconomic cycles, high inflation, volatile local currencies and illiquid capital markets, one may wonder what compels investors to make acquisitions in risky geographies to begin with? More often than not, the most gripping feature of emerging market investments is access to extraordinary growth that—if things go well—trickles down to investors in a form of eye-watering investment returns. Nobody would be keen to take excess risk, if it were not for the prospect of excess return.

  When tasked with valuing a company in an emerging market, my first instinct is to do as much work as possible on understanding the historic and projected macroeconomic environment: economic growth, inflation rates and the FX curve. If the macro forecast is poor, there is nothing more to do. If, by contrast, it looks rather promising, my next step is to perform a valuation analysis of the investment target. There is one key complication, however: the company's cash flows are denominated in a risky currency that won't match the currency of my investment fund. Also, the nominal growth rates may appear abnormally high to what we typically encounter in developed markets, given a more pronounced inflationary environment. What do we do?

Economic theory suggests that nominal cash flows discounted at nominal rates should be completely equivalent to the corresponding real cash flows discounted by the corresponding real rates. However, this might be rather confusing. When valuing an emerging market business, I follow two simple rules: I ignore real rates and I ignore the currency of my fund. In other words, I consider all valuation metrics and model operating cash flows in nominal terms in a local currency. If there is any significant debt in the business, it better be denominated in local currency to avoid a disastrous currency mismatch.[3] The final step is to calculate an investment return on the investment in a local currency as well, which—at this stage—I can translate in the currency of my fund.

For example, suppose I am investing out of a dollar-denominated fund and looking at an investment where the equity returns consists of a dividend payment in Year 3 and exit proceeds in Year 5. How do I get from a local currency return to a dollar return? I translate the initial equity investment into dollars using the FX rate that applies at the transaction closing date, followed by converting the dividend payment in Year 3 at the applicable FX forward rate for Year 3

---

[3]If this is not the case, I would probably drop the deal unless I can make my investment conditional upon repayment of this debt instrument or refinancing it into local currency.

and do it again for the exit proceeds in Year 5 (please note that you should expect the FX forward rate in Year 5 to be higher than that in Year 3 in most cases). The dollar return can be further adjusted to account for the sovereign risk that I am taking: I can look up the cost of a 5-year credit default swap ("CDS")[4] for the geography of the deal and subtract it from the dollar return. I can, of course, choose to hedge the sovereign risk explicitly by getting my fund to buy protection in the form of a 5-year CDS at the time of transaction closing as most private equity funds are allowed to hold derivative instruments for hedging purposes. There is no requirement to hold the CDS to maturity: if something goes wrong in the country because of the political or macro factors, the CDS will dramatically shoot up in value and will allow me to achieve a partially victorious outcome if I sell the CDS in isolation at that time and crystallize a substantial profit.

From Valuation to Pricing

Valuation talk is cheap, unless it helps you derive a price that wins the deal. And the winning price itself can turn out to be quite perilous: it can lead to gains or losses. How do you avoid the latter outcome? According to Howard Marks, the most dependable route to an investment profit is "buying something for less than its value" (Marks 2011). It does sound like a great strategy. However, had I followed it closely, I would have done very few deals. The world of private equity is fiercely competitive most of the time, and "buying low, selling high" is simply unrealistic to attain on a consistent basis.

---

[4]In the absence of a CDS for a country, the cost of sovereign risk can be approximated by the spread between the long-term dollar-denominated sovereign bond and the US Treasury benchmark of the same duration.

Since paying a price below the company's value all the time is hard to achieve in practice, how about paying fair value? Fair to the buyer and fair to the seller? This approach, in most cases, will enable the buyer to generate only a fair return that may not hit the outsized 20–25% IRR that private equity funds are targeting. What's the answer, then? In my mind, it is not worth putting a bid on a company at all, unless the value of the business to the buyer exceeds the value of the business to the seller. This scenario is possible when the seller desperately needs to sell the company. Alternatively, the buyer can engineer a situation of this nature by developing a unique deal angle that is capable of transforming the business in a manner that is simply not accessible to the seller.

How does one transition from valuation to pricing in practice? I start by plotting all the data points that I am aware of. What are the seller's pricing expectations? How realistic are they? What is the guidance from the deal advisers? Can they present the value ranges derived from the various valuation approaches on the "valuation football field"?[5] What's an affordable price range, as determined by my valuation work and, more importantly, my returns model? The considerations above enable me to triangulate toward a negotiation range, where additional deliberations might prove useful. Possible examples of points to consider include the following:

1. Does the deal command a premium because of a particularly attractive feature, such as access to a talented management team or a unique asset?
2. Does the deal command a discount because, for example, the company has recently underinvested in its business and, generally, is in some sort of disarray?

---

[5]The valuation football field is a conventional way of displaying visually the valuation ranges derived from all accessible valuation approaches.

3. How competitive is the sale process? Does the seller have many alternatives?

4. How attractive can this business be at exit: Will it appeal to many buyers?

5. Does the pricing range reflect the economic reality and current market sentiment appropriately?

6. Does the price need to be adjusted based on the stake that is being offered?

7. In a deal where the seller retains a stake, can my fund's strategic and operational insight add differentiated value to the seller? If so, has this been communicated appropriately?

8. Can I bid a bit lower and offer speed and transaction certainty to the seller?

9. Do I get paid for the execution risk in this transaction? Do I give up too much of my upside to the seller?

10. Is my fund too desperate to do a deal? Is the seller desperate to do the deal?

The considerations above represent a thought process that helps firm up the negotiation range: I typically know at this stage what price level represents the final stop. At times, it is possible to reach an agreement that feels fair to both parties and where the deal price falls within the acceptable limits. At other times, there is a persistent difference of opinion between a buyer and a seller about the company's worth. But all is not lost: provided that the seller is still willing to engage in further negotiations, there are a few deal structuring mechanisms that can help overcome valuation gaps and modify deal economics for both parties. To read more about what these deal structuring tools are, please refer to the next chapter.

9

Deal Structuring

Key Topics in Chapter 9:

- Capital structure considerations: what type of leverage to use and when it is too much
- Management Incentive Plans: target A, reward A and achieve A
- Enhance your deal through earn-outs, earn-ins, escrows and vendor loan notes
- Minority deals: negotiate robust exit rights or be held hostage by majority owners
- Advanced deal structuring techniques for minority investments

---

What is deal structuring, exactly? There are quite a few topics that fall within this realm, ranging from financing and governance considerations to the legal and tax aspects of a deal. This chapter will focus on what I regard as the three most crucial areas of deal structuring: the capital structure, the management incentive plan and the key deal structuring features that private equity sponsors might choose to employ in order to improve the risk and reward characteristics of a deal. Unlike valuation, the topic of structuring a private equity investment is scarcely covered else-where: while there is some information available about typical debt structures and management incentive plans, there is very little written about more advanced deal features, such as those involving performance-based value sharing or hybrid equity financing. This clear gap in the investment literature gives me an opportunity to say a few things about a variety of deal structuring tools that, in my experience, can help investors maximize returns, overcome entry valuation gaps, amplify upside or serve as a downside protection mechanism. I will focus on these more advanced deal features at the end of this chapter.

Capital Structure

As you no doubt already know, private equity investors most commonly use a mixture of debt and equity in order to purchase a business. Typical control deals require full repayment of the existing financing instruments, so investors start from a clean slate and make decisions relating to the company's capital structure completely afresh.

The first consideration in any leveraged acquisition is, naturally, debt. Employing leverage has its pros and cons. Thanks to several high-profile LBO fiascos, the private equity industry is often criticized for using too much debt. While I would argue that this statement is not universally true for all private equity deals, I admit that excessive leverage sends chills up my spine: it significantly increases the risk of financial distress for the target business and can magnify losses for the private equity sponsor. The concept of debt, more generally, has a stigma attached to it: in some societies, borrowing might still be associated with living beyond one's means and engaging in something self-indulgent. However, virtually no capital structure would be considered optimal without any use of debt, so it is generally a good idea for any business, whether it is a private equity target or not, to have an appropriate level of leverage.

The benefits of leverage in an LBO are evident: debt enhances equity returns and motivates the management team to cut organizational slack and focus on maximizing free cash flows. There is the added advantage of tax deductibility of interest expenses: the LBOs that I worked on typically would pay little to no taxes for the first 4–5 years. This, in effect, means that the value created in a leveraged structure also includes an implicit transfer from the government. Does this sound bad? Perhaps it does; however, the same tax saving is available to any company with a debt instrument in its capital structure. Let's leave it at that.

What is a typical capital structure for a leveraged acquisition? There are quite a few choices of financing instruments available to equity sponsors. Most commonly, an LBO features several tranches of debt, each with a decreasing order of priority and commensurately increasing cost. The larger the transaction, the more layers of different debt you will usually see within a single deal. The debt providers, such as banks and other institutional debt investors, impose a number of obligations on the borrower—known as covenants—in order to enforce financial compliance, identify early warning signs of a potentially deteriorating performance and maximize the chance of the loans being serviced and repaid.

Let me briefly run through a typical LBO capital structure:[1]

- *Senior secured debt.* Quantum: 50–55% of the capital structure or up to 5× LTM EBITDA (although senior debt providers might be willing to lend as much as 5.5-6× LTM EBITDA

---

[1]If you are looking for in-depth examples of typical LBO structures, please see Chapter 13 in Arzac (2007) for a worked example of an LBO; Chapter 9 in Ippolito (2020) for a typical debt structure, "back-of-the-envelope" LBO and full LBO model; and Chapter 5 in Rosenbaum and Pearl (2009) for a step-by-step LBO analysis. Please refer to Chapter 9 References for complete publishing citations.

for established companies with very stable cash flows). The senior debt package is often structured as several tranches of term loans: Senior A is an amortizing instrument with a typical cost of 250–275 basis points ("bps") over the benchmark rate and maturity of about 6 years; Senior B and Senior C are bullet tranches, where Senior B costs about 50 bps more than Senior A and has a longer tenor of 7 years and Senior C costs about 50 bps more than senior B and has a maturity of 8 years. Some capital structures will not have a Senior C tranche at all, so the senior debt package will consist solely of an amortizing tranche A and a bullet tranche B. You get the logic by now: for each subsequent debt tranche, lenders charge a progressively higher cost of debt—typically in increments of about 50 bps—to compensate for the lack of amortization, the longer tenor and lower ranking in the capital structure.

Senior debt providers require the strictest set of borrower obligations compared to lenders of other debt instruments. These obligations consist of *affirmative covenants* (such as regular reporting and specific application of loan proceeds), *negative covenants* (that will prevent the borrower from taking on additional liabilities or paying dividends to equity holders) and *financial covenants* (specific ratios to ensure sufficient headroom for interest and principal repayment).[2] The senior lenders will also typically extend additional debt facilities that allow multiple drawings (just like a credit card), such as a revolving credit facility, a working capital facility to finance the seasonal needs of the business, an expansion CAPEX facility and / or an acquisition facility. These

---

[2]For a detailed discussion of covenants, please see Chapter 4 in Rosenbaum and Pearl (2009) and Darley (2009). Please refer to Chapter 9 References for complete citations.

additional instruments will generally have the same ranking in the capital structure as senior debt and normally have the same maturity as the Senior A tranche.

Senior debt facilities are most commonly arranged by banks, and then subsequently syndicated to a broader group of institutional investors in order to spread the risk. The lead lenders who arrange the debt financing charge an underwriting fee of 2–3% payable at closing of the transaction—and this cost comes on top of the cost of debt that the company will bear in an LBO. The more holders of senior debt there are post-syndication, the better it is for the equity sponsors: if the company experiences a period of deteriorating performance down the road, the equity providers have a greater likelihood of productive negotiations with the lenders, who each hold a small sliver of the company's debt and who, therefore, might offer a sympathetic ear. This may be more difficult to achieve if the senior lending group is represented by one or two dominant lenders who run excessive risk on their balance sheets and who have the ability and the firepower to enforce on the loans and take control of the business.

Since senior secured debt is the cheapest form of financing, private equity funds will always try to maximize the amount of debt available from the senior lenders before considering other layers of more expensive debt in the capital structure. Also, there is one additional advantage: senior debt can usually be prepaid at par (i.e. refinanced before maturity without prepayment penalties), which provides the equity investors with additional flexibility in case the circumstances of the target business change in the future.

- *Second lien.* This instrument ranks as senior subordinated debt, has a maturity of up to 9.5 years, and costs anywhere between 450 and 650 bps over the benchmark rate. However, second lien debt may not always be widely available: it is highly dependent on market conditions and—in tight credit markets—may be offered only to those companies that, in the eyes of a lender, have a particularly attractive credit profile. The second lien debt market is active and competitive in geographies with well-developed capital markets, and may be practically nonexistent in places where the capital markets are fairly illiquid.

The quantum of this debt is negotiable and is specific to a particular borrower. The main advantage of second lien is that it is still relatively cheap compared to other financing options. It also typically features limited prepayment penalties compared to other forms of subordinated debt that we will discuss below. One major disadvantage of second lien is that in a lukewarm market it might only be available from a few aggressive and speculative lenders who might demand meaningful negative control rights in return for a relatively small investment. This might add tremendous constraints on the business as well as complexity and risk to the capital structure, so I would argue that this form of debt should be avoided altogether unless equity sponsors manage to run a competitive process and secure reasonable terms for this debt financing.

- *Subordinated debt.* Quantum: 20–30% of the capital structure, or around 1.5–2.5× LTM EBITDA. There are two main choices of instruments at this point in the capital structure: a high-yield bond or a mezzanine loan.

  High-yield bonds are typically 8- to 10-year bullet instruments, with a cost of 7–9% per annum, where interest payment can be structured either as a cash coupon or—for an additional premium of around 75 bps—as a payment-in-kind ("PIK") coupon that accrues over time. Compared to senior debt, high-yield bonds have less restrictive covenants and provide greater operational flexibility to the borrower. However, this instrument has two important caveats. First, there is limited ability to restructure and pre-pay high-yield bonds due to a set of non-call provisions that effectively commit the borrower to this instrument for the first 3–5 years. Second, high-yield bonds are listed instruments that need to be issued and marketed to investors in the public markets, subjecting the borrower to market capacity, timing and liquidity risk. This means that it might be hard to implement a high-yield bond financing for a hurried private equity transaction, as there may not be enough time to arrange a successful roadshow and ensure a full take-up of the bond issue.

Mezzanine loans represent an alternative form of subordinated debt: similar to a high-yield bond, they are also often structured as an 8- to 10-year bullet instrument. However, they are more expensive, with costs ranging from 8% to 12% per annum or higher. Annual coupons are structured either as an all-PIK coupon, or as part cash coupon of 4–5% per annum, with the balance accruing through a PIK coupon. Mezzanine loans are structured as private debt instruments sold to specialized debt investors, which makes their implementation fairly quick and straightforward. Some providers of mezzanine loans may ask the borrower to provide a so-called "equity kicker" in the form of equity warrants as a part of the financing, so that the mezzanine holder can achieve a higher all-in return, typically in the area of 12–15% per annum.[3] Compared to high-yield bonds, mezzanine loans feature less severe early termination penalties and can often be pre-paid without extra charges after Year 3. The

---

[3]Please see Chapter 13 in Arzac (2007) for a worked example of a mezzanine loan with an "equity kicker." Please refer to Chapter 9 References for a complete citation.

covenants that apply to mezzanine loans normally mirror those in place for the senior term loans; however, the key coverage ratios afford the company more flexibility and feature additional headroom of about 10%.

- *Other debt.* Apart from the most common debt instruments we discussed above, you may sometimes come across securitizations (ranking as senior debt); vendor loans (ranking as subordinated notes) or PIK notes (ranking directly above equity). There are no standard market terms for vendor loans as they are completely negotiable, although paying cash interest may not be allowed by the senior lenders. PIK, as the name implies, is a sliver of non-cash paying debt provided by adventurous debt investors targeting about 15% IRR. The inclusion of the PIK notes allows the equity sponsors to stretch the leverage ratio to the limit—at a cost which is still marginally lower than that of equity.

- *Equity.* In a typical leveraged transaction, the total equity contribution amounts to about 20–30% of the capital structure. What's a good way to think about the appropriate cost of the equity financing? Equity investors focus both on the IRR and the MOIC: when considering these two metrics, more attention is given to the total amount of capital gain. Therefore, it is fair to say that an appropriate cost of equity can be expressed as a return that enables investors to generate 2.5×–3× of invested capital over 4–5 years. The equity tranche most commonly features a more senior class, structured as a shareholder loan note or a preferred stock[4] with a rolling PIK coupon of 8–15% per annum, and a more junior class, common stock. Shareholder loan notes provide a form

---

[4]Preferred stock is a senior equity class that functions in the same manner as shareholder loan notes: it is structured as equity rather than debt and usually has dividend rights.

of return and liquidation preference to the equity holders, and also enable them to achieve an efficient structuring of the management equity award. Common stock—also known as ordinary equity—is the bottom layer of the capital structure, a modest portion of which is allocated to management equity and the rest is held by the equity sponsors. As a result, management equity represents the most leveraged position in the whole capital structure: not only is it subordinated to the LBO debt, it is further leveraged by the shareholder loan and its accruing coupon. We will look at the economics of the management equity award more closely later in the chapter.

Now that we have considered a typical capital structure in an LBO, let's pivot to the immediately practical questions. How do we know how much leverage to employ? What is an optimum split among the various debt and equity instruments?

The total level of debt depends not only on the specific credit profile of the business but also on the credit market conditions at the time of the transaction. In feverish markets, leverage multiples generally tend to rise—albeit to a lesser extent than the acquisition multiples. In terms of company-specific considerations, you have probably heard about the two major types of bank financing that may be available: asset-based or cash flow–based. Asset-based lending allows businesses—even those with poor earnings—to borrow against their hard assets based on a specific loan-to-value ratio (akin to a mortgage loan on a house). However, bank debt in a typical LBO is normally based on the expected cash flows of the business. A company with a steady and growing cash flow profile can usually borrow more than a business that generates cash flows that are uncertain or volatile. As senior term loans represent the largest share of the capital structure, the lending banks in charge of the senior debt package play a key role in determining the ultimate leverage multiple that is achievable for a given private equity transaction. Contrary to what one might expect, this is not a trivial matter: lending banks use a blizzard of ratios to estimate a probability of default and determine debt capacity that permits debt service without the need of refinancing during the period of senior debt amortization. What do the banks do in practice to determine the maximum amount of senior debt? They examine the company's business plan thoroughly, run a variety of adverse scenarios and determine a comfortable leverage multiple that allows the business to withstand the downside in the vast majority of cases and ensures adequate cash flow headroom even in a scenario where the company significantly underperforms.

Once the use of the senior debt facilities is fully maximized, equity sponsors use their best judgment in order to determine what other subordinated debt instruments might be appropriate given the specific context of the deal. Key considerations include cost, operational flexibility and execution risks. For example, if the private equity sponsors are under pressure to meet a particular deadline, they might prefer to go down the mezzanine loan route instead of trying to issue a high-yield bond in a hurry. Thoughtful private equity funds understand that as a part of the transaction, they accept responsibility to thousands of the company's employees and their families. Therefore, they would be minded to structure additional layers of debt carefully—especially for businesses with high operating leverage—and ensure that subordinated debt instruments meet the unique needs of the business during the private equity fund's investment horizon. Many would agree: it rarely makes sense to handcuff the target company with excessive leverage at the outset of the transaction and then lose sleep over its solvency. Instead, the equity investors in any leveraged acquisition are better off targeting a reasonable capital structure—the one that can withstand a few headwinds and will enable the private equity funds to maintain control of the business throughout the economic cycle: in good times and in bad.

Management Incentive Plan

As we already explored in Chapter 6, the private equity industry is known for its ability to hire, retain and motivate superb management teams. Most private equity investors will tell you that the value creation in their portfolio companies is driven by the quality and dedication of the managers who take responsibility for delivering on—and sometimes outperforming—the business plan. Private equity investors address the "agent-principal" problem head on: they make managers owners in the target business and ensure that their incentives are directly aligned with those of the shareholders. This is exactly what the Management Incentive Plan ("MIP") is designed to do.

While the exact structure of the MIP depends on the governing jurisdiction and local tax rules,[5] the majority of the management compensation packages follow the same logic. Incentive plans are most commonly offered to a small group of senior executives and a few other critical employees who take daily responsibility for driving financial performance. The size of the total management award often represents about 15–20% of the company's common equity. It is not unusual for about up to half of the equity pool to be allocated solely to the CEO: the aim here is to ensure that a successful private equity transaction translates into a meaningful step-up in the CEO's personal wealth.

---

[5]For a comparison of management incentive equity arrangements in private equity transactions across the United States, Europe and Asia, please see a paper prepared by Weil, Gotshal & Manges LLP (Weil, 2015). Please refer to Chapter 9 References for complete publishing information.

Management equity awards usually follow a vesting schedule in order to maximize retention and enable private equity funds to alter compensation based on individual performance. As a private equity–backed company embarks on its growth trajectory post-closing, it needs to think through how to incentivize new joiners: therefore, most private equity funds set aside about 3–5% of the equity pool for future hires.

The participation in the management equity award is not free and requires an upfront investment by the management team. How much should each key executive invest at closing? This sensitive discussion arises on every deal—and the truth is that there is no prescriptive answer. For a highly paid CEO who already built and sold a business in the past, a suitable level of investment might be in the millions of dollars. In fact, CEOs who are founders or significant owners in the company already will be expected to roll over between 80% and 100% of their stake into the deal. For more junior members of the management team—for example, for those who are newly promoted and have young families—the appropriate investment level might be a fraction of the CEO's investment amount and might equal about one year's gross salary. It is important to remember that private equity investors are not really looking for management to fund a sizeable portion of the deal: all they want is "skin in the game" and full alignment of incentives. The desired psychological effect can be described as follows: the senior management team should invest a meaningful proportion of their wealth to feel motivated to deliver on a business plan and earn a life-changing amount of money. Losing their personal investment in a transaction should definitely feel painful to them; however, it should not be so dramatic that they are lying awake at night worrying about their ability to pay the bills. Excessive worry might lead to a disproportionate amount of stress that will make management overly risk-averse.

Here is an example of a simple MIP structure that demonstrates the magnitude of the gain that management teams can
expect to earn in a successful private equity transaction:

a. A private equity fund acquires a business for $300 million,
   where $200 million is funded by debt. Therefore, the total
   equity requirement is $100 million.
b. A small group of top executives is offered to purchase 20%
   of the common equity. However, there is one problem: they
   are fairly young and not yet independently wealthy, so collectively they can't invest more than $2 million into the deal.
   This is an important structuring consideration: since you
   are now looking to allocate 20% of the equity upside in a
   $300 million company for $2 million, this means that the
   size of the total common equity needs to be $10 million.
   As you can see, the only way to get to a stake of 20% given
   the investment constraint of $2 million is to have a very thin
   capitalization in the common equity tranche.
c. Now we know that the required equity funding of $100 mil-
   lion will consist of $10 million of common equity ($2 million
   divided by 20%)—and the remaining amount of $90 million
   will go into the shareholder loan.
   i. The resultant equity structure will consist of a manage-
      ment stake in the common equity ($2 million) as well
      as the "institutional strip" financed by the private equity
      fund ($8 million of common equity and $90 million of
      the shareholder loan).[6]

---

[6]Please note that this simple structure won't work if the CEO rolls over a
significant stake into the deal and other members of the management team
are only able to invest modest amounts of capital. In this case, the CEO will
have to participate in the institutional strip, and the private equity fund will
have to work out the required capitalization of the common equity based
on the appropriate equity incentive percentage for other team members.

    ii. As discussed earlier in the chapter, shareholder loans always feature a fairly high coupon of 8–15% per annum in order to create a performance hurdle for management and provide the sponsor with a liquidation preference.[7] Let's assume that the coupon rate on the shareholder loan is 10% per annum in this example.

d. For the sake of simplicity, suppose the business is sold 5 years later and the value of the company's equity at exit is $300 million.

    i. The private equity investor receives total proceeds of $269 million: $90 million of the shareholder loan principal; about $55 million of the accrued interest on the shareholder loan; and about $124 million of proceeds for their 80% stake in the common equity.

    ii. The management receives $31 million of proceeds for their 20% stake in the common equity, a 15.5× return on their $2 million investment. As you no doubt understand, this is the type of payout that makes jobs at private equity-backed companies so popular with entrepreneurial executives who thrive in high-pressure environments.

    iii. You may have noticed that management's equity could also become completely worthless if the exit were less successful: since the shareholder loan principal and accrued interest rank ahead of the common equity, any exit equity value of $145 million or less will effectively mean that the common equity is wiped out and management will get nothing.

---

[7] In certain jurisdictions, there might be an additional benefit in that all or part of the interest on the shareholder loan may be tax deductible.

There are two further important aspects to remember about management equity plans. First, a management equity award is a long-term incentive tool that enables the team to acquire shares in a company at a relatively low price. Thus, it is only fair to expect that this arrangement comes with a number of strings attached, such as a tight vesting schedule, no voting rights and a number of clauses that will penalize behavior that private equity funds will want to discourage. Second, share incentive schemes typically are structured in a tax-efficient manner, enabling the capital gains achieved in a deal to be taxed at a rate which is lower than that applied to ordinary income. The various restrictions I mentioned above help justify the reasons why these shares can be sold to management at relatively lost cost. As the deal progresses, management may be awarded or invited to purchase more equity shares, so their eventual capital gain will be even larger.

Advanced Deal Structures

There are a number of structuring mechanisms available in virtually any private equity deal that can help reallocate risks, enhance liquidity options and, more generally, satisfy the varying needs of a buyer and a seller. The range of structuring tools that are both available and critical depends, to a large extent, on whether the investor ends up being a majority or a minority investor. Let's look at both scenarios.

In a full buyout of a company, investors get to control the business post-transaction: their investment represents nearly the entire position in the equity and entitles them to the vast majority of the upside. Since the position of majority investors is already quite favorable, there are relatively few structuring tools available that can further improve the deal. If you think about it for a moment, you will agree that majority investors don't actually require a lot of complicated structuring. They already own the two most valuable aspects of the deal: the majority of the equity upside and the ability to make all strategic, operational and financial decisions in the target business. Nonetheless, it is always worthwhile to consider whether additional deal features might improve the risk and reward profile of the transaction. I often start with the following three:

- *Earn-out.* In my view, this is one of the most effective tools that helps buyers and sellers to overcome an entry valuation gap. It also helps investors to protect their downside because an earn-out effectively transfers part of the risk of the business performance from the buyer to the seller. Owners of companies tend to be optimistic about the prospects of their business and tend to incorporate myriad rosy considerations to come up with their valuation aspirations—and some are more reasonable than others. If the buyer does not agree with the seller's overly ambitious price expectations for the company, an earn-out can still help achieve the seller's headline price by splitting the purchase consideration into a portion payable at closing and a contingent portion payable some time in the future provided certain specific targets are met.

  Suppose the seller is convinced that the business is worth $1 billion and the buyer can't get to a price above $800 million. The deal between these two parties can still go ahead for a headline price of $1 billion, where $800 million is paid upfront and $200 million is structured as a contingent payment that will be only become due if the business hits certain clearly defined milestones within a specified timeframe. Performance thresholds might include financial targets, such as specific levels of revenue, gross margin or EBITDA; or operational targets such as the completion of a specific project, finalization of a valuable contract or a successful product launch. Best practice is to avoid linking a fixed payment to a binary financial target, in order to discourage the company from manipulating the numbers and reduce the risk of potential litigation between the buyer and the seller. A superior alternative is to make the contingent payment variable and connect it explicitly to a range of outcomes, so that the seller can still be rewarded if the company is on the right track but can't quite reach its full target within the pre-agreed timeframe.

There is an inverse variant of this structure: *an earn-in*. In the example above, an earn-in would result in the buyer paying $1 billion upfront and getting $200 million back from the seller if specific performance targets are not met. However, earn-ins are far less common than earn-outs because they are less attractive, as the buyer will have to bear the credit risk of the seller and make a larger equity investment upfront—potentially completely unnecessarily.

- *Downside protection through an escrow.* This approach can often serve as an elegant solution in a situation where the buyer is very interested to do a deal with the seller, but is worried about a specific, clearly defined and quantifiable risk facing the business. For example, let's assume that the target company is facing a litigation claim that won't be settled until after the closing of the transaction. From the legal work done on the case, it is known to the buyer and the seller that the magnitude of a potential loss to the business can range from zero up to $10 million. The buyer can still proceed with the deal on the condition that the vendor funds an escrow account in an amount which is equivalent to the best estimate of the maximum value of the claim—$10 million in this illustrative case. Once the claim is settled, the funds in the escrow account get released either to the purchaser or back to the vendor, depending on the outcome. For this structure to work well, it is important that the risk that the buyer is trying to manage is known, quantifiable and has a high probability of materializing fully or being resolved in the near term. No vendor will want to lock up a large sum just to cover a buyer's concern about a highly unlikely, unknown or unquantifiable risk that may potentially emerge in the future.

- *Vendor loan note.* This mechanism has a number of attractive features that apply to a whole spectrum of investment scenarios. Vendor loan notes essentially allow the buyer to defer a part of the purchase consideration by asking the seller to finance a part of the deal. As a result, the buyer of a business is able to reduce the upfront equity investment. Since vendor loan notes typically have reasonable pricing, no covenants and extremely limited negative control rights, they serve as a safe and efficient way for the equity holders to stretch subordinated debt in a transaction further. Moreover, there is one additional advantage: vendor loan notes can function in a similar manner to the escrow account arrangement we discussed above. Any future claims brought against the business can potentially be offset against the vendor loan note: in other words, the principal of the note is reduced by the amount which is equivalent to the value of any claim that materializes down the road. This approach ensures a form of a continued alignment between the seller and the target business; and, most importantly, it enables the buyer to manage a variety of risks that are hard to quantify during the transaction process but nonetheless remain present in a company post-closing.

While there are only a few potential modifications to the deal structures that work well in majority control transactions, the structuring options in minority deals are far more plentiful. And why is that? First of all, minority investors find themselves

in an inherently vulnerable position by ceding valuable governance rights and allowing the majority equity holder to control
their destiny. Therefore, minority investors—by default—need
to think upfront about a number of structural features in a
transaction in order to protect their investment, avoid falling
prey to the potentially unreasonable behavior of the controlling
investor and ensure an eventual exit from the deal at fair market
value. Second, the fact that minority investments represent only
a portion of the equity capital structure opens up a number
of alternatives around how the deal economics can be shared
among the deal participants. Finally, minority and majority
investors might be driven by completely different priorities and
motivations in the context of the same deal, so avoiding disputes in the future and aligning incentives upfront through specific structural arrangements is particularly important in every
transaction featuring several shareholders with varying degrees
of influence.

What exactly can minority investors do to protect themselves and achieve greater alignment with other shareholders?
The initial step is to negotiate a robust list of negative control rights that will allow the minority investors to gain influence over critical decisions affecting the target business, such as
changes to the composition of the board or the senior management team, significant acquisitions or disposals, incurrence of
major CAPEX and changes to the company's capital structure.[8]
The next step is to ensure that minority shareholders can actually exit their investment at fair market value within a specific
time horizon.

---

[8]Please note that this list is illustrative in its nature and, therefore, incomplete. Your transaction lawyers are best positioned to advise you on a more
detailed list of negative control rights that may apply to a specific deal.

I can't stress enough the importance of exit rights in a minority private equity deal. Minority investments—even those made in thriving businesses—can be doomed to fail if the minority shareholders can't monetize them. Without structuring a range of liquidity options upfront, exits for minority investors in private equity transactions could end up either significantly delayed or achieved only at extremely unattractive terms. After all, most private equity investors operate investment vehicles with a finite fund life: therefore, they need to avoid the nightmare scenario whereby they become forced sellers simply because their funds can't hold the investments any longer. Boston Consulting Group conducted an interesting study of minority private equity deals above $100 million that took place between 2003 and 2014, which found that in nearly 60% of all exits the minority investor was the only selling party (Boston Consulting Group, 2015). What do we conclude from this information? If you are a minority investor, never trust a majority shareholder who might be promising that both of you will exit together: instead, structure on your own exit arrangements at the outset of the deal. Otherwise, you may end up in a situation where the majority shareholder has you over the proverbial "barrel" and you may be forced to sell your investment at a material discount to fair market value.

Here is a blueprint of a potential *exit roadmap for a minority investor* in a private equity deal. It is typically designed as a staged approach that starts with those liquidity mechanisms that are easiest for the majority shareholder to accept and control. If and when those fail, the arrangement proceeds toward solutions that become more cumbersome for the controlling investor. The staged sequence provides the majority shareholder with an incentive to organize a timely exit for the minority investor at a reasonable valuation and may include the following steps:

a. First, the majority shareholder will have a Right of First Offer ("ROFO"),[9] which means that the majority shareholder has the right to offer to purchase the shares of the minority investor at a price they propose. The minority investor has the right to say yes or no. If the offer is rejected, the minority investor is free to sell its stake in a business to a reputable third party, but only at a price that exceeds that offered by the majority shareholder. That way, the majority shareholder has an incentive to bid a reasonable price to begin with, since the shares can always be sold to another buyer who might be willing to pay more;

b. If the option above fails to work (for example, if the majority shareholder decided not to exercise their ROFO or because the minority investor declined the offer price yet could not find another buyer), the two parties will agree to "work together in good faith" for a period of time to effect an exit for a minority investor through raising sufficient debt (via a refinancing) or to achieve a successful IPO. The benefit of an IPO is that the minority investor can exit while the majority shareholder can decide to retain its control position;

c. If that does not lead to an exit, the two parties will "work together in good faith" to either find a buyer for the minority stake or for the company in its entirety;

---

[9]It is far better for minority investors to give another shareholder a ROFO as opposed to a Right of First Refusal ("ROFR") because that can make it very hard to attract buyers. In effect, a ROFR will enable the other shareholder to step into the deal if it decides that the minority investor agreed a deal with the third party at a price at which they would rather buy the shares themselves. As you can imagine, any third party will be reluctant to engage in due diligence and deal negotiations if they know that the transaction can be taken away from them by an existing shareholder at the last minute.

d. If the above fails to deliver an exit, the minority investor can ask for a put right: i.e. the right to sell its stake to the majority shareholder at fair market value ("FMV"). Should the parties fail to agree on the appropriate level of FMV, they will appoint an independent third party to determine the valuation of the business; and

e. If the majority shareholder does not honor the put right within a pre-agreed timeframe, the minority investor then finally has a drag-along right that will entitle it to sell 100% of the business.

Would you rather avoid detailed negotiations of exit rights, such as those above, in a minority private equity deal? Then you can consider structuring your minority investment in a slightly different manner.

- *Convertible note.* There is no particular requirement to make a minority investment in a company in the form of equity shares. Instead, you can opt to structure your investment as a convertible note: it acts as a debt instrument that earns a coupon and can be converted to equity upon exit. A convertible note entitles the investor to either get a debt return or an equity return, whichever one works out to be higher. In other words, if the business does well, you convert your note into equity; if the business does badly, you stick with a convertible note that earns you an annual coupon. The immediate benefit of a convertible note in this scenario is that this instrument will have a maturity date, which makes a realization event relatively straightforward.

    However, some controlling shareholders may not be willing to entertain a minority investment in the form of a convertible note: it is easy enough to see that there is meaningful embedded downside protection for the note holder—and the majority shareholders may not want to extend that to another investor (or at least not without charging a significant valuation premium). There are further options that can be considered, all of which are designed to improve the risk and / or reward of a transaction.

- *Guaranteed minimum return.* In these structures, you invest in ordinary equity at the outset of a transaction, but negotiate to get a guaranteed minimum return on your investment at exit. This can range from a simple liquidation preference, whereby you get just the cost of your investment back before others receive their investments back, and the excess return is shared across all equity holders. Another option would be to negotiate a specific minimum return hurdle for your investment. This can be achieved by adjusting the number of shares you hold so that you are entitled to a greater share of exit proceeds and therefore can generate your minimum return hurdle. Alternatively, you can replicate the same economics through a preferred coupon that accrues over your investment period. This instrument will work in a similar manner as a convertible note.

There are two other structures I will mention briefly:

- *Value sharing arrangements.* If you are looking to lower your entry valuation price in a minority private equity deal, you can explore a structure whereby you give up a part of your investment upside above a certain predetermined level. For example, once your investment generates a MOIC of 2×, you can agree a split of the remaining upside above that level with the majority shareholder.
- *Upside amplification mechanism.* On occasion, you might find yourself in a situation of a value-added minority investor who brings the last slice of much-needed capital in order to get

a deal done. As a result, you may try to use your strong bargaining power to negotiate either a valuation discount, or an additional package of out-of-the-money warrants that will enhance your returns if the business outperforms.

This chapter described the main deal structuring features that I came across during my own work experience. I recognize that the material we covered here is rather dense. I hope that the dullness of the content in this chapter will be compensated by the potential benefit that the various structuring aspects might bring to your transactions in the future. Even if not all of the tools I mentioned in this section apply to your day-to-day work, I hope that you will nonetheless use every chance you can to show off your deal structuring knowledge to your team as well as your deal lawyers.

10

Deal Execution: Transaction Process and Due Diligence

Key Topics in Chapter 10:

- What to expect in a typical private equity transaction process
- Don't "boil the ocean": ten principles of a well-managed due diligence effort
- Who does what and why you need it: an anatomy of the key due diligence workstreams

---

D
eal execution processes are filled with thrills. Scarcely an hour goes by without a conference call, a meeting or an internal discussion focusing on a specific aspect of the transaction. I thrive when I find myself immersed in a deal execution process: I can feed on deal adrenaline alone and am content sleeping little, provided that the transaction is progressing, step by step, to the finish line. I relish the deeply analytical

work on the investment target that gets compressed into a couple of critical weeks. And, of course, I enjoy observing some of the theatrical action that inevitably takes place when worn-out deal participants get completely caught up in deal fever. The most fascinating places are the conference rooms where the negotiations take place. While the initial discussions are often calm and civil, fast forward to the third meeting between the buyer and the seller, and you won't be too surprised to see some anxious people banging on the table and ruffled counterparties accusing each other of re-trading the deal terms. When sleep is but a distant memory and emotions run particularly high, you are likely to observe someone losing their last bit of patience and storming out of a negotiation session.

From what I have seen, most transactions, even those that are completed successfully, tend to "die" at least once during the deal execution process. Any transaction could be temporarily or permanently terminated because vendors change their minds; or management teams get cold feet about working under private equity ownership; or the investment committee loses its decisive spirit because of particularly challenging due diligence findings; or there is a sudden onset of a global crisis that comes out of the blue and freezes all market activity. Given how many things can go wrong and can do so virtually at any moment, I always need to remind myself that it is worthwhile to balance the deal team's collective endeavors aimed at progressing the transaction with the best estimate of the most likely return on these efforts. At times, the most reasonable decision is to stop spending time and money on a transaction that no longer looks promising: the deal team and the transaction advisers simply "down tools." Is it a pause or is it a total halt? Good question. If the deal can't be revived in the next several weeks, more often than not, the precious deal momentum with the seller is lost and the deal is gone for good. That is painful, but may well be the right decision.

Transaction Process

Not all deals are destined to advance all the way to the execution stage. In fact, most do not. There are important precursors to successful deal closings that form a fairly structured deal process. Let's consider the various stages of a typical private equity transaction:

- *Preliminary discussions.* In a heavily competitive process, the only information that might be available to the private equity funds about the investment target at the initial stage is a deal teaser. It is a short, 2- to 10-page summary document about the deal providing high-level company information. The sell-side advisers retained by the target business might make themselves available for a brief conversation with potential investors, but typically won't provide access to management and certainly won't deviate much from the message already provided in the teaser. If the deal is proprietary, the process tends to be less prescriptive and will most likely consist of a few meetings between the investors and the target business.

- *Review of high-level confidential information and first-round bid.* In the event that the investors are interested in proceeding and learning more about the company post-teaser, they will be asked to sign a Non-Disclosure Agreement ("NDA"), so that they can receive confidential information about the target business. Most commonly, sell-side advisers share a formal transaction document, a Confidential Information Memorandum ("CIM"), with those investors who sign the NDA. Every potential bidder knows that the CIM is effectively a marketing document. It depicts the company and its prospects in glowing terms: it is prepared by the company's advisers who endeavor to portray the company as a highly desirable asset and stir up the excitement via a competitive auction.

Even though investors realize that the CIM might understate some of the challenges that the business might be facing and overstate the quality of the company as well as its future prospects, they nonetheless use the available information to learn more about the industry, the company, its operating environment and its business model and—most importantly—its historical and projected financials. If you are lucky to work on a deal that is not intermediated by a company's advisers, you will have to submit your own data request to the investment target: upon signing of the NDA, you can typically get ahold of a company presentation and a business plan with financial projections.

This is the stage when investors are offered restricted access to management as well: they will be invited to attend a call or a meeting with the existing management team. It is a good opportunity for potential bidders to expand their knowledge of the company and its business model, ask questions and evaluate the strategic thinking and the management style of the CEO. Many investors choose not to drill the existing team much on the matters that may come across as negative or contentious, given that potential bidders find themselves in intense competition with each other and, therefore, will work hard to come across as likeable and charming at this stage of the "courting" process.

Following the management presentation, potential buyers are asked to submit their first-round bids for the business. Most interested investors will endeavor to supplement the information provided in the CIM and the key takeaways from management meeting with any additional background analysis that can be conducted within a limited timeframe. Apart from filtering the public domain for nuggets of relevant data, reading broker reports and studying market research, the most competitive bidders will also take the time to hire industry experts and appoint main transaction advisers, such as consultants, accountants, lawyers and buy-side M&A bankers. The parties engage in a short period of intense work in order to develop an overall investment thesis, generate a differentiated deal angle and come up with a valuation range for the first-round bid.

There is frequently not enough time at this stage of the process for any meaningful interaction with the financing banks in order to calibrate the leverage assumptions that are needed to support the offer price. Some investors resort to relying on using leverage multiples recently seen in other comparable transactions. The bidders who aim to outperform, however, manage to line up their key relationship banks in order to obtain one or two support letters that are attached in the appendix of the first-round offer letter. Despite a stressful timetable, most private equity funds who compete in the first round will typically prepare a preliminary investment proposal for their investment committee to provide a transaction overview and obtain permission to spend money on transaction advisers.

- *Subsequent bidding and the final round.* Potential investors who pass the first round of bidding are granted access to the company's data room that contains extensive information covering multiple domains, such as sales, operations, finance, accounting, legal, tax, property, intellectual assets, human resources, risk and insurance.

  In competitive auctions, it is not uncommon for 3–6 bidders to participate in the second round. Given the fairly large number of parties involved, the seller might be feeling nervous about disclosing particularly sensitive information about the target company in the data room: after all, there is a chance that one of the bidders might be a shareholder or an operator in another business that competes with the target. Therefore, any documents that might make the target business vulnerable may not be disclosed in the data room. Examples of sensitive information that may not be readily available include customer lists, contract terms with large suppliers, joint venture agreements with important business partners or special compensation arrangements with top managers. If potential investors require certain information that is not available in the data room, they typically submit a separate information request to the company's advisers.

Apart from gaining access to more confidential information about the target business, potential investors are typically allowed to conduct site visits and arrange further meetings with management. Visiting the head office, meeting additional members of management, touring the company's facilities and getting a glimpse of the operational processes provide investors and their advisers with additional insights about the target business in advance of the next bidding round. Depending on the number of interested parties at this stage of the process, the company's advisers conduct one or two additional bidding rounds in order to narrow down the list to only one or two potential investors.

This is a busy time for deal teams. Together with their consultants, accountants, lawyers and industry experts, they have to identify priority areas of the initial company due diligence, with a view to develop and validate their investment base case. This is also the right time to involve a number of lending banks and run a competitive process in order to secure one or two leverage proposals with the best financing terms. Before bidding in the subsequent rounds, the deal teams need to prepare an updated investment proposal for their investment committee. The work on the investment proposal should not be underestimated: it is a detailed document that provides the most up-to-date view of the company, the investment thesis and deal angle, the proposed valuation and deal structure, the summary of findings from the initial due diligence, the key assumptions in the investment base case, the exit analysis, investment returns and sensitivities. The deal teams also discuss bidding tactics and the likelihood of a successful completion. The investment committee approval enables the deal team to incur additional due diligence costs and compete in subsequent bidding rounds.

This is also a busy time for the seller and the company's advisers. After taking considerable time to organize site visits, provide additional access to management and address information requests from the remaining bidders, they prepare to receive final bids from the investors. Once the final offer letters are in, the seller reviews the investment proposals and selects just one party for further deal negotiations. The winning bidder is typically granted a period of exclusivity to complete all outstanding due diligence, finalize financing arrangements and agree definitive transaction documentation with the seller.

What happens at this stage of the process if the transaction is proprietary? Well, life feels so much more straightforward! The deal team takes responsibility for sending a detailed information request to the company and organizing its own site visits and additional meetings with management. The aim is to achieve the same outcome—albeit without having to endure the frustrating distraction of a competitive auction: the deal team submits a credible offer to the company on the back of the initial due diligence and hopes to unlock the deal by agreeing a period of exclusivity with the seller.

- *Deal execution and closing.* Transaction execution feels like a special time for any investor. This is what deal fanatics—myself included—live their life for. Even though achieving this stage of the transaction feels rewarding and exhilarating, it is wise to suppress emotions and retain intellectual sobriety: after all, the deal is still far from being done. There is always a risk of discovering an unexpected deal-breaker issue in further due diligence, or ending up in a deadlock with the seller during final negotiations. In other words, until the transaction closes, there are plenty of scenarios that might compel the buyer or the seller to walk away from the deal.

Once the seller identifies a preferred buyer and grants a period of exclusivity, the deal counterparties will then move to drafting definitive transaction documentation. The legal documents that the investor needs to negotiate on every acquisition represent an extensive list: the buyer needs to agree the purchase agreement with the seller, finalize all equity documentation (including the shareholders' agreement and the management incentive plan) and settle on the final terms of the financing by agreeing a suite of debt documentation with the lenders. I will discuss the main transaction agreements in Chapter 11.

In conjunction with the ongoing work on the definitive transaction agreements, the deal teams and their advisers work hard on completing any outstanding company due diligence. At this stage of the process, the seller should be comfortable sharing any sensitive information about the target business that has not been disclosed in prior rounds. When deal closing is in sight, the buyer will commence work on setting up a legal and tax structure to effect the acquisition. Once due diligence is complete, debt financing is in place and all negotiations between the buyer and the seller are finalized, the deal team submits a final investment proposal to the investment committee. After receiving investment committee approval to execute the transaction, the investor gets the green light to sign a binding purchase agreement with the seller. Following signing, there is a period of time until transaction completion, so that the various pre-closing conditions can be satisfied by the deal parties. Finally, the deal closing date arrives: that's when the money changes hands between the buyer and the seller.

Due Diligence: Introduction

No transaction process can succeed without an efficient and thorough due diligence of the target company. At the start of my investing career, I did not really appreciate the true meaning of a well-executed due diligence process. I naively assumed that conducting great due diligence was all about being exhaustive and leaving no stone unturned. I thought that a high-quality "health check" of a target business could only be achieved if the deal team prepared detailed questionnaires about the company's operations and financials, and sent an army of advisers to the data room to perform a compliance-like "box-ticking exercise" until any transaction issues surfaced.

Having been a deal leader on several dozens of deals during my career, I can confidently tell you now that what is described above is a really bad approach to due diligence: it will waste time as well as money, and potentially leave you with only a few valuable insights about your investment case. Jumping to the other end of the spectrum and pursuing "light" due diligence is not a good option, either—it is simply dangerous. After all, we—as fiduciaries—vow to our LPs to conduct a thorough analysis of every company that we invest in. When I worked for a private equity fund focused on large LBOs, one of our investment committee members used to say to the deal teams embarking on a due diligence process, "Go and find all issues before deal closing, or they will find you after closing." What a powerful statement: it is both frightening and motivating, isn't it? Now that you know that I believe that both approaches—an overly exhaustive one and an insufficiently detailed one—are deficient, you may wonder, what actually works? In my opinion, a well-executed due diligence process starts with developing a clear strategy and thoughtful tactics.

The Ten Principles of a Good Due Diligence Process

1. *Be strategic about which advisers to use.*

    The truth is that deal teams compete not only for an acquisition target, but also for great teams of advisers who can help execute the transaction. It is not uncommon for the vendor of a target company to grant access to the data room to 8–10 serious bidders who are asked to perform preliminary due diligence and "sharpen their pencil" on their initial offer price. Since there are only a handful of reputable strategy consulting firms, accountancy and law firms with relevant experience, you might discover that your usual service providers are conflicted and can't help you because they are already engaged by other bidders. While in a perfect world our LPs expect us to get the best terms from our advisers by considering 2–3 pitches for each due diligence work stream, this approach may not always be realistic in practice, especially in a highly competitive auction scenario. Therefore, it is good to make an effort and engage key advisers as early as possible in a transaction process. When you choose whom to appoint, it is frequently more productive to focus on the track record of concrete individuals rather than place excessive focus on the firm where they work. In other words, you need to ensure that your advisers have the specific experience that you require on a given transaction: moreover, it is important to check that these people will actually be working on the due diligence for your firm and won't delegate this assignment to other colleagues.

2. *Invest time upfront in briefing your advisers.*

The more your advisers know about the transaction, the more effective they can be in helping your deal team. Once they sign the relevant confidentiality agreements, you should feel comfortable having a frank discussion with your advisers about why your fund is interested in the transaction. Advisers should clearly understand your fund's investment thesis, proprietary deal angle and key value creation drivers in the business plan. Even though you might be tempted to regard particular aspects of the deal as your fund's "secret sauce" and keep certain information close to your chest, there is really no point in being cryptic with your advisers: from now on, they become an essential part of the wider deal team. Therefore, it makes sense to invest some time upfront in briefing your advisers thoroughly to allow them to understand your investment rationale.

3. *Be clear about what you require from your advisers.*

Ultimately, your advisers should aim to provide commercial input and help your deal team compete with other bidders. It is imperative that they adopt an investor's mindset (as opposed to a service provider's mindset) and treat the due diligence process as a highly strategic exercise aimed at prioritizing, identifying and analyzing key pockets of the most useful information about the company. Your adviser's input should help your fund explore creative deal angles, differentiate your bid early in the process and allow the entire deal team to become aware of the potential deal hazards. Demand a clear view from your advisers: their work should be capable of generating transaction advice that is actionable and specific. Resist getting caught up in inconclusive discussions with your advisers: "on the one hand. . ., on the other hand. . . ." Everyone working on a transaction should understand that private equity funds don't expect to find a 100% trouble-free company because they put capital at risk and get paid for taking this risk. Therefore, the due diligence process should enable the deal team to develop a clear perspective on major issues, quantify possible downsides and understand what, if anything, can be done to mitigate these risks. Your advisers should appreciate the importance of open and clear communication with your fund: the early stages of due diligence are absolutely critical because they can generate valuable insights that will assist the deal team members to determine their level of comfort with the transaction. If the first few weeks of work produce due diligence findings that are not satisfactory, your deal team may decide to pull out early in order to minimize broken deal costs, save everyone's time and remain credible in the market. However, it is important to remember that advisers are there solely to provide assistance, resources and insights: the deal team is responsible for making the decisions. "Our advisers told us. . ." is not an acceptable excuse in your conversation with your investment committee or the LPs when the time comes to write down the investment.

4. *Consider the vendor due diligence ("VDD") report with a healthy dose of skepticism.*
   Treat any market data, company information or financial analysis that you receive from others with caution, especially if they are sitting on the opposite side of the negotiating table. It is worth remembering that vendors and their advisers have only one goal in mind: to sell the business for the highest possible price. Therefore, it is logical to assume

that whatever information you get from the seller will typically present the company in the best possible light and downplay some of the challenges faced by the business. Don't get me wrong: the vendor due diligence pack is unlikely to contain facts and figures that are outright incorrect or fraudulent. However, most VDD reports are likely to be biased and might display a number of obvious deficiencies. The most common problems, in my experience, include the following: a) using simplistic extrapolations of historic performance into the future without a rigorous thought process to support these assumptions; b) choosing a nonstandard, "custom" time period for the historic analysis in order to capture the best performance of the business; c) inflating projections and making qualitative statements that are not adequately supported by the hard facts and numbers; d) relying on market research or customer analysis data that originates from third-party sources that you may not consider sufficiently solid, reputable or reliable; and e) using inconsistent definitions of a relevant market in order to make specific statements more convincing: for example, many companies like to showcase their dominant market share in the context of a very narrowly defined industry or product category, yet proceed to describe future growth opportunities within a market which is far broader. Overall, while the VDD reports often help interested bidders to get up to speed on a transaction very quickly, they are not really considered to be a reliable substitute for a proprietary due diligence process performed by a skeptical buyer.

5. *Approach due diligence in phases and don't "boil the ocean."*
The due diligence process allows investors to acquire more knowledge about the target and mitigate key areas of deal uncertainty. If private equity deal professionals faced no

deal competition, had access to an infinite budget and could dedicate unlimited time to each transaction, any of them could simply "boil the ocean" and churn out a decent due diligence output. I doubt that even this kind of process is capable of taking investors to a position of total certainty about the deal. In my mind, complete certainty is simply unattainable. It might be useful to remember a quote attributed to Voltaire, "Uncertainty is an uncomfortable position. But certainty is an absurd one." There are not enough resources and time available in a competitive deal situation to engage in an overly meticulous and exhaustive due diligence exercise that will attempt to eradicate all uncertainty. A more effective approach, in my opinion, involves bifurcating the due diligence process into a preliminary stage (Phase 1) and a confirmatory stage (Phase 2). For Phase 1 to be fruitful, it should focus on several well-articulated objectives, such as validating the investment thesis, examining the main assumptions and key value creation drivers in the investment base case, assessing the key components of value as compared to the deal price, investigating the main downside risks and ascertaining that the company generally comes across as an investable entity with no obvious deal breakers. By front-loading Phase 1 with a finite list of the most critical items, the deal team can deploy just enough resources in order to find out quickly whether or not there is sufficient conviction about the transaction. I personally try to resist engaging in the much more detailed and expensive Phase 2 due diligence until the deal team progresses to a more advanced stage of the transaction and agrees a period of exclusivity with the vendor. Even though Phase 2 is often referred to as a "confirmatory" due diligence, I find that the process nonetheless is capable of revealing a number of new insights, both positive and negative. Confirmatory diligence, in other words, is not mere "box-ticking": it might give you enough reasons to walk away from the deal—and do so with confidence. I incorporate any worrying due diligence findings into an investment process by analyzing them with the deal team and deciding together whether we believe they constitute an outright deal breaker, or if they can be addressed through a price adjustment, an earn-out or a specific provision in the legal documentation.

6. *Be prescriptive about the format of the due diligence findings.*
Does this sound to you like an unimportant housekeeping point? I can't stress enough how crucial it is to agree upfront an exact format of the due diligence reports with all of your advisers. The most helpful due diligence reports provide clear and succinct advice which is adequately supported by facts and relevant analysis. The views of the advisers need to extend beyond the scope of the proposed transaction and capture any issues that are likely to impact the investors' eventual exit from the deal. Since most deals tend to move rather quickly, advisers need to keep up with their clients and release their due diligence findings within a pre-agreed—and often highly compressed—timetable. What does that mean in practice? In my experience, due diligence reports tend to arrive at 11pm on a Friday, or some time over the weekend, and the deal team typically gets only a few days to study the findings in detail, ask follow-up questions, conduct additional analyses, adjust the investment base case, update the investment committee and get to a consensus view on how the latest due diligence information might affect the final offer, deal structure or legal documentation. Given this challenging backdrop, it is always extremely disappointing to receive due diligence findings in an undecipherable format that makes it very

difficult for the deal team to process quickly: Who needs
a 700-page legal due diligence report that comes across
as very comprehensive yet fails to highlight and prioritize the most critical issues? Having been burned by prior
experience, I now resort to being fairly prescriptive with
all advisers about the format of the due diligence reports.
Moreover, if I work with a new firm, I might go as far as
sharing a dummy template with them in advance in order
to avoid any potential misunderstandings during transaction crunch time. As a deal captain, I expect the advisers
who work with my deal team to deliver a high-quality,
easily digestible end product by going over the available
company information in a detailed and systematic manner,
conducting thoughtful analyses, developing clear opinions,
summarizing key issues and providing adequate context to
support any critical findings.

7. *Control due diligence costs.*

We all know that transactions might be terminated unex-
pectedly by a buyer or a seller, for a number of reasons and
at any time. You need to be fully prepared for this even-
tuality and, therefore, incur due diligence costs—which
can easily surpass many millions—carefully. Since the costs
of aborted deals are borne by the fund, they have a direct
negative impact on the fund's net IRR, which is a key
performance metric that your LPs focus on. Splurge on
the advisers unwisely on a few occasions, and the fund's
performance might be under pressure! Upon engaging
advisers, it is good practice to price different phases of
work separately as well as agree specific budgets and fee
caps early on. If you can't agree to a fixed fee figure for
a specific segment of work and have to settle on a pay-
as-you-go approach, it is important to get updates about
what costs are incurred with each service provider on a

weekly basis. Your advisers should tread carefully in the early stages of the process and avoid staffing large teams in the first weeks of the transaction, especially if the deal team is still considering whether or not to go ahead. There has to be an explicit arrangement regarding abort costs, too: if the deal is unsuccessful, it might be appropriate to ask upfront for a degree of risk-sharing and a fee reduction from your advisers.

8. *Remember that advisers are human.*

   As transaction timeframes get compressed and deal issues get more complex, it is important to appreciate that your advisers may not know all the answers. It is the responsibility of a deal team to manage advisers, communicate with them frequently and understand their level of confidence in their own due diligence findings. If something does not make sense, question your advisers' conclusions, try to understand their logic and ask for supporting facts and figures. Examine raw data, not just the advisers' conclusions. Since you are a paying customer, you have the right to be demanding. It is also important to remember that advisers are not invincible: they can occasionally make a mistake in their work, especially when writing their due diligence reports under time pressure. Each deal team member should cast a critical eye on the output presented by the advisers and ensure that any potential errors are spotted and corrected as quickly as possible. If you simply can't get to the bottom of an important issue or begin to doubt the competence of your advisers, it is prudent to seek additional sources for input, such as an industry expert or even an alternative due diligence provider.

9. *Remember that you are human.*

   Investors like doing deals. It is hard not to: investment professionals are directly incentivized by their funds to get deals done. As a result, it is difficult for any deal-hungry brain to process due diligence findings dispassionately. Falling in love with a potential investment and getting emotionally attached to the management team will make it virtually impossible to conduct a thorough and objective analysis. Just like any other human immersed in a transaction for multiple weeks, you may find yourself gradually succumbing to all sorts of cognitive biases. Apart from getting too emotionally involved with the investment target, there are two other common pitfalls that you may encounter during any due diligence process. The first is confirmation bias: when reviewing due diligence findings, you may feel that you are specifically seeking out any facts and figures that support your investment thesis and choose to downplay or ignore any information that undermines it. The second is the sunk cost fallacy: having spent considerable time and money on a long due diligence process, you might feel compelled to proceed with further work, even if there is sufficient evidence of negative trends in the target business. To avoid falling prey to my own overoptimistic mind, I try to retain an objective perspective by increasing my own self-awareness. I document the decision-making process and keep a list of positives and negatives relating to the potential investment. I try not to internalize the transaction and preserve an outsider's point of view. Finally, I might solicit advice from colleagues who are not involved in a deal: sometimes it is helpful to get someone you trust to critique the proposed investment and provide constructive feedback to the deal team.

10. *Don't get lost in detail and keep the big picture in mind.*
Since a typical due diligence exercise is likely to generate many hundreds of pages of findings, it is very easy for anyone to get lost in small details. Some of them are

important and some of them are not. Avoid falling into a deep rabbit hole! Even though every due diligence process feels different to investors because target companies and their challenges don't fit the same pattern, it is worth remembering that the issues that need to be checked over carefully on every transaction are not that unique. Personally, I have come to the view that a comprehensive due diligence process needs to deliver solid answers to only a short list of big-picture questions:

a. Is our initial understanding of the *business model* accurate? What factors might make this company vulnerable in the future?

b. Given what we know about the market and the company post-diligence, does our *investment thesis* still stack up?

c. Is the *business plan* in our investment base case achievable within our investment horizon? If so, do we have adequate comfort in our assumptions relating to projected revenue growth, margin expansion, cost reduction, cash conversion and reinvestment requirements? Moreover, do we have a backable *management team* to deliver this business plan?

d. Do we have any reasons to suspect that the company's *financial statements* might not reflect reality, for example, due to aggressive accounting choices, manipulation or fraud? More broadly, do we have any concerns about the business that might give rise to a *reputational risk*?

e. Are we completely clear about *what assets are included* in the perimeter of the deal (e.g. brands, trademarks, patents, proprietary technology, tangible assets and human capital)? Are these assets sufficiently unencumbered to ensure a smooth transfer of ownership?

f. What current and future *liabilities* of the company are we buying? This might be a broad list that might include any potential liabilities arising for a number of reasons, ranging from litigation to social obligations. Do we understand the expected impact of these liabilities on the projected cash flows in the business plan?

g. How will the *change of control* impact the company and its business model? What material agreements might need to be renegotiated? Are we confident that the change of control won't cause the company's business model to dissipate (for example, due to potential losses of dominant customers or suppliers)?

h. Is the company likely to be a desirable investment target at *exit*?

Due Diligence: Key Workstreams

Anyone new to due diligence might ask a very good question: Where and how does one start? I was fortunate to be introduced to due diligence early in my career during my work for a large private equity fund that had already developed a systematic approach to due diligence, so I could benefit from the existing library of standard questionnaires and checklists. Moreover, I could access files relating to my fund's prior transactions, review a number of relevant deal precedents, study the due diligence reports of past investments and talk to colleagues involved in those deals. As the years went by, I felt the need to cross-check my own knowledge against additional external sources and stumbled upon several useful business books on the subject.

    Should you be interested in furthering your knowledge about transaction due diligence, I wholeheartedly recommend an anthology by Rosenbloom (2002),[1] where each due diligence workstream is explained clearly and thoroughly. I particularly appreciate that each segment of the book includes contributions

---

[1]Please refer to Chapter 10 References for a complete citation.

of the senior experts with relevant expertise: the commercial due diligence chapter is written by strategy consultants from a top-tier firm; the financial due diligence is addressed by a partner from a global accounting firm; and the legal due diligence matters are discussed in depth by real lawyers with immense cross-border transactional experience. Even though this book was published some time ago, I would argue that the majority of its content is evergreen, which makes it a relevant source for present-day deal-making. Other books that I consider useful include an M&A due diligence guide by Gole and Hilger (2009) and a simple collection of transaction due diligence checklists by Howson (2008).[2]

As you probably already know, each due diligence process is structured in distinct parts exploring specific areas of the transaction. Let's go over the key due diligence workstreams and discuss what investors typically aim to learn from each of them.

Commercial Due Diligence ("CDD")

<u>Who does the work</u>: In-house deal team, in-house operating partners, an external strategy consulting firm, external industry experts and the buy-in management team (if it is known upfront that the existing management is going to be replaced shortly after closing).

<u>What is included in the full scope of work</u>: Analysis of the external environment (including macroeconomic considerations), market size and growth, industry trends, market structure and competitive environment, the company's strategy and business model, perception of the brand and product/service quality, customer value proposition, core competencies, competitive

---

[2]Please refer to Chapter 10 References for complete publishing information.

positioning and benchmarking, profit pool analysis, key sales and profitability drivers, price optimization strategies, cost structure and supply chain, customer acquisition models and distribution channels, effectiveness of sales and marketing, risk of a competitive raid on the company's core markets, risk of disruption, and exit analysis.

Priority issues for Phase 1: Validation of the investment thesis; analysis of key value creation levers; verification of key assumptions in the business plan relating to projected revenue growth, margin improvement potential, cost optimization and required reinvestment; business plan execution risks and the attractiveness of the target business at exit.

Additional considerations: If the investment target is a consumer company or an e-commerce business, your CDD will be considered deficient unless you also perform a "digital due diligence." This includes data mining of the company's online records and digital footprint, evaluation of customer sentiment via online reviews and analysis of social media ratios, influencer metrics and search trends.

Financial and Tax Due Diligence ("FDD")

Who does the work: An external accounting firm and the in-house deal team.

What is included in the full scope of work: Accounting policy review, assessment of reliability and integrity of the financial statements, evaluation of potential risks relating to aggressive accounting practices, earnings manipulation and "window dressing." Detailed examination of historic financial results and current trading, analysis of budgeted versus actual performance, reconciliation of audited and unaudited financial information. Quality and visibility of earnings. Breakdown of sales into organic and non-organic growth. Breakdown of sales and profitability by product, customer account, distribution channel and geography. Detailed analysis of fixed vs. variable costs and unit economics. Correlation of revenue and earnings to the economic cycle. Analysis of non-recurring items, foreign currency effects and hedging. Balance sheet review, including net debt, accruals, provisions and trapped cash. Detailed review of contingent liabilities, employee benefit provisions and off-balance-sheet items. Normalized levels of earnings, target working capital and sustainable levels of maintenance and expansion CAPEX. Detailed analysis of business plan projections and key sensitivities. Detailed examination of historic and projected cash flow profile. Analysis of historic and current tax position and preparation of the tax model and transaction structure.

Priority issues for Phase 1: Reliability of the financial statements; assessment of historic budgeting accuracy; positive and negative trends in historic financial results; key drivers of historic revenue, profitability and cash flows; analysis of relevant KPIs and unit economics; cost analysis; quality of earnings; review of significant extraordinary items; calculation of normalized, pro-forma and LTM EBITDA (or other most relevant measure of earnings); high-level analysis of CAPEX, working capital, and net debt; verification of key business plan assumptions against historic trends; and an EBITDA bridge between historic and projected performance.

Additional considerations: If there is one thing to remember about financial due diligence, I would choose a quote by Andy Grove, the Silicon Valley legend and Intel co-founder: "Only the paranoid survive" (Grove, 2002). Therefore, if you want your deal to succeed, it pays to be extremely paranoid, especially when it comes to analyzing the target company's financial statements. In my experience, aggressive accounting, earnings manipulation and even fraud are not that rare, sadly. Don't take my word for it: instead, look around. Do you notice accounting scandals everywhere? General Electric, once a posterchild of management excellence and still a household name today, agreed to pay a $200 million penalty in 2020 as a result of a probe into the company's accounting treatment of certain costs and profits (Michaels and Gryta, 2020). Wells Fargo, a prominent financial institution in the US and, incidentally, the bank where I opened my first checking account as a college freshman, also recently made the news. The company was charged a $3 billion fine in early 2020 to settle a civil and criminal probe into the bank's use of fictitious customer accounts that were opened by rogue salespeople in order to bump up their revenue targets (Kelly, 2020).

The list of creative accounting examples goes on and on. There is Tesco, a supermarket giant in the UK. And the Italian subsidiary of British Telecom. If big brand industry champions dare to manipulate their financial statements and do so regularly, what can I assume about the integrity of a much smaller business that might be on my investment radar? While I have not yet lost my faith in humanity completely, I do believe that it is important to be extra vigilant when conducting financial due diligence. Next time you work on a transaction, ask your FDD advisers to examine in detail any issues in the financial statements that you may consider odd,[3] such as: inappropriate or obscure revenue recognition; understated cost base due to aggressive capitalization policy; cash flow smoothing by manipulating CAPEX, delaying payments to suppliers or failing to restock inventory; write-ups or impairments of significant assets or liabilities; suspiciously low effective tax rates; sudden changes in the accounting methods or the company's auditors; and—perhaps most importantly—any

---

[3]Spotting odd entries in the financial statements requires practice. I found it helpful to read several books about creative accounting: in particular, Mulford and Comiskey (2005), Shilit et al. (2018) and Fisher and Hoffmans (2010). Please refer to Chapter 10 References for complete publishing information.

discontinuities in the financial statements, especially those that result from the extraordinary charges and restatements due to acquisitions, disposals or business restructurings.

Operational Due Diligence ("ODD")

<u>Who does the work:</u> The in-house deal team, the in-house operating partners, an external management consulting or specialist firm (e.g. focused on operational turnarounds or IT systems), external industry experts, and the buy-in management team (if it is known upfront that the existing management is going to be replaced shortly after closing).

<u>What is included in the full scope of work:</u> Analysis of the organizational layout, product or service delivery protocols and internal operating procedures; assessment of the infrastructure and core assets supporting the company's operations; detailed review of current asset efficiency, capacity utilization, age, performance and quality of manufacturing facilities and equipment, real estate and digital assets, including software and IT systems; assessment of the company's culture, ethics and business conduct as well as employee satisfaction; analysis of management style, experience and track record of key line managers, recruitment and retention programs, workforce churn and union issues; detailed analysis of current inefficiencies and identification of potential areas of cost reduction and operational improvement; assessment of company's current competencies, resources and assets against what may be required to implement the business plan.

<u>Priority issues for Phase 1:</u> Verification of key assumptions in the business plan relating to asset efficiency, capacity utilization, availability of human capital, required CAPEX, cost reduction and operational improvement opportunities; and screening

for serious issues relating to the company's reputation, unethical business conduct, inappropriate treatment of employees or unsustainable operating practices.

Legal Due Diligence ("LDD")

<u>Who does the work:</u> The in-house deal team, the in-house legal counsel and an external law firm.

<u>What is included in the full scope of work:</u> Review of corporate history, group structure, historic acquisitions, disposals, restructurings and any current transitional issues; ownership structure, corporate governance and legal agreements among key stakeholders; background checks on current owners; compliance with laws and regulations; any history of criminal, commercial or financial misconduct; analysis of known and potential liabilities, litigations and disputes; change of control clauses; material contracts; intellectual property rights; compliance with environmental and social obligations; quantification of potential risks and liability exposures.

<u>Priority issues for Phase 1:</u> Summary of the information provided in the data room to identify important disclosure gaps; change of control clauses; material contracts; identification of any issues that might have a reputational impact or result in a material cash outflow; summary of all material items that might require a price adjustment or an indemnity from the seller.

Other Due Diligence

There are a few additional due diligence workstreams that zoom in on particular deal issues. *Insurance due diligence*, for instance, includes an analysis of historic and future insurance costs and a review of material claims, damages and liabilities. Since investors need adequate insurance coverage as of deal closing, it is important to quantify what is deemed a sufficient and robust insurance package in the context of the company's likely exposures going forward. Don't forget this due diligence item! More likely than not, the company's existing agreement with an insurance provider will lapse automatically due to change of control provisions—and not having appropriate insurance coverage on the day of deal closing is considered a breach under the financing agreements with the lending banks.

Some investors prefer to separate *HR due diligence* as a distinct workstream, rather than include relevant matters in the ODD or LDD. In this case, this process will cover any issues relating to compensation and benefits, workforce training and retention programs, and employment contracts (including those with key members of the management team). To the extent this area is not already covered by the LDD, the HR workstream might involve referencing, background checks and verification of prior employment and educational credentials of the top managers.

Environmental due diligence has become more critical over the years: as sustainability issues gain prominence with the private equity investors and their LPs, there is a trend among investors to investigate upfront a wider scope of ESG issues during the transaction due diligence. Apart from establishing that the business is not in outright breach of the applicable environmental laws and regulations, many investors will spend some time understanding the company's present attitude and standing in key ESG matters such as carbon emissions, waste management, employee diversity and inclusion programs, workplace health and safety as well as compliance and governance protocols.

Other potential due diligence workstreams are highly dependent on the nature of the company's business. In some cases, you may find it useful to commission additional reports from consultants who can provide expertise on highly specialized matters that might play a critical role in your transaction, such as the assessment of a proprietary technology, a review of cybersecurity risk or the valuation of esoteric intellectual property assets.

Once all due diligence workstreams are complete, investors find themselves in a far more comfortable place: they are relieved that the information asymmetry between them and the seller is finally reduced. A well-executed due diligence of an investment target is vital because it allows deal teams to refine their investment base case and make an informed decision about the appropriate price and terms of the transaction. And, inevitably, some due diligence processes go beyond that: certain findings about the company might convince investors that the business should not be bought at all. At any price. Don't despair if this is the outcome. Avoiding losses is as important as doing deals. I said this already in Chapter 5 and I am going to repeat it here: sometimes the best deal of your career is the one that you never actually do.

11

Deal Execution: Legal Documentation

Key Topics in Chapter 11:

- Why you don't need to be a lawyer to provide valuable input in legal negotiations
- How to translate due diligence findings into legal clauses in the deal documentation
- My cheat sheet summary of common issues in the key transaction agreements

---

L et me begin this chapter by making two statements. Both may be obvious: nonetheless, since I believe they are important, I am going to put them in writing anyway. First, the topic of transaction agreements is a fairly dry legal matter that inevitably involves the use of legal language that may be tedious to absorb. I wish I could make this chapter more amusing but the subject of my writing simply does not provide me with enough room to maneuver. I can only sympathize with all my brave readers who decide to work tirelessly through this section of the book. Second, I would like to state upfront that I am not a lawyer. Yet, I will devote a whole chapter to key legal issues that frequently arise in transaction agreements on a typical private equity deal. Should you rely solely on anything I say in this section of the book? Please don't. All transactions are different: you should always seek professional advice from experienced lawyers who are familiar with the legal framework of the jurisdiction that applies to your deal. Some of the areas that I cover below may not be that pertinent in the context of your deal, and some legal provisions may even be unenforceable in your geography. My sole aim in this chapter is to provide directional feedback on where to look for potential issues and pitfalls. My personal (and subjective) experience with legal documentation stems from my work on deal executions in my capacity as an investment professional—not as a lawyer. Therefore, let's agree that nothing in this book can substitute for the professional advice of an experienced lawyer.

Before we go into the key aspects of each transaction agreement, let me say a few words about some of the lessons I learned from working on deal executions.

- *The role of deal teams.* Investment professionals are not lawyers, yet they get very involved in drafting and negotiating transaction agreements. Why? Well, the members of the investment team are closest to the transaction and can provide important commercial input to their lawyers. Also, they are best placed to understand the main risk areas of a deal following due diligence and enable the lawyers to negotiate meaningfully better, so that possible future negative eventualities are covered off upfront. Deal teams also need to take responsibility for checking every number in the transaction agreements because lawyers tend to get carried away with crafting complex legal constructs and may not be careful[1] with numerical figures in the legal documents.

- *First draft advantage.* Lawyers know this one very well: whoever "holds the pen" in producing the first draft of a legal agreement gains an advantage over the other party. The first drafts set the ground rules: make sure you take every chance you can to volunteer your legal team to take responsibility for the initial drafting process.

- *Non-binding vs. definitive agreements.* It sounds very easy: a signed definitive agreement represents a solid commitment of a transaction counterparty. A non-binding agreement signals the positive intent of a counterparty to proceed with the transaction. However, there is another factor: credibility. Therefore, it is not sustainable for investors who care about their reputation to pull out of transactions a few hours before signing—even though they are not legally obliged to commit to a deal. Initial drafts of key transaction documents serve as a fairly good barometer of how far the deal counterparties are from reaching an agreement. If the deal looks unlikely, it might be best to pull out as early as possible in the drafting process.

- *Risk management.* When you encounter risk areas in the transaction, there are a number of legal tools that might help you mitigate some of these risks. For example, *indemnifications* enable indemnified parties to receive damage payments from the counterparty in the event of losses; *representations and warranties* compel the parties providing this undertaking to state a specific fact and make a commitment that this fact is true; and *covenants* are promises of specific future behavior that

---

[1] *Ludex non calculat* is an expression in Latin: it originates from the Roman times and can be loosely translated as "lawyers cannot count." As such, don't be surprised if you find obvious errors in the calculations of financial ratios, covenants, earn-out and ratchet mechanisms in draft legal agreements produced by your legal advisers.

restricts the parties from doing something that the other side will regard as disagreeable.

- *Narrow vs. wide definitions.* When drafting a right, make sure that it applies in the broadest set of scenarios. When drafting an obligation, you want to narrow its application as much as possible. Your deal counterparty will probably use the same tactic; however, it is always worthwhile to pay attention to the scope of specific definitions in the legal agreements.

- *Expect the best, plan for the worst.* Ideally, when the deal teams get involved in drafting definitive transaction documentation, they should have clear views about their desired level of risk, investment time horizon and preferred exit route. Well-drafted legal agreements should reflect the base expectations of the deal team in the context of a transaction, align the interests of the deal participants and allow for some flexibility due to uncertainty about the future development of the business. However, transaction agreements should also be robust. They need to cover a variety of scenarios, no matter how unlikely, by seeking to minimize potential disputes between the deal counterparties in the future. Apart from providing a solid legal framework for the investment in the expected base case, transaction agreements need to state explicitly what actions will be taken in certain grave circumstances, such as a bankruptcy or the sudden death of a key executive.

On this gloomy note, let's jump to the transaction agreements. In a typical private equity transaction, a deal professional will encounter the following legal documents:[2]

---

[2]Transaction agreement requirements differ across jurisdictions: please refer to the *Global LBO Guide* published by Baker McKenzie (2015) for a high-level overview of key legal considerations in leveraged buyout transactions in 34 geographies. Please refer to Chapter 11 References for a complete citation.

1. Non-Disclosure Agreement;
2. Engagement Letter(s);
3. Offer Letter(s);
4. Sale and Purchase Agreement;
5. Articles of Association;
6. Shareholders' Agreement; and
7. Debt Documentation.

Let me go through key issues[3] in each legal document.

1. Non-Disclosure Agreement

<u>Purpose of the document:</u> The NDA is a legally binding agreement that places an obligation on the private equity fund and its deal advisers not to disclose confidential information about the investment target.

<u>My approach to key issues:</u> Some private equity funds take a tough stance on every NDA they sign, whereas others choose a relaxed approach because they believe that "nobody gets sued over an NDA." My personal approach is somewhere in between. While I haven't heard about any lawsuits that relate to the NDA breaches in a private equity context, I personally don't want to be the first one to make the newspaper headlines. Since the NDA is signed at an early stage of the deal, I think it is important not to overnegotiate and risk coming across to the seller as a difficult and unreasonable counterparty. Therefore, I tend to focus on just a handful of critical items listed below.

---

[3]For alternative views of key issues in private equity transaction documentation, please see Chapter 10 in Zeisberger et al. (2017) and Chapter 12 in Ippolito (2020). Please refer to Chapter 11 References for complete publishing information.

- *Who is covered by the NDA.* To the extent the agreement asks the private equity fund to take responsibility for breach of confidentiality obligations by third parties, such as the deal advisers and lenders, it is important to have complete clarity about who is included in the NDA and get back-to-back undertakings from these parties.
- *Definition of confidential information.* It is good practice to check that the NDA does not have any nonstandard clauses in the definition of confidential information and explicitly mentions typical exclusions, such as any information about the company that the private equity fund already possesses (obviously, legally) before entering into the NDA, anything already available in the public domain, or anything that can be derived independently by the private equity fund or its advisers.
- *Indemnity.* If the NDA asks the private equity fund to indemnify the company for any losses that might be incurred as a result of a breach of the agreement, I typically start by striking out this clause because any disagreements between parties can be resolved in court. However, sometimes my resistance is not acceptable to the seller, in which case a good compromise might be to agree to an indemnity as long as it is defined very narrowly and is limited to actual damages suffered by the company as determined by a court.
- *Term of the agreement.* Typical NDAs expire either at the consummation of a transaction between the parties, or after a standard period of time, such as 1 or 2 years. If the NDA does not have any language about the duration of the agreement, there is a reason to worry: it means that the agreement binds the private equity fund and its advisers forever. Obviously, that is not a reasonable position, so it makes sense to include a clause that will limit the term of the agreement to 1 or 2 years. Sometimes the seller is particularly nervous about sharing highly sensitive information about the company and

insists that the NDA should last for a very long time, such as 5 years. In my experience, it is usually possible to agree to something in between, such as a period of 3 years by arguing that any information about the company beyond this time-frame is likely to become stale anyway and, therefore, should be considered less sensitive.

2. Engagement Letters

Purpose of the document: Engagement letters are retention agreements with professional advisers, such as consultants, accountants, lawyers and investment banks.

My approach to key issues: Each engagement letter should typically cover the following areas: scope of work; fees and expenses; indemnification; timing of deliverables and duration of the advisory relationship. The scope of work should reflect the areas that the advisers are expected to cover; however, it is marginally helpful to the deal team if the scope is defined in somewhat broad terms, so that it does not have to be amended every time a new due diligence issue arises. Virtually all advisers will demand an indemnification: while this is typically accommodated as a matter of standard market practice, it is always a good idea to check that the indemnity is defined in terms which are not considered to be too extensive or unreasonable. Conversely, your fund may ask for an indemnity from the adviser in case of negligence. In Chapter 10, we discussed the importance of documenting a clear agreement on fees: investors are keen to control deal costs and will negotiate intensely on the overall fee, as well as fee budgets and caps that may apply to a given due diligence workstream. Some advisers, especially those who agree to work on a success basis or on a weekly retainer, will expect their expenses to be covered: in this case, it is important to agree specific budgets and notification periods for any allowable expenses. Finally, there has to be a clear framework of compensation for the advisers in case the deal is aborted or fails to close.

3. Offer Letter

<u>Purpose of the document:</u> This is an indication of interest that the private equity fund submits to the seller. The first offer letter at the beginning of a transaction is a non-binding legal document that a private equity fund uses to express its enthusiasm about the investment target and communicate its first-round bid to the seller without being overly specific on key terms of the deal. The final offer letter at the end of a competitive process includes a final offer price and outlines the main terms of the transaction. This document is also non-binding and subject to a number of conditions, as the private equity funds still needs to complete any outstanding due diligence, agree definitive transaction documentation with the seller and confirm the final terms of debt financing.

<u>My approach to key issues:</u> A well-written first-round offer letter is essential in any competitive deal process: apart from informing the seller about the level of the indicative bid, the buyer has a chance to position itself favorably against other bidders by means of clever marketing. I believe it is always worthwhile to put substantial effort into producing a high-quality indication of interest document: the deal teams that have this mindset can instantly differentiate themselves against those competitors who believe that charm is not important and, therefore, might resort to using generic letter templates to bid in the first round. What should the offer letter say? Apart from being clear about the price, key assumptions, deal structure and

main conditions to closing, there are a few additional rules that I try to follow.

First, I think it is important to sound upbeat about the acquisition target and mention something distinctive about the company that signals to the seller that our fund is a credible bidder and the deal team has already done substantial work on the acquisition target. Second, I want to make sure that the letter explains how our fund is going to add value to the company as a responsible shareholder and mentions our relevant sector expertise, track record and past transactions. Finally, I believe it is crucial to telegraph upfront our fund's willingness to move quickly: this can be achieved by pointing out that the deal team already completed preliminary analysis of the target, appointed transaction advisers, and received non-binding financing proposals from the lending banks (with one or two indicative financing letters attached in the appendix). Ultimately, most vendors are looking for three things: price, deliverability and a timely transaction completion.

As the deal progresses to the final round and a few remaining bidders are asked to submit final offers, I have to admit that charm and charisma become less helpful. The final offer letter is typically drafted in a manner that is reminiscent of a legal agreement, such as a Letter of Intent ("LOI") or a term sheet:[4] it outlines the main pricing assumptions and terms of the deal. It is best to submit a proposal that is crisp, comprehensive and not misleading: the deal team needs to set out the final bid price, ask for exclusivity and outline a process, timeline and conditions to a successful closing.

---

[4]Term sheets are more common in minority equity transactions and hybrid financings. Please see Chapter 12 in Ippolito (2020) for an example of an equity term sheet. Please refer to Chapter 11 References for a complete citation.

4. Sale and Purchase Agreement ("SPA")

<u>Purpose of the document</u>: The SPA is the most significant legal agreement in every acquisition process: once signed, it binds the buyer and the seller to execute a transaction. The SPA defines exactly what is being bought, sets out the headline price with all relevant adjustment items and describes the closing mechanism for the deal parties to follow on a transaction completion date. The buyer and the seller use the SPA to document the detailed terms of the deal, reflect specific outcomes of their commercial negotiations and address any future risks and liabilities.

<u>My approach to key issues</u>: Given the prominence and the consequential nature of the SPA, it always takes a small army of lawyers from both sides of the deal to draft and negotiate this vital transaction document. However, this agreement is far from being strictly a legal matter: the deal teams are expected to take full responsibility for the SPA and provide specific commercial input to lawyers during the negotiation process. In my opinion, it is good practice for all members of the deal team—even those who have no prior experience with legal documentation—to read through every clause of the SPA and develop a good level of understanding and comfort on the most critical aspects of the deal. While the document is important in its entirety, there are a few specific areas that I believe are particularly essential.

- *Transaction perimeter.* The purchase agreement will provide a precise definition of what is being bought depending on the nature of a deal: the buyer might purchase some or all of the company's shares or some or all of its assets. In a corporate "carve-out," the buyer might be acquiring only a particular business line or a specific division from a larger group of companies. In every transaction, the deal team needs to ensure that the perimeter of a transaction is articulated appropriately in the SPA, with correct legal entities and assets included in a deal. It is crucial that any transitional issues are addressed explicitly, so that the company can continue operating in the ordinary course of business post-closing (in other words, it is not missing critical functions, services, IT systems and software, brands, licenses and other key assets). One notorious example of a deal where this went awry is the acquisition of Rolls-Royce by Volkswagen Group ("VW") in 1998. VW paid over $700 million for the luxury automaker; however, the acquirer discovered after closing that the Rolls-Royce trademark and logo were not in fact included in the deal (Buerkle, 1998).

- *Purchase price and deal structure.* This can get quite complicated. Arguably, defining the purchase price properly is the most important aspect of the SPA. The document sets out the headline price of the transaction and details how the purchase consideration will be funded with the various financing instruments in the deal structure. Since the headline price is expressed on a debt-free, cash-free, tax-free basis, with a normalized level of working capital and no underspent CAPEX, this headline number is subject to a number of adjustments that the buyer and the seller need to document explicitly in order to arrive at an appropriate cash consideration payable at closing. These adjustments inevitably are subject to exhaustive negotiations between the deal parties, as there is no market standard to rely upon in order to define the concepts of debt-like items and normalized working capital objectively. In addition, the buyer and the seller have to agree a specific price adjustment mechanism: one option is to set a preliminary purchase price that will be modified at completion through a "closing accounts" approach, and another option is to agree to a fixed purchase price through a "locked box" mechanism.

- *Closing mechanics.* To resolve the challenges described above and avoid potential disputes post-closing, the buyer and the seller document all necessary adjustments that will take place between the signing and closing of the transaction. Under the "closing accounts" mechanism, the preliminary purchase price is determined based on a pre-closing balance sheet. As the company continues to operate between signing and closing of the transaction, its levels of cash, inventory, receivables, payables and other items change every day. To account for these differences, the preliminary purchase price is then adjusted based on a balance sheet prepared in the completion accounts as of the closing date of the transaction. In this scenario, the buyer assumes economic ownership of the company at closing. Under the "locked box" approach, the parties agree a fixed purchase price based on a pre-closing balance sheet, and the ownership of the business is then effectively transferred to the buyer as of the "locked box" date. Interestingly, the seller remains responsible for running the company until the closing date of the transaction; the buyer, therefore, needs to ensure that the seller operates the business in the ordinary course and does not cause any leakage of cash or value in the company between the "locked box" date and the transaction completion.[5]

- *Protection mechanisms.* In every transaction, the buyer seeks to cover potential risk areas as broadly as possible, whereas the seller aims to limit any reductions to purchase price or potential reimbursement claims as much as possible. The buyer's

---

[5]The buyer will subject the seller to a number of restrictive covenants that will apply between the "locked box" date and closing to prevent the seller from "looting the firm." If there is a significant delay until transaction completion, the seller might demand interest payments from the buyer to reflect the time value of money of the sale proceeds.

protection mechanisms consist of getting the seller to provide representations and warranties, indemnities and covenants: if those are breached, the buyer might be entitled to a variety of remedies, ranging from the right to terminate the transaction to the entitlement to a specific monetary compensation. The seller's warranties consist of a long list of statements that describe the overall condition of the investment target, including its legal title, assets, intellectual property, indebtedness, financial statements, employees, tax, litigation and insolvency. Indemnities are used to address any specific known and near-term risks and liabilities identified in the due diligence: if any indemnified issues arise in the future, the buyer is typically entitled to dollar-for-dollar reimbursement by the seller. Covenants are designed to impose specific restrictions on the behavior of the seller before and after closing. In effect, they help the buyer to prevent the seller from taking specific actions that might impair the investment target. For example, pre-closing covenants help to restrict the seller from making material changes to the business, such as paying itself a dividend, incurring debt, changing auditors, amending material contracts or replacing senior managers. After closing, covenants can prevent the seller from doing anything that can be viewed as value-destructive to the investment target: for example, the seller is typically restricted from poaching key company employees or establishing a new company that will be in direct competition with the target business. Since the seller might be responsible for future liabilities, it is customary for the buyer to pay a specific amount of the purchase price into an escrow account in order to ensure that there are sufficient funds available to cover future claims if and when they materialize.

- *Conditions of the transaction.* The SPA sets out a list of events that need to take place before and after closing. Conditions precedent ("CPs") are specific actions and events that need to be satisfied prior to a transaction completion. For example, CPs typically include final approval of debt financing from the lending banks, receipt of required regulatory approvals and confirmation from key customers that they won't invoke a change of control clause and cancel their contracts with the company. Conditions subsequent ("CSs") include actions and events that are not critical enough to justify a delay in the transaction completion. However, they are nonetheless important enough for the buyer to insist on getting a formal written commitment from the seller to satisfy the CSs within a pre-agreed timeframe from closing.

- *Termination rights.* The parties to the SPA detail a number of provisions that could allow each side to terminate the agreement prior to closing. The buyer will often want the option of walking away from the deal in the event of a material adverse change ("MAC"). While the exact definition of what might constitute a MAC is subject to lengthy negotiations between the buyer and the seller, typical events include death or incapacity of key managers, sudden loss of a major company asset, *force majeure* or terrorism. It is worth noting that there are significant differences in the use of the MAC language in the purchase agreement across jurisdictions, so it is prudent to take legal advice about the applicable local rules. Apart from the MAC clause, other provisions that might allow the parties to terminate the purchase agreement consist of material breaches of representations and warranties or failure to satisfy certain CPs. Unless the buyer and the seller jointly decide not to proceed with the transaction, a signed SPA is a binding contract. Nonetheless, on occasion, the SPA might include specific break fees payable by the terminating party, in case the buyer or the seller decide to walk away from the transaction between signing and closing.

5. *Articles of Association ("Articles")*

<u>Purpose of the document:</u> The Articles are the by-laws of the company that represent a contract between the company and its shareholders. The document specifies the company's constitution, its share classes and its approach to handling key governance and financial matters. Depending on the geography of the investment target, the Articles might be referred to by a different name, such as the Certificate of Incorporation or the Legal Charter. Unlike other legal documents in a private equity transaction, the Articles are typically filed with the relevant government body and are often available in the public domain.

<u>My approach to key issues:</u> Since the Articles are a public document, the company and the shareholders will often choose to limit disclosure solely to the information which is required to be disclosed by the local law. Additional rights, obligations and specific arrangements among the various parties are discussed in more detail in the Shareholders' Agreement, a private document that governs the relationship between the company and its shareholders. In my opinion, the most important areas of the Articles are the items below.

- *Share classes and the associated rights.* The Articles set out the share structure of the company by share type, number, price and ranking. Since management and the investors often hold shares of different classes, their entitlements differ in terms of voting as well as preferential liquidation and dividend rights. As we discussed in Chapter 9, most private equity funds allocate their capital to the senior share class, with only a small proportion invested in the common equity. By contract, management teams typically invest all—or the majority—of their capital in common equity. The Articles specify how the proceeds are allocated among the various share classes following a liquidity event: senior shares receive their proceeds ahead of the common equity holders. In addition, senior share classes are often entitled to a preferred dividend, which enables private equity investors to receive a minimum return on their investment before any remaining proceeds are distributed to common equity holders.

- *Pre-emption rights, transfer provisions and exit.* Most share classes will have pre-emption rights: when new shares are issued, existing investors will be entitled to purchase their pro-rata portion of the new shares in order to maintain their shareholding in the company. The Articles set out the transfer rules among the shareholders, including the order, transfer mechanism and determination of the price. In addition, except for any pre-agreed lock-up period, the drag-along right entitles the majority shareholders to sell the entire company and "drag" other shareholders in the event of a sale to a third party or a listing. Conversely, minority shareholders (including management) have a tag-along right, which entitles them to sell their pro-rata shareholding alongside the selling shareholder. Typically, management shares are non-transferable, except for provisions specified in the transfer rules, drag-along and tag-along clauses. The Articles will also include specific provisions to describe any other exit arrangements that might exist among the shareholders, such as the ROFO or ROFR we discussed in Chapter 9.

- *Governance.* The Articles outline the company's governance framework, such as the composition of the Board of Directors, frequency of meetings and required voting thresholds for key decisions. The document also specifies a list of major actions that will require shareholder and / or board approval. Among many others, major actions include approval of the budget, significant changes in the business plan, appointment or dismissal of the auditors, approval of new employment contracts of key employees, major acquisitions or divestments, changes in the company's capital structure or amendments in the main legal agreements.

6. Shareholders' Agreement ("SHA")

<u>Purpose of the document:</u> The SHA is a private document that supplements the Articles and details the obligations of all shareholders in the company. This is a key transaction agreement that needs to be signed by all shareholders of the company, including senior management (to the extent they own shares).

<u>My approach to key issues:</u> While the SHA is more flexible in its format and is far more specific than the Articles, both documents feature a number of overlapping areas. For example, the SHA also contains provisions about the share classes, liquidation and dividend preference, share transfer rules (including ROFO and ROFR), pre-emption rights, drag-along and tag-along clauses. There is also a section on governance that is more detailed than that in the Articles: there is more specificity provided about the conduct of the board meetings, required voting thresholds as well as the roles of the various board committees (such as the Audit Committee and the Remuneration Committee). There are a number of additional areas covered by the SHA, such as those listed below.

- *Management equity.* The SHA sets out the composition of the management incentive plan (such as common equity, ratchets and co-investment in the senior share classes) and outlines the vesting schedule of the management shares. In addition, the SHA also addresses the circumstances of potential departures of those managers who are also shareholders in the company. "Good leavers" are typically those who die, become critically ill or incapacitated, retire at an appropriate age or who are deemed to be good leavers by the Board of Directors. Upon their departure, good leavers most commonly sell their shares at market value. "Bad leavers" are those managers who resign for any other reason than stated above, or who are dismissed for cause. The shares of bad leavers are bought at the lower of cost or market value. Please note that the SHA contains provisions relating to managers solely in their capacity as shareholders: detailed terms of service, benefits and severance entitlements are agreed separately in the management employment contracts.

- *Restrictive covenants.* The SHA includes a number of restrictions, such as "non-compete" and "non-solicit" clauses aimed at preventing key executives from joining a direct competitor and poaching the company's employees or clients after their departure. These clauses are considered to be easier to enforce in court if the key members of the management team agree to them in their capacity as shareholders of the business (as opposed to in their capacity as company employees).

- *Protection of minorities.* The SHA contains a number of clauses aimed at providing protections to minority shareholders. Apart from pre-emption rights and tag-along provisions, other protections typically include board seats or board observer rights; information rights; and the requirement of a super-majority voting threshold for certain key decisions (such as an exit). Occasionally, the definition of a board quorum might include the minority board director, so that the majority shareholder cannot make decisions without the minority shareholder present.

- *Restricted matters.* The SHA specifies a number of decisions that require super-majority shareholder approval. Typically, these matters include selling or liquidating the company, incurring material debt, pursuing major capital expenditure or M&A, appointing or dismissing senior executives and engaging in litigation.

7. Debt Documentation

<u>Purpose of the documents:</u> The main legal agreements that relate to debt financing represent a suite of documents that include a mandate letter to appoint a lead underwriter; loan agreements for each type of debt facility in the capital structure (e.g., senior debt, second lien, mezzanine[6] and other tranches); transaction security documents to create appropriate loan guarantees; intercreditor agreements that govern the rankings and security subordination among the various lenders; a hedging side letter (in case equity investors choose to hedge floating interest rate risk); and—if the deal includes the issuance of a high-yield bond—a "highly confident" letter from the appointed bond underwriter and a preliminary high-yield bond offering memorandum.[7]

<u>My approach to key issues:</u>

The bad news is that debt legal agreements are both quite technical and long. The good news is that during the definitive documentation stage, deal teams benefit from working alongside experienced lawyers. If you work with a law firm that is active in the credit markets, your legal advisers will be able to dissect the core debt documents relatively easily and opine quickly on whether the terms of the financing are appropriate in the context of the transaction. Before commencing work on the full debt documentation, it is also helpful that most members of the deal team are well aware of the main terms of the financing: at an earlier stage of the deal, lending banks usually

---

[6]Chapter 10 in Nijs (2014) provides a helpful discussion of the main issues relating to mezzanine financing, including key terms, covenants and credit agreements. Please refer to Chapter 11 References for a complete citation.
[7]Chapter 6 in Bagaria (2016) provides a comprehensive overview of the high-yield bond documentation. Please refer to Chapter 11 References for a complete citation.

provide commitment papers—consisting of a commitment letter and a term sheet—that outline the key terms of the debt package. It is worth noting that there might be pronounced differences in standard loan terms across jurisdictions, so it is very important to get appropriate legal advice from lawyers who are familiar with the local legal framework. Deal teams are expected to review and provide input on the following key aspects of the debt documentation:

- *Debt terms.* The main areas of focus are the loan amount, interest rate, term and amortization schedule, fees and prepayment penalties. Is there a "market flex"? The lead underwriters of debt might have the right to change the terms of the bank debt if the syndication is not going as well as expected. "Flex" provisions might include the right to increase margin, increase the prepayment premium on the junior debt, or reallocate amounts between different debt tranches. Conversely, if the syndication is well-received and the loans are oversubscribed, the lenders might be able to improve the terms of the financing package by applying a "reverse flex."
- *Covenants and cures.* We already discussed covenants in Chapter 9. Loan agreements for each type of debt facility will set out the applicable affirmative, negative and financial covenants.[8] Although the approach to covenants varies by the specific debt instrument and jurisdiction, the most common financial covenants that you will come across are: leverage ratio; interest coverage ratio; fixed-charge coverage ratio and liquidity to minimum cash balance. It is also important to understand (and negotiate) what happens in the event of a covenant breach: in certain cases, the shareholders might be

---

[8] In addition to references already provided in Chapter 9 of this book, please refer to Chapter 16 in Pignataro (2014) and Chapter 10 in Nesbitt (2019) for an in-depth overview of covenants. Please refer to Chapter 11 References for complete publishing information.

offered a grace period to provide a deliverable that is over-due, or be allowed to inject additional equity to provide a "cure." Finally, covenants rely on the highly specific calculations of a "normalized" EBITDA and financial indebtedness, and the deal teams (together with the company's CFO) need to ensure that they understand and agree with the definitions provided in the loan agreements.

- *Events of default.* When the borrower triggers an event of default, the lender has the right to accelerate the loan, demand immediate loan repayment and potentially enforce on its security. While loan agreements feature a fairly typical list of circumstances that will constitute common events of default, there is some room for negotiation in the form of cure periods and materiality thresholds. Another tricky area is a MAC clause: while this feature is less common in US transactions, many European loan agreements will include an event of default due to a broadly defined adverse change that—in the opinion of the majority lenders—makes the borrower less likely to meet its payment obligations.

- *Permitted actions.* Certain terms of the debt financing have a direct impact on the company's operations and its ability to make payments to equity investors: in particular, the deal teams should study carefully any restrictions relating to minimum cash balance, permitted distributions to the shareholders, maximum CAPEX, permitted CAPEX as well as permitted acquisitions and disposals.

- *Terms and conditions of the financing.* It is essential to understand how the representation and warranties, CPs and CSs in the SPA interact with the relevant clauses in the debt documentation. Apart from the seller's representations and warranties provided at the outset of the transaction, the borrower will have to provide its own representations and warranties at specific future dates during the term of the lending agreement in order to reassert the accuracy of the company's reporting and reconfirm the overall state of the business. In addition to CPs and CSs already articulated in the SPA, the lenders will typically demand that the parties satisfy additional conditions, such as those involving the timely delivery of the due diligence reports and the financial model, as well as a confirmation of no events of default at closing. There is a good reason to be very careful in ensuring that all CSs are satisfied within the agreed time period from closing: any CS not fulfilled by the deadline might constitute an event of default!

12

Adding Value Through Active Ownership

Key Topics in Chapter 12:

- Develop your own success formula with a Value Creation Plan
- Four value-accretive actions for every portfolio company to consider
- Create powerful performance improvement momentum with a 100-Day Plan
- Governance and reporting: strategic priorities of a well-run private equity board
- When things go wrong: spot the first signs of company distress and take radical action

---

When the ink on the signed transaction documentation dries, it is very tempting for deal teams to get into full-on celebratory mode: the deal is finally done! While a closing dinner (or two) is a nice way to honor this important milestone for the deal team, transaction advisers and the newly acquired portfolio company, any prolonged festivities might be premature. Guess what: if you just acquired a struggling business with significant improvement potential, the company will still be underperforming on the first day of your ownership—and it will continue leaking value until you roll up your sleeves and do something about it. Henry Kravis of KKR famously said, "Don't congratulate us when we buy a company. Any fool can buy a company. You just pay enough and that's the easy part. The hard part is, what do you with the business once you've made your investment? How do you create value? What do you do to make that company much more efficient?" (Goldman Sachs, 2017).

Private equity investors tend to differ in how they engage with their portfolio businesses post-acquisition. Certain players choose to standardize their approach in managing investments and deploy their own formulas for value creation. For example, Vista Equity Partners follows a fairly regimented playbook that consists of applying more than 50 proprietary operating procedures aimed at benchmarking and improving each portfolio company in the areas of product development, sales and marketing, customer support, professional services and general administration (MacArthur et al., 2017). Platinum Equity implements its trademarked M&A&O® strategy that marries an operational business turnaround with steady growth from a stream of bolt-on acquisitions. Another example is KKR: the firm enlists a number of the dedicated operating professionals from its in-house consulting group, KKR Capstone, to assist deal teams in managing portfolio companies throughout their lifespan under KKR ownership. Adopting a proprietary value-creation method appears to be an effective strategy for these investors, as all of them were able to generate a track record of solid investment performance.

Regardless of the pronounced differences among investors in their approach to day-to-day operational execution within their portfolio companies post-closing, the private equity model broadly follows the same logic. New owners aspire to create lasting value during their investment horizon and turn their portfolio companies into thriving businesses by aiming to deliver on specific targets in terms of revenue growth, margin improvement, overhead reduction and capital efficiency. In Chapter 7, I argued that potential sources of value creation in a private equity-backed company are finite and can be boiled down to a list,[1] with a typical investment thesis relying on the successful execution of several critical value drivers. Having a list of broad actions, however, is insufficient: to accelerate implementation post-acquisition, each value-creation lever needs to be translated into a series of targeted steps that represent a unique path to value within each company's post-acquisition strategy. Since the value-creation plan is designed to be delivered within the compressed timeframe of a 5-year investment horizon, companies need to set clear priorities, address the most pressing needs of their strategic agenda and dedicate most effort to the areas where upside can be captured quickly.

As such, some businesses may choose to focus on improvements in organic revenue growth, while others may be best positioned to increase their top-line sales entirely through add-on acquisitions. Some companies will aim to unlock considerable value through better supply chain practices and eliminating pockets of waste in procurement, whereas others won't even look into this area—simply because they might have a more urgent need to address customer churn, improve sales effectiveness, build average transaction values and capture adjacent

---

[1]Please refer to Chapter 7 of this book for a detailed discussion of my *Master List of Most Common Drivers of Value Creation.*

market segments. Although private equity owners hope to achieve the same set of broad objectives—such as high cash-on-cash return through value creation and growth in their portfolio businesses—each company will take a different route and will follow its own bespoke Value Creation Plan.

Active Ownership: Value Creation Strategy

A Value Creation Plan is a roadmap to the company's future. It delineates a set of initiatives that a portfolio company needs to pursue in order to realize its strategic agenda and fulfill its potential under private equity ownership. A typical Value Creation Plan encourages the company to adopt a methodical approach and carry out the following actions over a 5-year horizon:

1. Establish a culture of performance and accountability to challenge the *status quo*.
2. Overinvest in early wins in the first 100 days of ownership.
3. Strengthen existing capabilities and deliver operational excellence.
4. Pursue profitable growth through new products or markets.
5. Consolidate success and position the business for exit.

How does one design a Value Creation Plan in practice? Perhaps I can share my own experience. None of the funds where I worked had a "pre-baked" value-creation strategy or a replicable formula that could be applied to every transaction. Instead, it was the responsibility of the deal team to sit down with company management on each transaction and map out the strategic direction of the business, complete with critical milestones, relevant KPIs and explicit links to the investment base case. Since most members of the deal team had financially oriented skillsets, we often sought specific operational input from external industry experts or in-house operating partners who had first-hand knowledge of best practices in procurement, sales and marketing, working capital management, technology and international expansion. Their perspective was invaluable in sense-checking the assumptions of the management team and setting robust—yet realistic—targets to drive implementation.

The most opportune time to design a Value Creation Plan is straight after signing: there is often a delay of multiple weeks before deal closing that can be used productively to engage in a comprehensive planning process, with a view of hitting the ground running on Day 1 after deal completion. At that stage, you have the benefit of your investment base case that provides a rigorous quantification of the planned cost savings and revenue enhancements during your holding period. In addition, you can synthetize the findings from the final due diligence reports that highlight the company's current process inefficiencies and key areas of value leakage. It is hard to translate an investment thesis into a formal plan without pressing the management team to give a lot of thought to the optimal operating structure and required resources post-acquisition. Does the company have sufficient capabilities and assets to deliver the Value Creation Plan? Who will own each value-creation activity and are there any obvious talent gaps? Armed with this knowledge, the deal professionals and the management team should be able to create a shared vision of critical priorities, set out implementation steps and agree on milestones and KPIs.

The planning session around the Value Creation Plan is often a good opportunity for investors to create a deeper bond with management and clarify mutual expectations in advance of the exciting adventure that lies ahead. If the management team is new to the private equity ownership model, it might be appropriate for the deal team to reiterate some important principles that matter to financial investors, such as a relentless focus on cash management as well as careful and disciplined capital allocation. Especially in a levered acquisition, the Value Creation Plan should be tilted toward de-risking the transaction as soon as possible after closing: the management team should prioritize any value-creation levers that can generate cash quickly in order to build a cushion against an unexpected downturn, pay down debt early or deploy more capital toward business growth.

While the specifics of the value-creation blueprint depend on the particular circumstances of the acquisition target, I believe there are some actions that every portfolio company should consider during the 5-year horizon under private equity ownership.

- *Embrace digital tools.* No company operating in the 21st century should require any convincing of the merits of exploiting the latest technology in order to enhance its operational agility. Entering private equity ownership represents a perfect opportunity for any portfolio company to assess its digital literacy, review legacy IT systems, identify existing gaps and invest in a state-of-the-art technology infrastructure. Astute private equity investors increasingly turn to digital tools in their value-creation playbook[2] and guide their portfolio companies through a targeted adoption of systems that help businesses generate quantifiable benefits across the value chain. Advanced technological, data and analytics capabilities improve the company's proficiency in tracking customer footprint and engagement, delivering consistent purchasing experience, capturing operating performance data from business units across numerous locations, automating supply

---

[2]For an example of digital approaches to value creation in a private equity–backed business, please refer to an article by Boston Consulting Group (2017). Please refer to Chapter 12 References for a complete citation.

chains and optimizing logistics networks. The companies armed with first-class digital expertise and access to real-time data analytics can compete better by responding quickly to address shifts in customer preferences and manage their value chain in an evolving market.

- *Optimize product pricing.* Outright price increases may not be appropriate or even possible for every business: after all, company executives rightly fear upsetting their long-term customers, inducing churn and suffering from an aggressive competitive response. However, price optimization is an effective value-creation lever for businesses that historically lacked pricing discipline. Every additional dollar captured through pricing falls straight to the bottom line: for a typical mid-size US company with revenues up to $1 billion, a 1% improvement in pricing raises profits by 6% on average, whereas a 1% reduction in variable cost produces an increase in profits of 3.8% (McKinsey, 2019). Unless the business can demonstrate that it has already built superb commercial capabilities that allow it to execute on pricing with precision and consistency, there might be select pockets of opportunity to implement a price optimization program. At times, companies with complex business models and sizeable product portfolios— especially those serving B2B customers—may be guilty of leaking value by relying on outdated price lists, differentiating insufficiently among their customer accounts and applying variable discounts and rebates at the discretion of the sales force. In circumstances where profitability varies significantly by customer group and product type, one of the suitable post-acquisition strategies for a new private equity owner might be to introduce greater pricing discipline in order to maximize the margin potential of a portfolio company. What can one do? Possible initiatives might include a thorough data-driven assessment of the product value against customers' willingness to pay; enhanced customer segmentation to determine the right price for each customer group; greater differentiation by upgrading product features; improved product mix tailored to maximize profitability; and an introduction of a consistent policy on rebates and discounts.

- *Grow the moat.* Every good private equity due diligence process reveals a company's strengths and weaknesses. While the first instinct of a new private equity owner might be to launch a series of initiatives post-closing aimed at addressing the portfolio company's shortcomings, another option is to empower the business to double-down on its strengths. Most private equity professionals are familiar with the "whale chart"—a simple visual analysis that dissects the company's metrics into performance segments. What does the "whale chart" look like when you rank the company's customers, products or locations by their profitability? It is not uncommon to discover that a modest proportion of customers or products accounts for a major share of the company's profits. What does the top quartile look like and what attributes make it special? This is the quartile that demonstrates what works well in the company's customer value proposition. This is the area where the company has an economic moat. What should you prioritize in your post-acquisition strategy: bringing the bottom quartile to average, or focusing on the top quartile to make its performance skyrocket during your investment horizon? Good question. Perhaps it is worth thinking about what the private equity owner might find easier to sell at exit: a business that is average in five areas, or a business that is superb in only two? To me, it seems that focusing on the top quartile of the company's strengths, enhancing its customer value proposition in that target area and growing its existing moat is a much safer strategy.

- *Enhance the company's ESG standing.* Producing and measuring positive ESG outcomes is no longer reserved to companies with a clear sustainability mandate. A company-wide ESG program does not need to be viewed as a purely philanthropic activity either: sustainable business practices are capable of attracting and retaining customers, improving operating efficiency, enhancing returns,[3] limiting risk and making the company more valuable at exit.[4] While there is no "one-size-fits-all" ESG strategy, portfolio companies can often discover tangible ways to create value from commanding a price premium on products with sustainability features, reducing costs through eco-efficiency, eliminating waste and building sustainable supply chains (WWF and Doughty Hanson, 2011). The savviest private equity investors already explicitly embed ESG value creation levers in their deal calculus and empower their portfolio companies to deliver an attractive financial return alongside a positive social or environmental impact.

---

[3]Friede *et al.* (2015) conducted an analysis of more than 2,200 individual studies investigating the link between the ESG factors and corporate financial performance ("CFP"). The researchers found a positive ESG-CFP relationship in 63% of the meta-analyses and a negative ESG-CFP relationship in 8% of the meta-analyses in the data set. Please refer to Chapter 12 References for a complete citation.

[4]McKinsey & Company surveyed 558 investment professionals and C-level executives on the value of ESG programs in July 2019: 83% of respondents indicate that they would be willing to pay about a 10% median premium to acquire a company with a positive record relating to the ESG issues over one with a negative record (the result holds true even for those skeptical executives who say ESG programs have no effect on shareholder value). McKinsey & Company (2020) published an article to describe detailed findings of "the ESG premium." Please refer to Chapter 12 References for a complete citation.

From Paper to Action: 100–Day Plan

As a statement attributed to Thomas Edison goes, "Vision without execution is a hallucination." The 100-Day Plan is the first step in making the Value Creation Plan execution a reality. What is so special about the first 100 days post-acquisition? That's the time when the transaction reaches its maximum momentum and the company is most receptive to implementing changes. The most effective 100-Day Plans focus on producing quantifiable improvements in EBITDA through a limited set of actions aimed at capturing near-term value through selective optimization and redesign of the portfolio company. While there is no industry standard in private equity that governs the conceptual framework behind 100-Day Plans, most of the plans I have seen typically address the aspects below.

- *Communication.* Nobody likes uncertainty. As soon as the transaction is announced, it is important to build support for the deal and preserve good relations with key stakeholders of the business. The CEO, together with other members of the senior management team, should prepare a series of communication scripts—both formal and informal—to address employees as well as major customers and suppliers. An effective communication plan will describe the business opportunity in compelling terms, signal change and set out future expectations. It will clarify the strategic direction of the business post-acquisition and define the role of the stakeholders in the successful implementation of the planned changes. The CEO needs to convey empathy, honesty and trust without creating unrealistic expectations: if the business is ailing and needs to undergo a painful restructuring in order to return to stability and growth, the employees need to hear this first-hand from the leadership team. Soft issues such as the strategic vision and company culture need to be discussed, so that people across the organization gain a shared sense of purpose and feel aligned around common goals. The CEO needs to watch closely how the news is received across the business, act promptly to mitigate uncertainty and aim to safeguard the company's most valuable assets, such as its human capital and its key customers.

- *Employees.* A change of ownership is often an emotionally charged experience for the company's employees. They find it hard to partake in the excitement of financial investors and the senior management team about the transaction until they understand fully what it means to them. Will they stay? Will they leave? Excessive worry due to uncertainty may lead to reduced productivity and diminished morale. Any delay in managing employees' expectations might result in defections of the most talented contributors to the organization, which—no doubt—will undermine the company's performance. The CEO needs to move decisively with planned changes during the first 100 days: if the Value Creation Plan assumes a new organizational layout and a different reporting structure, these adjustments need to happen quickly. What does the leadership structure look like just below the senior management team? Is the talent matched appropriately to the demands of the value creation strategy? Existing and newly appointed line managers need to decide on the optimal structure for their business units, so that the employees across the board can be informed as soon as possible post-acquisition about any decisions relating to their titles, responsibilities and work assignments. Any lay-offs or rationalizations need to happen quickly as well by following a fair and transparent process. Once the organizational boundaries are re-drawn, the employees should feel engaged and empowered to deliver on ambitious targets. The culture of ownership and accountability should extend to the deepest layers of the organization by linking compensation to individual performance.

- *Reporting*. Once the deal team gains full access to the company post-acquisition, the finance function is the first area that investment professionals investigate as a matter of priority. How strong are the reporting capabilities at present? Does the finance team use business analytics to produce insightful analyses of the company's operations? Finally, does the finance department have adequate resources, both in terms of capable people and efficient systems? More often than not, the company is already generating a battery of regular financial reports and an abundance of KPIs; however, there are probably only a few metrics that measure what financial investors really need to know. Further, the reporting capabilities frequently require strengthening: we often find that there are quite a few members of the finance team who simply push data around and spend too much time on the low-value-added activities that can be automated. Without effective tools that aid finance reporting, planning, budgeting and forecasting, it's very difficult for the company to track its performance against the investment base case. This is an area where the private equity deal professionals—as opposed to the senior management team—can roll up their sleeves and add real value: we typically lead the thinking on the required metrics to ensure that the company is focused on cash, return on investments and covenant headroom—and not merely on paper profit. If we identify skillset gaps, we can resort to using external consultants until new team members are recruited and onboarded. I worked on several transactions where one or two investment professionals were seconded to portfolio companies for a period of several months in order to drive the transformation of the finance department. Overall, we do whatever it takes to bring the finance function to complete fluency when it comes to producing timely and accurate monthly reports that align the financial and operating perspectives of the company performance and use business analytics to generate valuable insights.

- *Objectives, milestones and KPIs.* What does the company really need to do in the first 100 days post-acquisition? Well, it should certainly not pursue every initiative laid out in the Value Creation Plan: instead, the business should target only what's critical and is likely to produce tangible near-term gains. Broadly speaking, the company should take steps toward becoming a best-in-class organization in terms of its operational performance and focus on the core business before adding new capabilities. In addition, most businesses will need to be selectively upgraded and retooled to support future growth. Where is the low-hanging fruit? What creates the most impact and produces early wins? Typical initiatives in the first few months under private equity ownership include optimization of the working capital, IT upgrades, improvements in the supply chain and purchasing arrangements, as well as re-deployment of spare capacity and other unproductive capital assets. To avoid overwhelming employees who are engaged in the implementation of the 100-Day Plan, it helps to break down each initiative into detailed step lists, with interim milestones and specific dollar targets. I have found it helpful to represent the plan as a list of line items—complete with target dates and names of the responsible individuals—that detail specific actions, success criteria, milestones and the associated KPIs.
- *Program office.* The CEO and other members of the senior management team need to run the day-to-day operations of the business as the main priority and may not have the bandwidth for detailed tracking of the various assignments included in the 100-Day Plan. It is in nobody's interest to cripple the core

business and overburden the leadership team with enormous to-do lists. If a 100-Day Plan is fairly extensive, it might make sense to set up a Program Office that will be responsible for coordination and control of the implementation progress. The Program Office needs to be run by an experienced, motivated and energetic executive who will be capable of prioritizing, making cross-functional decisions as well as anticipating and mitigating risks. From what I have seen in various portfolio companies, most Program Office leaders are hired externally and typically come from a strategy consulting background. The management team can leverage the Program Office to ensure that there are tools in place to measure progress, capture value and provide frequent updates to all stakeholders, including investors, employees and senior managers.

- *Reward system.* The implementation phase of 100-Day Plan is a busy time. However, it should not feel like a labor camp to the company's employees. In fact, they should feel rejuvenated by the positive changes and motivated to deliver on their targets. How can one inject some joy during this demanding and stressful time? In my experience, it is effective to award a one-time bonus or additional equity in the company linked to the successful execution of the plan and delivering quantifiable EBITDA improvements. It is also nice to celebrate interim accomplishments that help sustain momentum among the employees and serve as a source of further confidence in achieving the full targets.

Governance and Reporting

The private equity governance model is one of the major value-creation levers in any transaction. Controlling financial investors have the resources and capabilities to monitor the performance of their portfolio companies carefully, make critical decisions, execute on requisite changes and ensure continued support for the businesses they own. What is the typical structure of a private equity board? How do board members interact with management teams post-acquisition? What do private equity boards need to measure in order to keep on top of their investments? Let me share my thoughts on the main aspects of the private equity governance mechanism.

- *Composition.* Private equity boards tend to be small, averaging about 5–7 board members. A controlling investor will typically take at least 3 board seats, with 2 seats allocated to the company's Chairman and the CEO. The CFO of the business attends most board meetings by invitation without being a formal member of the board. If the acquisition was executed by a consortium of investors, every shareholder representing at least 20–25% of equity will be entitled to a board seat and any shareholder with around 10% holding in the company will typically have a board observer right. Some board observers choose not to attend board meetings; however, they never fail to show up when the portfolio company is in trouble! As I mentioned earlier in this chapter, I never worked for funds that had a dedicated portfolio group of in-house operational consultants. The funds I worked at were reluctant for the management team to develop a sense of dependency on external resources that will be pulled away at exit. However, my deal teams always executed transactions in tandem with in-house operating partners, who would in most cases join the company's board post-acquisition alongside the key investment professionals. It is always reassuring to have our firm's operating partners serving on the portfolio company board, as they are well-positioned to track the state of the company's operations, evaluate markets and opine on whether the business has the required capabilities to respond to headwinds. Moreover, an operating partner is someone who can step up to the role of interim CEO in case of illness or prolonged underperformance of the incumbent CEO until the board recruits a new business leader. If the management team that we are supporting in a transaction lacks private equity experience, we would often recruit a seasoned industry executive—ideally someone who has worked for a private equity–backed business in the past—to assume the role of Executive Chairman. This person needs to have a good chemistry with the CEO and will typically play the role of a *confidante*, coach, challenger, firefighter and a disciplinarian to the senior leadership team. The Executive Chairman needs to believe in the deal thesis and is required to invest in the business upon joining to ensure full alignment of interests.

- *Board cycle.* In my experience of serving on boards of both publicly listed companies and private equity–backed businesses, I find that private equity boards require more time and greater engagement from their members. There are around 10–12 formal board meetings a year; however, the time commitment does not stop there. The controlling shareholder interacts with the CEO and other members of the senior management team almost daily immediately post-acquisition and during the implementation phase of the 100-Day Plan. The deal partner who led the transaction on behalf of the controlling financial investor is the person who is best positioned to develop the closest relationship with the CEO: both of them will be talking outside board meetings at least weekly for the duration of the transaction.

- *Board dynamic.* Effective boards strike the right balance of supporting and challenging the portfolio company. They set out clear expectations for the business and create a disciplined framework that allows the company to make progress toward its stated goals. They act as a sounding board to the management team and a steering committee for making critical business decisions. The CEO of a private equity–backed business is often an ambitious and decisive individual who dislikes seeing the senior management team micromanaged by the board. A well-run company frequently strives to build sufficient capabilities within its business to be able to handle most of the challenges on its own. To ensure good board chemistry, it is important that the operating partners on the board don't jump in and try to fix every problem themselves; they are better off adopting the mindset of senior advisers to the business as opposed to company executives. The CEO, in turn, needs to understand that controlling investors will be directly involved in the decision-making process when it comes to significant matters: the company's budget, changes in the senior management team, an acquisition or a disposal, changes in strategy or operations as well as any major capital investment will need to be reviewed and approved by the company's board of directors. There are some areas where financial investors are especially well-positioned to add value to the portfolio company: they are likely to take a prominent role in the ongoing discussions with the lenders and will probably lead the workstreams relating to any refinancings, restructurings, the company's M&A program and the eventual exit.

- *Management reporting.* "What you measure is what you get," say Kaplan and Norton, the architects behind the balanced scorecard approach. Further, they urge every company to develop a set of metrics that will enable it to assess business performance along the following four blocs: 1) financial perspective; 2) customer perspective; 3) internal business perspective; and 4) innovation and learning perspective (Kaplan and Norton, 1992). In other words, the balanced scorecard method urges every company to ask itself four key questions. What are our main financial targets? What do we need to offer our customers in order to achieve these targets? How do we need to run our internal processes so that we can provide the requisite customer value proposition and hit our targeted profits? Finally, how can we make continual improvements to our key human, systems and (where relevant) production assets?

Let's think about what implications this advice has in the context of a private equity portfolio company's monthly management reporting to the board. Perhaps we can take a step back and consider what the board members really need to know in order to be able to discharge their duties properly and provide adequate oversight to the portfolio business. First, they need to track the company's performance against the investment base case and the Value Creation Plan. Second, they require timely and accurate data about the past performance against budget and forecast data for the future period: this information needs to include relevant operating and financial company KPIs— including covenant headroom—as well as key leading indicators (industry-wide or macroeconomic) that can serve as an early signal of any potential future change in business performance. Third, they must be aware of key areas of risk and evaluate whether there are sufficient controls and risk mitigation mechanisms in place. Finally, they should be presented with an integrated view of business performance across the main pillars of the organization that include operations, sales and marketing as well as human resources and leadership. It is good practice for the management report to include an executive summary that highlights current market trends, key insights about the business and main challenges faced by the company.

- *Management performance.* As we discussed in Chapter 6, one of the major benefits of the private equity ownership model is the ability to attract and retain talented management teams who are directly incentivized to achieve ambitious targets. Another benefit is the ability to react quickly to underperformance and replace one or more members of the senior management—without engaging into an extended and bureaucratic process—when they fail to deliver on their goals. It is productive for the board to reserve some time at least every quarter when the management team is not present in order to talk openly about the performance of the Chairman, CEO, CFO and other senior managers holding mission-critical positions in the portfolio business.

When the Deal Goes South

One day you might arrive to work and discover that one of your portfolio investments is underwater. This makes you look like a submariner of sorts—operating in harsh conditions in deep-water territory. While real submariners receive hardship payments for their hard work, you are more likely to get stern reprimands from the members of your investment committee, endless phone calls from the lenders and cries of desperation from the portfolio company management team. What do you do? I have been there and done that. I have been involved in difficult transactions, some of which subsequently returned to good health and some of which ended up generating abysmal returns for my fund. Along with other deal team members, I had to take meetings with LPs and explain what went wrong.

I remember this experience vividly: it is a difficult situation that will make you feel like your entire career is on the line. While I can't offer an effective remedy for all companies in distress,[5] I can share some of my learnings that you may find helpful.

- *Look out for signs of trouble.* The first clue might be a change in the behavior of the senior management team. Do you feel that they are distracted? Do you sense that they might be filtering information or holding back important data from the shareholders? Does the CEO act differently by suddenly becoming too conservative or too risk-prone? Are there any management resignations in the senior team? Other early warning signals may include:

  a. political or regulatory changes;
  b. macroeconomic or industry-wide challenges that hit the newspaper headlines;
  c. too many new entrants in the core market of your portfolio company;
  d. an unexpected liability claim against the business;
  e. a period of unprofitable revenue growth due to business overexpansion;
  f. increasing customer churn;
  g. high-profile flops of new products;
  h. loss of a big customer or a large contract;
  i. deterioration in supplier relationships or terms of trade;
  j. poor cash generation and inability to cover costs or near-term obligations;

---

[5]Please see a great book by Slatter and Lovett (1999) for useful advice on managing corporate turnarounds. Please refer to Chapter 12 References for a complete citation.

k. reduction in covenant headroom or an outright covenant breach;

l. unexpected extraordinary items in the financial statements;

m. the management report to shareholders is either missing or late; and

n. the auditors raise concerns about the business.

If you are worried, it is alright to be paranoid and arrange a meeting with the company or go on a site visit to see first-hand what may be going wrong.

- *Understand the causes.* If the business is indeed in trouble, you need to understand why and assess the severity of the problem. Is there a deterioration in the underlying business performance due to external factors, such as changes in market demand or an industry-wide slowdown? Are the causes of the decline purely internal, such as managerial errors, lack of discipline due to inadequate controls or an overly complex business model that seems to be ineffective? Do you suspect that the company could be the victim of reporting manipulation or fraud? In a levered acquisition, a sound business may begin to struggle simply because of the excessive leverage and the overoptimistic projections in the business plan. You need to understand if this could be the case in your portfolio company.
- *Prepare to fight.* Once you are certain about what's happening, don't deny the problem. Also, don't succumb to fear. You need to compose yourself and maintain a positive mindset. Are you worried that your fund's equity investment will be wiped out? When I was in this situation, I always reminded myself that many others—including the most successful private equity investors—had faced similar situations in their careers. Blackstone lost its entire investment in Edgcomb Steel and

Stephen Schwarzman candidly shares this story in his memoir (Schwarzman, 2019). KKR made a number of bad investments, such as Eaton Leonard and Bruno's; there is an entire chapter describing the fund's setbacks in a book by Baker and Smith (1998). I can go on and on. If you are paralyzed with fear, perhaps you can look at how the US Navy SEALs are taught to act in highly stressful situations. When they jump from an airplane and their parachute does not open, they are trained to remain in full control and follow a standard procedure in the next 40 seconds: "Assess the situation, decipher the problem, decide which skill is needed to solve it, implement that skill, then evaluate whether that solution worked" (Diviney, 2021). This is roughly the same approach that private equity investors ought to follow when their portfolio companies are in trouble—although they are lucky to have more than 40 seconds to act and they won't be required to jump out of a military aircraft to solve the problem.

- *Communicate.* Sooner or later, you will understand the full extent of the difficulty in your portfolio company and will need to share this information with others. Who are the important stakeholders? First, it is your fund, your investment committee and the portfolio company board. Second, it might be the company's lenders. Depending on the nature of the business challenge, you might also require a communication plan aimed at the company's key customers, suppliers and employees. In my opinion, it is best to talk straight and deliver a transparent message. What can be worse than bad news? More bad news later. Therefore, it makes sense to tell the whole story all at once rather than opt to deliver bad news piecemeal.

- *Act quickly.* Don't ignore the early warning signs and move decisively while there is still some cash left at the portfolio company. Convey a sense of urgency to the senior management team. What can be done to fix the fundamental issues of the business? Possible options include implementing short-term operational improvements, revamping the sales process to generate additional customer demand or refining business strategy. Does the management team need to be replaced or supported by bringing someone new onboard? Depending on the nature of the problem, consider whether the external support of strategy consultants, turnaround specialists or forensic accountants might be a good idea. What is the near-term funding strategy? If the business is cash-constrained, act swiftly to implement emergency cash management controls. According to Jeff Sands, a corporate turnaround expert, there are at least 30 ways for any troubled business to generate cash quickly: while we won't go into all of them, potential opportunities might include selling inventory, renegotiating supplier terms, rationalizing product lines and disposing of equipment or other capital assets (Sands, 2020). Whatever route you decide to take, make sure that you gain full stakeholder support and create a crisis taskforce to oversee the implementation of a turnaround.

- *Consider restructuring options.* By now, it is fairly clear that the investment base case failed to materialize. You need to develop a new game plan and—depending on the severity of the problem—your new objective will probably be just to recover the cost of the investment. First of all, is the company still a viable entity? Does its core market still have potential? If this is the case, you need to go through all possible options. Can you sell the company early? While a struggling business may not appeal to many buyers, it might be an attractive M&A target to a few direct competitors. Further, in a levered acquisition, you will inevitably have to consider the company's debt and its capital structure. If the business is undergoing a temporary challenge that will be rectified quickly, it might be possible to convince the banks to reschedule the liabilities. In case there is a sudden economic downturn or an industry-wide slowdown, the lenders might—just might—relax covenants for a period of time and extend debt maturities, as they might have many companies in their bank portfolios facing similar challenges and it may not be practical for them to enforce on their loans. Your fund might be able to inject more capital into the business and provide an "equity cure": however, your investment committee will want to make sure this does not mean throwing good money after bad. Other possible scenarios might include purchasing a company's debt at a discount or pursuing a complete financial restructuring that will involve the renegotiation of the company's debt structure to alleviate the financial distress. In all of these scenarios, you will need to work with the company on a new business plan that will be conservative and focused on corrective actions. You will need to structure a new incentive plan for the senior management team, as they won't be motivated to work hard unless they feel that they still have something to gain. Should you hit a brick wall in your restructuring efforts and the banks end up enforcing on their loans, there is no other option other than preparing to transition the company to the lenders.

- *Learn from your mistakes.* No matter how this arduous journey ends, try to make the best out of this situation. Your deal team may find it helpful to hold *a postmortem* meeting to discuss what went wrong and determine what all of you can do to avoid this challenging scenario in the future. The worst investment mistakes enable private equity funds to refine their investment strategy and succeed in the future.

13

Exit Strategies and Deal Monetization

Key Topics in Chapter 13:

- How to exit a minority investment (effortlessly)
- Exiting a majority transaction: Should you time the market?
- Conventional exit routes: an IPO, strategic sale or sponsor-to-sponsor buyout
- Can't exit your investment? Alternative deal monetization strategies to the rescue
- The finishing touch: exit preparation roadmap for every portfolio company

---

E very story needs a good ending; and every private equity investment needs a profitable exit. Although quarterly valuation uplifts of a portfolio business during the holding period may be comforting to your LPs, these interim estimates merely represent "paper gains." Nobody really knows for sure how well any private equity deal will work out until the investment is fully monetized. While quarterly valuations serve as a useful directional guide to your investors, they will be primarily concerned with the return of capital and excess profit distributions from each transaction in your portfolio. The timing and the magnitude of these payments form your fund's investment track record—a critical measure of performance that will directly influence investors' decision whether or not to commit to your firm's future fundraisings. Private equity sponsors are well aware that their very livelihood is contingent upon delivering a solid stream of timely and profitable exits from their portfolio. Moreover, as regular sellers of businesses, financial investors are regarded as important and sophisticated capital markets players capable of delivering smart paths to liquidity—even for the most difficult investments—with one goal in mind: to maximize cash returns to their LPs within the fund's 10-year life.

Exiting a Minority Transaction

How do you exit a private equity transaction if you are not a controlling shareholder? In minority deals, there is not that much that financial investors are expected to do at exit, other than express their thinking on the appropriate exit route and timing. In Chapter 9, I emphasized the importance of negotiating and documenting a suite of robust exit rights that, in my mind, represent an absolute "must" in every minority private equity transaction. Without those, your investment may be doomed: if the majority shareholders do not have an interest in creating a liquidity event for the portfolio company, there is virtually no way for you to get your hands on your capital, let alone your share of excess profits from the transaction.

If you do have solid exit rights, the best scenario is still to be completely aligned with the majority owners on the intended exit route and timeframe from the outset of the deal: this way, the controlling shareholders will do the bulk of the work in engineering a liquidity event for everyone in the equity capital structure. As we discussed in Chapter 9, your exit rights will come in handy in case of exit delays. There are several tools that you can turn to in order to create a path to liquidity for your equity stake, ranging from an ROFO arrangement with the majority shareholders to your eventual right to drag everyone into a sale. I hope that you won't find yourself in these circumstances, however; enforcing your liquidity rights as a minority shareholder will take time and effort—in fact, it might be years before you manage to effect a complete exit from your investment on acceptable terms.

Exiting a Majority Transaction

It is far more straightforward and potentially more exciting to be a controlling shareholder when it comes to private equity exits. Assuming that your portfolio company remains a viable business under your ownership, you can choose when to sell it. There are many complex elements that underpin a majority investor's decision to exit a portfolio company. When is the most opportune time to exit? What is the most appropriate exit route? What can you do in order to maximize the portfolio company valuation at exit? We will consider these points in subsequent sections. For the remainder of this chapter, I will adopt the perspective of a controlling shareholder who is at liberty to determine the optimal exit strategy for its investments.

Exit Timing

I believe that there are at least three factors that need to be evaluated by private equity owners when considering a portfolio company exit. First, what is the current state of the portfolio business: Is it exit-ready? Second, do the market multiples look attractive in the context of recent history? Finally, is this an optimal time to return cash to LPs from the sponsor's point of view? Let us examine each of these factors in detail.

- *Current state of a portfolio company.* At the beginning of your ownership, the business may not look very appealing to others: it might be in the middle of a complex restructuring, with an unstable workforce, constrained growth and volatile cash flows. This is the reason why most owners will most likely opt to keep the early phases of the value-creation magic out of sight of prospective buyers. As soon as a significant part of the business plan is delivered and the company can demonstrate a consistent positive trend in its revenue growth, profits and cash generation, your portfolio company turns into a desirable asset—even more so, if it is led by an experienced and capable management team. There is no need to wait for the portfolio business to reach its maximum level of performance: in fact, a far better tactic is to "leave some money on the table," so that potential buyers can get excited about their own equity story that will include taking advantage of the remaining upside opportunities or strategic add-on acquisitions for the business during their period of ownership. In my experience, the time when the majority of the value creation story is visible—and not yet fully exhausted—might be precisely the best moment to consider an exit.

    Beyond this window of opportunity, you ought to ask yourself a question: Does it make sense to wait another

6–12 months before selling the business? What is the expected trade-off between the money multiple and the IRR on this investment? After all, the longer the holding period, the higher the required exit price will be to hit your target return. Carl Thoma, a well-respected private equity investor and the founder of Thoma Bravo, said, ". . .time is the enemy. The difference between delivering outstanding returns to our investors and falling short is all related to how long we own the company" (Finkel and Greising, 2010). In other words, waiting too long is dangerous due to the possible erosion of the realized IRR on the investment. Moreover, there might be another culprit: if you delay an exit for a well-performing portfolio company, the business could take a turn for the worse, or the market might make the assumption that you own a problematic asset. Therefore, the only rational reason for you to defer a sale of an exit-ready business is an unassailable conviction of a superior outlook in the near future—for example, due to higher expected market multiples or meaningfully improved EBITDA growth in the portfolio company.

- *Market environment.* You are no doubt aware of the aggravating market cycles that finance professionals have to grapple with: one day, capital markets participants are optimistic and awash with cheap excess capital. The next day, they expect the worst and hold every investment dollar close to their chests. When the economic outlook is uncertain and publicly listed companies are trading at historic lows, it makes little sense to attempt to find a sensible buyer who will pay a fair price for even the most attractive and resilient private equity asset.

  While valuation multiples are known for reaching perilous troughs at times, they do rise eventually in response to improved market conditions. According to McKinsey (2019), there has been significant volatility in global private equity exit valuations for assets sold during the period between 2007 and 2018: depending on the year of the divestment, median EV/EBITDA multiples at exit ranged from 7.5× to 13.7× for consumer businesses; from 5.8× to 10.9× for operators in the B2B sector; and from 6.0× to 13.8× for technology companies. Looking at these highly unstable valuation metrics, one may wonder, "When the market is tough, why rage against the machine? Why not time the economic cycle instead?"

And that's exactly what the majority of private equity sponsors attempt to do to the best of their ability. One study of global buyouts reveals a striking finding that multiple expansion at exit is not in fact as illusory as deal teams are often led to believe by their own investment committees. This analysis of 1,090 realized and 890 unrealized European and North American buyouts completed between 1986 and 2010 provides evidence that "multiple expansion is a manageable skill that can be influenced by a PE sponsor and is not only driven by luck" (Achleitner et al., 2011). In other words, private equity investors are capable of timing their exits and capturing higher multiples by selling a greater number of investments during a market boom. From what I have seen, some sponsors also manage to charge a handsome premium for those investments that attain superior positioning during their private equity ownership and re-rate to higher multiples by demonstrating clear leadership in terms of market share or an unbeatable cost position at exit.

- *Sponsor considerations.* As we discussed in Chapters 7 and 8, most private equity funds underwrite their investments on the basis of a five-year business plan and evaluate estimated exit returns assuming a holding period of three to five years. As it turns out, the assumed investment horizon resonates with what tends to take place in reality—at least, on average:

Bain's research of global buyout divestments between 2004 and 2020 demonstrates that the majority of deals were exited well within five years. Moreover, the median holding period for exited assets for each year ranged between 3.3 and 5.9 years, exceeding the five-year mark only in four years over a 17-year period (Bain, 2021). Based on this analysis, one would think that an ordinary fund LP is strongly anchored to expect distributions for each portfolio company at some point during the three- to five-year horizon after the initial investment.

While this is precisely what seems to be happening on average, private equity investors often incorporate clever tactics in timing their exits in order to accommodate their institutional interests. The portfolio companies that are acquired at the early stages of the fund's investment period are often exited quickly because private equity sponsors are eager to return cash to the LPs earlier than expected in order to crystallize a track record of realized investments in the existing fund in advance of the looming fundraising for the next fund (Zeisberger et al., 2017). Once investors are on the road for fundraising, it is unlikely that they will be seeking to squeeze every last cent from the companies that they sell during this time: it is more probable that they would rather sacrifice a bit of MOIC in return for an accelerated exit and an IRR that will look good for marketing purposes. Conversely, businesses that are purchased later in a fund's life are typically held for longer, as the sponsors are strongly incentivized to maximize money multiples on each investment and, as a result, boost their own financial reward in the form of carry distributions (Zeisberger et al., 2017).

As you can appreciate, there is a lot of complex thinking involved in settling on the most favorable exit timing that allows private equity investors to fulfill their various objectives. The exit has to happen at the right time for the

portfolio company, in a benign market, while also supporting the institutional goals of the private equity sponsors.
All of this complexity, however, goes out of the window
in the relatively rare, but fortunate case where a portfolio
company becomes the subject of an unsolicited approach
from a credible buyer at a premium valuation—and, indeed,
this could happen at any time. That's why they say in private equity, "Everything is potentially for sale if the price is
right." When someone offers you tomorrow's price today,
why would you turn them down?

Conventional Exit Routes

The main three routes to achieve a full exit from a private equity
investment include an IPO on a stock exchange, a sale to a strategic buyer or a sponsor-to-sponsor buyout. Although there are
a number of alternative deal monetization strategies that I will
present later in this chapter, the lion's share of private equity
transactions will be exited through a listing or a sale to strategic
or financial buyers. From what I have observed, a typical buyout
fund is likely to exit half of the portfolio to strategic corporates, sell about a third of portfolio businesses to other financial
investors, and take only 2 or 3 companies public. Private equity
funds that focus on smaller businesses will most likely have to
rely predominantly on the strategic and sponsor-to-sponsor exit
channels for their investments, as the majority of their portfolio
companies will generally lack the required scale for a successful
listing with sufficient liquidity post-IPO.

While there are no explicit rules that allow private equity
investors to predict the likeliest exit route with any degree of
precision, it is fair to say that specific company characteristics
tend to entice a particular category of potential acquirers. For

example, IPOs are most appropriate for large-scale players with a stellar financial track record, a compelling growth profile and a simple, well-articulated equity story that will appeal to public investors. Strategic buyers are less concerned with the sheer scale of a portfolio business and could potentially be interested in acquisition targets of all sizes. Corporates are looking to purchase companies with strong brand power, defensible market positions and an attractive geographic footprint that are capable of delivering strategic value and synergies to their core business. Finally, financial investors are mostly drawn to companies with clear levers for future value creation and solid cash conversion profiles to support a leveraged acquisition. Financial buyers can be quite forgiving of the recent operational hiccups in the businesses they acquire—and this is something that IPO investors or corporates might find more difficult to digest.

Despite the apparent differences in preferences among the potential acquirers, it is common for the exiting private equity sponsors to organize an exit process that will target as many categories of buyers as possible. In advance of a sale, the owners meticulously package their portfolio business in a way that produces maximum appeal for any acquirer, so that both strategic and financial buyers can be lured to compete in the same auction. If the portfolio company is working toward an IPO, the listing process will most likely be conducted as a "dual track" route alongside a traditional sale. This approach enables the sponsor to optimize the exit valuation for the portfolio company as a result of the competitive tension between public and private investors. In addition, in case the IPO fails to materialize due to a sudden deterioration in the stock market, the traditional sale process has already been fully prepared and becomes the logical alternative exit scenario. Let's look at each of the main exit routes in more detail.

IPO

An IPO allows a private equity owner to monetize its investment by offering shares in a portfolio company to public market investors through a stock exchange listing. This strategy works particularly well when market sentiment is positive and the target business fits the criteria of the public investors: the most attractive IPO candidates are sizeable companies that operate in an industry with strong fundamentals and possess a solid track record of sustainable and increasing earnings. To maximize the chances of a successful listing, the senior members of the company's management team need to prepare a compelling equity story for IPO investors and demonstrate their capability to handle the pressures of the stock market once the company operates as a listed entity. Moreover, the management team ought to be completely comfortable with the ongoing disclosure requirements, the public exposure of the company's potential blunders in the future and—perhaps most importantly—intense scrutiny of every quarterly report by the analysts, investors and the general public.

The company needs to look, feel and act like a publicly listed business in advance of the IPO, with an effective and well-staffed finance function, a professional investor relations department capable of addressing complex queries from analysts and investors, as well as a high-quality board of directors that satisfies the requirements of a stock exchange. Not every private equity–backed portfolio company is suited for an IPO—in fact, most are not. According to Bain (2021), IPOs accounted for less than 20% of the total value from global buyout exits that took place between 2005 and 2020. Moreover, listings of private equity businesses tend to have a mixed record of trading performance, with more than 70% of the IPOs led by global buyout sponsors in 2010–2014 underperforming their relevant public benchmarks over the following five-year period (Bain, 2020). Therefore, the decision to pursue an IPO as an exit route requires a careful analysis of its potential merits and drawbacks. What are they?

Advantages of an IPO:

- *Visibility and public awareness.* Given the extensive media coverage of new listings, every sponsor-led IPO is often perceived by the public as a triumphant way to exit an investment. A public listing is often considered to be a marker of the company's unquestionable success and this perception, no doubt, brings personal satisfaction to the senior management team. This exit route also produces tangible reputational benefits to the private equity sponsors, who are viewed by their LPs as sophisticated capital market players capable of professionalizing their portfolio companies to make them IPO-ready and effectively navigating the complexities of a listing process to deliver high-profile exits from their investments.
- *Attractive exit valuation.* Successful IPOs often enable private equity investors to generate better investment returns from their portfolio companies compared to alternative exit routes. There appears to be sufficient empirical evidence from several research studies of global private equity exits to suggest that public listings led by sponsors are generally priced at median multiples that are higher than those achieved in sales to strategic buyers or financial investors (Pérez Navarro, 2018 and Chinchwadkar and Seth, 2012).
- *Access to long-term liquid capital.* By converting equity into publicly listed shares, the company benefits from generating a liquid and diversified capital base that will support its subsequent funding needs. Listed shares serve as a valuable acquisition currency in a potential M&A activity and provide the company with the ability to structure attractive employee

retention and benefits programs. Management teams also often enjoy the independence that they gain from having to report to a widely dispersed group of passive shareholders, instead of a small group of hands-on control investors.

Disadvantages of an IPO:

- *Pressure on short-term company performance.* Public market investors and analysts covering the company's stock are mostly preoccupied with the quarter-on-quarter performance of the business. Once the company goes public, it loses its operating confidentiality and may find it difficult to pursue risky product launches or embark on new ventures—no matter how lucrative in the long run—where upfront losses might adversely affect the consensus earnings trajectory. The stock market demands steady increases in sales, earnings and dividends and is likely to punish those companies that can't deliver them on a consistent basis.

- *Not a full exit for the sponsor at an IPO.* Private equity investors do not benefit from immediate liquidity in an IPO; instead, they are able to dispose of only a part of their stake in a portfolio business upon listing. They continue holding a large portion of the company's publicly traded shares at least for the duration of a mandatory "lock-up" period, typically lasting up to 12 months. As a result, sponsors are exposed to the stock price performance of the business during the mandated holding period, which introduces uncertainty to their eventual returns from the investment.

- *Market risk.* Since markets are unpredictable and volatile, sponsors bear significant risks during the multiple stages of an IPO process. Once the private equity sponsors decide to take a portfolio company public, they have to take a number of steps, such as selecting an underwriter, preparing a prospectus and sending the company management on a roadshow to meet with investors. Inevitably, there is a gap of several months between the decision to go public and the IPO pricing day, which means that the initial valuation target for the business may not be achieved due to changes in market conditions or operating performance. Moreover, the strength of post-IPO stock performance partly depends on the allocation of the IPO order book: there is a chance of excessive downward pressure on the stock price if the order book includes too many speculative investors looking to "flip" the company's stock in a short-term trade. Also, persistent stock price weakness or pronounced deterioration in the markets may force the private equity funds to hold the remaining shares post-IPO well beyond the expiry of their "lock-up" period: in this case, the full exit may not be achieved[1] for several years after the listing.

Strategic Sale

Corporate acquirers represent by far the most vibrant and important exit channel for private equity sponsors, with strategic sales accounting for about half of the total value generated from global buyout exits that took place between 2005 and 2020. Strategic interest is an important pillar of strength for the private equity industry in tough times: when the IPO window

---

[1]Some sponsors get frustrated with poor stock price performance post-IPO and decide to reacquire the portfolio business they recently listed. For example, see a transaction by CVC buying back construction tools distributor Ahlsell in 2018, just two years after the IPO: at the time of the public-to-private, CVC was the largest shareholder with a 25% stake in the company (Reuters, 2018).

is closed and other routes to liquidity are not achievable, sales to corporates might account for as much as two thirds of the total value of exits that occur in difficult years (Bain, 2021). Corporate buyers are generally content purchasing a wide range of assets—including mid-tier performers in a private equity portfolio—as long as the target company has no significant operational issues and can demonstrate a strong strategic fit with the acquirer's core business.

Most corporations experience ongoing pressure from their boards and shareholders to deliver consistent top-line growth and stay ahead of the competition. As a result, they might feel the need to complement their principal business strategy with acquisitive growth by hunting for attractive targets—including those that reside in private equity portfolios. Strategic buyers often view M&A as a fast and effective way of enhancing their present operations by integrating assets and capabilities that they consider to be valuable—such as strong brands, access to new markets and products, or additional sources of organic growth. To take full advantage of strategic interest in a private equity sale process, the portfolio company should position itself as a desirable target by highlighting the exclusive market segments that it serves and emphasizing its distinctive capabilities that others may lack—in particular, unique expertise, superior resources, outstanding customer service, or better commercial execution.

The price that a corporate buyer might be willing to pay for a private equity asset depends on the target's strategic value to the acquirer and the presence of potential synergies. This type of buyer most often comes from the same industry and will be predominantly focused on potential value creation opportunities in the combined business. If tangible synergies can be extracted by generating substantial cost savings and creating extensive cross-selling opportunities, a corporate acquirer might be compelled to offer a very attractive price to the private equity owner of the target company.

A sale to a strategic acquirer has its merits and drawbacks, which I will discuss below:

Advantages of a Strategic Sale:

- *Attractive cash consideration.* Corporate acquirers may be willing to pay a premium for a private equity asset that, in their view, will deliver potent synergies and clear strategic benefits. Strategic sales enable the private equity owners to realize their investment in cash and enjoy a clean exit—subject to customary representations and warranties—by transferring all assets and liabilities of a portfolio business to the new corporate owner.
- *Speed of execution.* Since corporate buyers are likely to have extensive first-hand knowledge of a portfolio company's key markets, they won't spend much—if any—time on conducting industry due diligence. They also typically don't need to raise acquisition leverage, which enables the deal parties to run an efficient transaction process and engage in negotiations of critical items fairly quickly.

Disadvantages of a Strategic Sale:

- *Employee resistance.* The management team and other employees of the target business might be fearful of restructuring initiatives post-acquisition that are likely to result in extensive job losses. In certain scenarios, senior management of the portfolio company might be openly opposed to a sale to specific acquirers or insist on retention agreements or exit arrangements that might complicate an exit process.
- *Disclosure of confidential information to a competitor.* The strategics who are best-positioned to acquire a portfolio business might

be its closest rivals. Inevitably, they will gain access to sensitive commercial information about the company's operations during the sale process and might be tempted to engage in aggressive competitive behavior in the future, in the event the exit fails to go through.

- *Antitrust approvals.* A merger of companies operating in the same industry often requires regulatory approval, which might create uncertainty and delay closing. Moreover, antitrust consent might be granted subject to a number of conditions—such as mandatory divestitures—that may not be acceptable to the buyer or may take months to complete.

Sponsor-to-Sponsor Buyout

As the private equity industry matures, it has become increasingly common for companies to undergo several rounds of ownership by different financial sponsors. According to Bain (2021), sponsor-to-sponsor exits accounted for 10% to 30% of total value from global buyout exits each year between 2005 and 2020. Although private equity buyers are highly price-sensitive and unlikely to be overly generous, they nonetheless are capable of offering an attractive valuation to the exiting sponsor, especially if the market environment permits them to finance the acquisition with high levels of debt. While much of the low-hanging fruit of operational improvements in the target company might be fully harvested by the initial private equity owner, other financial investors might still be interested in the business due to its strong growth potential.

What are private equity buyers looking for? I believe this topic has been extensively covered in prior chapters, so it is my hope that you feel well-equipped to answer this question yourself. In general, financial investors require a compelling investment thesis to support the transaction and will certainly be exploring all possible avenues of value creation during the period of their ownership. Further, they will examine the company's existing track record of operating in a private equity setting, driven by cash-focused KPIs and an emphasis on debt paydown. Compared to other buyers, private equity investors are not always looking to invest in a flawless asset, as long as it has a promising upside potential. They tend to be more operationally openminded and are unlikely to be turned off by the fact that the target company might still be undergoing a restructuring: in fact, most will gladly roll up their sleeves and help the business to reach its peak performance—albeit for a price.

As you already know, companies that appeal to private equity investors are likely to have a strong market position, an attractive cash profile and clear growth prospects. The best way to position a portfolio company as a desirable asset to financial buyers is to address upfront the information needs that arise in most typical private equity transactions. Financial buyers will require extensive data about the external environment, including industry outlook and competitive dynamics in the key market and product sectors; a compelling narrative about the target's customer value proposition; and a value-creation plan supported by clear implementation milestones and detailed financial projections. Anyone wishing to impress a potential private equity buyer should consider preparing a comprehensive analysis of the company's unit economics, working capital cycle, cash generation and conversion as well as returns on investment from prior CAPEX spend.

One of the main advantages of exiting an investment to a financial investor is an inherent understanding between the buyer and the seller who share the same mindset and focus on similar financial and operational metrics. However, private equity buyers are often difficult to deal with during the exit process because they—rather unsurprisingly—tend to engage in exhaustive negotiations of every critical item along the way, require a long and comprehensive due diligence of the target and are likely to come up with a complex proposal—full of ratchets, earn-outs and escrows—that may reduce the upfront cash consideration payable to the seller at deal closing.

Alternative Deal Monetization Strategies

What happens if private equity sponsors are either unwilling or unable to exit their investments by taking one of the conventional routes described above? They are very likely to be evaluating possible paths to achieve a partial exit in order to fund an interim cash distribution to their investors. One option might be to refinance debt in the portfolio company and generate a payment to the equity holders through a leveraged recapitalization. Another option is to reduce the equity holding in the portfolio business by selling either a minority or a majority stake in the investment to another party.

Alternatively, private equity sponsors could engineer a full exit from an investment by considering fairly unorthodox structures, such as selling a portfolio company in a cross-fund secondary transaction or setting up a continuation fund to acquire one or more portfolio investments from the main fund vehicle. These two exit models may appear aggressive because private equity sponsors end up exiting their investments to funds they control: in other words, they effectively sell their portfolio businesses to themselves. Does it sound like an obvious conflict of interest, if someone is both a buyer and a seller? Indeed, these exit strategies were initially considered to be controversial, although many LPs have grown to accept them over time. A number of large and reputable sponsors, such as Blackstone, EQT and Hellman & Friedman, became early adopters of "selling-to-own-fund" strategies and achieved high-profile exits for some of their investments (Wiggins, 2020).

Let's step back and explore alternative deal monetization routes in greater detail.

- *Leveraged recapitalization.* The aim of this strategy is to accelerate equity distributions and, as a result, improve the investment's IRR. A leveraged recapitalization enables a portfolio company to increase its leverage by replacing its original acquisition debt with new and larger loans, or supplementing the existing capital structure with an additional debt tranche, such as a high-yield bond or a securitization. The proceeds generated from increased leverage are used to purchase a portion of the equity and pay special dividends to the owners. This approach might be considered when a portfolio company has de-levered significantly through debt paydown, or when debt providers become willing to extend higher leverage to the business based on its improved financial performance or more favorable conditions in the credit markets. Private equity sponsors rely on leveraged recapitalizations to decrease their equity exposure and achieve partial liquidity without having to reduce their ownership. Since the portfolio company has to service an increased debt load and bear higher financial risk, aggressive leveraged recapitalizations may lead to a bad press for the sponsors, particularly if the company subsequently files for bankruptcy.
- *Partial sale.* This route might be appropriate when private equity investors wish to return a portion of the capital to their LPs and lock in an attractive rate of return, while retaining exposure to the long-term upside potential of a portfolio business. For instance, sponsors may choose to maintain majority control in a portfolio company and sell a minority stake to a likeminded partner midway through the holding

period in order to de-risk the transaction, crystallize an attractive valuation for the portfolio business and make an early distribution to their investors. Another option is to sell a majority stake in a portfolio business and keep a hand in the game by retaining a minority position in the target's equity. This approach might make sense when private equity sponsors are under pressure from the LPs to deliver a successful exit from a well-performing investment they've held for a long time: if they are reluctant to sell out completely, a workable solution might be to sell most of the company and keep a small stake in order to maintain exposure to an asset that is likely to keep growing and generating attractive returns in the future.

- *Cross-fund secondary transaction.* This exit model enables private equity sponsors to sell a portfolio company from the original vehicle to another fund they control through a cross-fund secondary deal. When a private equity fund approaches the end of its 10-year life and the investment professionals are busy exiting the remaining deals in the portfolio, it might be tempting to hold on to a particularly attractive business with significant value-creation potential by reallocating the asset to a new-generation fund. The most contentious aspect of this approach is determining a fair price at which an investment can be passed from an old fund to a new fund controlled by the same private equity firm: therefore, ordinary cross-fund secondaries tend to happen in conjunction with selling a minority stake in a portfolio company to an outside investor in order to establish the necessary arm's-length valuation.[2]

---

[2]For example, see EQT's 2020 transfer of ownership in software developer IFS from EQT Fund VII to EQT Funds VIII and IX, while also selling a minority stake to TA Associates (Mendonça, 2020).

Cross-fund secondary transactions are seen as increasingly acceptable forms of exit for private equity firms that manage a number of funds with multiple investment strategies targeting different investment returns, such as growth equity, buyouts and long-term value. These players find it easier to explain to their LPs why it might make sense to provide long-term support to a portfolio company throughout its lifecycle by moving the maturing asset from the original fund to another vehicle with a less risky investment strategy and a lower expected IRR.[3] In this scenario, the sponsor might avoid having to bring in an outside investor and instead opt to conduct a "go-shop" process, in which independent deal advisers are instructed to solicit higher bids for the portfolio company from outside parties to see whether the proposed valuation of the sponsor's acquiring vehicle can be beaten (Wiggins, 2020).

- *Continuation fund.* There is yet another way to resolve the "end of the 10-year fund life" conundrum for the last few assets in the private equity portfolio. The sponsor can set up a continuation fund, identify investors to back it and sell one or more portfolio companies owned by its old fund to the new vehicle. This exit strategy may be used to dispose of a single portfolio company[4] with a strong upside potential, or several assets[5] with divergent investment performances, so that

---

[3]For example, see Blackstone's 2020 reallocation of its investment in life science office platform BioMed Realty from Blackstone Real Estate Partners VIII to its new permanent vehicle with a "core plus" return strategy (Campbell, 2020).

[4]For example, see BC Partners' sale of academic publisher Springer Nature to its own continuation fund in 2020 (Wiggins et al., 2020).

[5]For example, see Hellman & Friedman's 2020 transfer of the three remaining portfolio companies in its 2009-vintage Fund VII to its own continuation vehicle (James, 2021).

a struggling portfolio business can be bundled up with several star performers to create an appealing overall investment proposition.

Continuation vehicles are typically backed by specialist asset managers—such as private equity secondary players, sovereign wealth funds or pension managers—who expect to earn quicker returns compared to those generated by a traditional 10-year fund structure. These investors provide cornerstone commitments to a continuation fund and set the key terms of the transaction, such as the valuation of the assets to be transferred and the level of the sponsor's management fee and carried interest allocation. The LPs in the original fund can then review the proposal and decide whether to cash out or roll-over their interests into the continuation fund (Wiggins, 2020).

The Finishing Touch: Ensuring a Successful Exit

There is nothing quite so disappointing as snatching defeat from the jaws of victory. Any private equity exit can get derailed suddenly for reasons outside of your control, such as an unexpected reversal of investor sentiment due to an industry-specific event or a general deterioration in the economic environment. It is, therefore, all the more important to have a firm grasp on the critical factors that you can actually influence in the exit process. Yet, from time to time, sophisticated investors—who have spent years trying to maximize the value of their investments—trip themselves up by being poorly prepared to handle the pressures of a portfolio company sale.

I have experienced my own share of setbacks that happened on a few transactions right at the finish line. One time, my deal team was running an exit process for a rapidly growing telecommunications business, when the CEO and the CFO became too distracted by meetings with potential buyers and, as a result, found it difficult to maintain the appropriate discipline in the day-to-day company operations. As a result, the business experienced an embarrassing drop in trading performance—right in the middle of a sale process—which severely undermined the credibility of the company's projections. Several high-profile acquirers assumed a catastrophic scenario, lost faith in the asset and abandoned the auction process, leaving our deal team with just a few interested parties. Even though we did manage to sell the company, we missed our chance to crystallize a premium valuation: in fact, we could barely achieve a market-conforming multiple for what we thought was a highly sought-after business!

Another time, my deal team was involved in the sale of a consumer company that fetched an attractive bid from a Japanese strategic buyer in the final round. We were too quick to grant exclusivity to this party, without carrying out detailed checks on the managerial style of the acquirer, who ended up moving frustratingly slowly and failed to meet our timetable. In that process, we misjudged the cultural differences that would influence the negotiations: the Japanese counterparty was used to operating in a consensus-oriented business environment, requiring numerous board meetings to approve every little change in the SPA. After a few months of exasperating back-and-forth with the buyer, it became clear that the market conditions were weakening and the deal could only be completed at a reduced valuation. We ended up declaring defeat, pulling the sale and opting for a leveraged recapitalization instead—which delayed our eventual exit from the business by about 18 months.

Can you avoid last-minute disappointments when exiting a portfolio business? I believe you can. A successful exit process rests on detailed planning, clever positioning, intelligent tactics, sensible negotiation and timely compromise. Let's review a number of best practices that you should consider in order to strengthen your position in advance of a portfolio company sale and optimize your exit outcome.

- *Start early.* As we discussed in Chapter 5, every thoughtful investment underwriting process requires a careful analysis of potential exit options. Consequently, you are very likely to have already developed a vision for the likely exit route and timing before transaction completion. It is paramount to revisit a portfolio company's exit options at least every 6 months post-closing by keeping a regular dialogue with corporate finance advisers and conducting your own valuation analyses, so that you are able to maintain complete clarity on the market environment and form realistic expectations about the exit price. You need to take action about 24 months before the planned liquidity event to ensure that you can exit a portfolio company from a position of strength. What do you need to do exactly?

  First, package the business for sale to make it attractive to potential buyers. Consider all areas of potential value leakage by addressing the company's operational weaknesses and mitigating known risk exposures. Always assume that any material issues will be uncovered during the exit process. As such, don't leave any problems—such as customer churn or operational delays—unresolved, as potential buyers will simply assume the worst and offer a reduced price, or walk away altogether. Enable the business to generate a consistent performance track record, with no sudden spikes in earnings or cash generation, as they may be deemed unsustainable and, as a result, will be discounted by potential acquirers.

  Second, tidy up the business and relieve it of any clutter that may complicate the buyer's analysis. Consider settling historic tax liabilities, repatriating trapped cash in a tax-efficient manner, selling obsolete inventory, collecting bad debts and disposing of excess non-operating assets. If a portfolio company operates a difficult division, it might be a good opportunity to contemplate a separate sale process—or even a liquidation—for this business line.

Finally, warm up the market by making the company more visible in its industry in advance of the sale. Engage in subtle PR by reporting new product launches and significant contracts to the business press and encourage senior management to attend relevant conferences and trade shows. Network within the industry to ensure that main sector investors, competitors and vertical integrators are aware of the company's accomplishments and view it as a desirable target.

- *Get management onboard.* The top management team you backed needs to be completely aligned with your exit goals. What will happen to them? Are they buyers or sellers? Engage the members of senior management in a frank discussion about their exit mindset. If they are leaving the company, you need to develop a succession plan and appoint new people to all key positions. It is easier to sell a business that has a complete, well-rounded and experienced management team, supported by a stable and competent talent pool. Consider implementing an employee retention program for key business line managers in the company to avoid sudden departures during the exit process. If top managers are intending to stay in the business under the new ownership, you need to take into account their preferences in terms of your exit route and timing, as they will have significant influence on the exit outcome. In this case, prepare for the possibility of top management "going native"—in other words, developing a close affinity with one particular buyer during the exit process and advocating for that counterparty to win the deal. This is unacceptable behavior that nonetheless occurs frequently, and can be managed by supplementing the existing Management Incentive Plan with an exit bonus or a performance-based ratchet that will pay off only if you achieve your target exit valuation.

- *Dedicate sufficient resources.* Let's face it: every exit path requires a considerable commitment of time and resources. An IPO is perhaps the most onerous route and will put tremendous pressure on both the sponsors and the company executives. Even worse, a public listing is likely to be combined with a traditional auction in a dual-track process, making the exit experience particularly challenging and demanding for everyone involved. Once you settle on an exit plan, carefully think through the process requirements and timing. Remember that the senior management will need to allocate significant time to preparing and delivering company presentations, meeting with potential acquirers and furnishing follow-up analyses, all of which will come on top of their primary duty of running the day-to-day operations of the portfolio business. Consider splitting the top management team for the duration of the exit process into two groups: for example, the CEO and the CFO can take responsibility for presenting the company and selling the business to prospective investors, while the Chairman, COO and the deputy CFO can stay firmly on the ground minding the day-to-day operations to ensure that there is no slippage in company performance.

You will need to make sure that the business is trading in line with projections that are being presented to prospective buyers, as any shortfall will cost you dearly. Therefore, it is sensible to check that near-term projections are realistic and budgeted numbers are achievable in the sale period. Finally, don't underestimate the burden of the exit process on the finance function: the team needs to be well-staffed and capable of producing reliable, rock-solid numbers, especially when working under time pressure. To support the exit process, the finance team will be responsible for maintaining a granular financial model of the business, with five years of historic and five years of projected financials.

- *Appoint first-class advisers.* Your choice of advisers can easily destroy or generate value in the exit process. While it might be tempting to save on fees, I do not recommend embracing an overly cost-conscious strategy during exit. High-quality advice comes with a hefty price tag; however, first-class advisers will pay for themselves by allowing you to maximize the valuation of your portfolio company at exit. Conduct beauty parades well in advance of the planned exit so that you can select an outstanding team of lawyers, accountants and bankers to guide you and your portfolio business through the complexities of the exit process. Your advisers need to regard your firm as an important client and possess solid industry expertise gained through similar deals they have done in the past. Be choosy when appointing a sell-side M&A adviser or an IPO underwriter: the best firms need to demonstrate strong execution capabilities and access to a large pool of potential buyers. If you are following a dual track exit process, you will need to appoint at least two separate investment banks: one will advise you on a traditional sale, and another one will be the lead underwriter on the IPO, possibly supported by additional firms in the syndicate.
- *Create a compelling equity story (or two).* You won't be able to sell your portfolio business unless you can convince prospective investors that they will make money. A well-articulated equity story includes a persuasive narrative of the company's unique customer value proposition and its future growth prospects, linked to past financial performance. Moreover, the

next owner should be excited about a pipeline of potential value-creation opportunities in the company's projections. What actionable strategies does the business intend to pursue? Is there strong and credible evidence to support future earnings growth potential? Since public investors, strategic acquirers and financial sponsors tend to appreciate different business characteristics, tailor the equity story in order to highlight specific company capabilities that appeal to each type of buyer. Include customized supplemental analyses that you share only with specific categories of acquirers. Apart from preparing *what* to say to prospective investors, focus on *how* the story is delivered. In my experience, it is worth considering public speaking training for key company executives and conducting a number of management presentation rehearsals to enable the top managers to articulate key messages effectively and convince the buyers to pay a premium valuation.

- *Target an uneventful due diligence process.* As you may be aware from your own investing experience, the quality of bids in any acquisition process is directly proportional to the quality of company data provided by the seller. The more useful information you can share with prospective buyers, the better they will be equipped to conduct their own analysis of the target. Allocate a fair amount of time to producing high-quality company data that satisfies the documentation requirements of the exit process. You will need historic audited financial statements (in a public company–style format if an IPO is on the cards); sound financial projections that are supported by hard, credible facts; a persuasive teaser that captures key selling points; and a well-articulated CIM or prospectus that provides the most important facts about the business, explains key value drivers and excites the buyer about the company's future. Some company auction processes also provide a staple financing package to prospective buyers of the business. Personally, I don't believe it is necessary: sophisticated financial investors are more than capable of negotiating their own acquisition leverage, whereas strategics rarely rely on LBO-style debt to finance an acquisition. I also think that having a staple financing package in place potentially sends an unhelpful signal to potential acquirers that the deal is "over-baked" and marketed too widely.

As I stated in Chapter 10, I am a VDD skeptic in my own due diligence process. Yet, I am a firm VDD believer when it comes to selling a portfolio business, since many buyers believe that a detailed VDD report reduces potential areas of uncertainty about the target business. Get your VDD report finalized in advance of a sale and consider sharing it with prospective buyers early in the process, especially if you are selling a complex business: this way, you will see fairly quickly who is doing real work and who is just fishing for information about your portfolio company. In addition to the VDD, you will need to set up a data room with comprehensive company information that enables the bidders to conduct their own due diligence of the target business. Before opening up the data room to others, visit it yourself. Is it user-friendly? Does it contain the appropriate level of detail? Does it signal to potential buyers that the company operates effective business systems, with sufficient oversight and accountability?

Finally, no matter how well you prepare your portfolio business for sale, every company is likely to have a few remaining operating issues, performance anomalies or material risks that will become apparent to potential buyers in the exit process. Don't conceal potential problems in the portfolio company, as they will likely come out as unpleasant unknowns post-due diligence! It is your job to anticipate difficult questions from buyers and prepare well-thought-out answers supported by credible evidence. Clarify your position upfront on key problem areas with the management team and coordinate a consistent message, aiming to explain coherently the nature of each issue and possible mitigating actions that could help alleviate the concerns of prospective acquirers.

- *Maintain competitive tension.* Keep all exit options open for as long as you can in the process: acquisition targets appear attractive and fetch the highest bids when there is a degree of healthy competition among serious buyers. If one of the exit routes is a public listing, it makes sense to press on with the required IPO preparation until the very end, as it is fairly easy to pull an IPO at the last moment when the business is fully prepared to list. By contrast, abandoning an IPO early will make it difficult for the company to step back into the listing process late in the game.

Theoretically speaking, the more prospective buyers there are evaluating your portfolio company, the better it is for the seller. However, there is a limit to this theory: you certainly want to avoid coming across as too desperate or creating the impression that your asset is being marketed too widely. I once worked on the sale of a very difficult portfolio company and our advisers were instructed to contact over 70 prospective buyers because our ultimate exit seemed highly uncertain. Our deal team was truly worried about the exit outcome; however, we maintained ambiguity throughout the exit process and never disclosed to anyone—other than our advisers—the number of parties involved in the first bidding round. We also decided to progress 8 bidders—which is a very high number, in my view—to the second round and tried to negotiate key deal parameters and critical contract terms during the period of intense competition.

Be skeptical when one of the buyers is trying to pre-empt the auction and asks you for an exclusivity period to complete due diligence ahead of everyone else. This one buyer, no matter how committed, can deter other parties evaluating your portfolio business and wreck the entire exit process. You can't take this risk after all the preparation work you've done! In my experience, truly serious buyers have the confidence to compete until the very end and are unlikely to walk away from a good deal simply because there are other bidders in the process.

- *Nail it (. . .or have a backup plan)*. Sooner or later—unless you are pursuing an IPO—you will have to conduct the final round of bidding, choose one transaction counterparty, grant them a period of exclusivity and try your hardest to complete the sale. Tread very carefully when assessing the few remaining parties in the exit process. Should you go with the highest bidder? Or should you choose the most logical buyer of your portfolio business? And what do you do if both of these parties have done significantly less work on the deal compared to others? There is no way to answer this question, unless you opt to be quite prescriptive in the final round and ask the remaining bidders to submit final offers in a format that enables you to carry out a detailed side-by-side comparison. For example, you can ask the bidders to specify their position on the following items:

a. headline price;
b. structure of consideration: cash vs. deferred or conditional payments;
c. financing structure: debt and equity;
d. reasons for acquiring your portfolio business and a statement of future intentions (including those relating to company management and the employees);
e. work done to date and summary of any outstanding items;
f. timetable to closing;

g. key SPA issues, such as:
    i. required representations and warranties;
    ii. required indemnities;
    iii. escrow period;
    iv. intended normalization of earnings, working capital and other cash items;
    v. conditions to offer (especially MAC, financing-out, antitrust approval);
    and
    vi. suggested closing mechanism.

This information should permit you to compare final offers on the same basis, understand the likely implications of the sale for your portfolio company and calculate the expected returns for your fund. Before making a final decision, do your own due diligence to ensure that you are likely to be content with the exit outcome. Who are the buyers and are they well-capitalized? Who owns them and do they have a good reputation? Do they have a track record of acquiring other businesses? If so, what is their business character and managerial style? Are they likely to dismantle the business or undertake enormous layoffs?

You may conclude that none of the offers on the table represent good value to your fund or shield you from potential reputational damage if you suspect that your portfolio business is likely to endure considerable hardship under new ownership. Do you need to compromise? You probably shouldn't. Have a backup plan instead: scrap the exit process, wait for better times ahead or pursue one of the alternative deal monetization strategies we discussed earlier in this chapter. Since you have gone very far in the exit process, I'd like to think that it is far more probable that you will actually be excited about the level and terms of the final bids and manage to identify the most committed buyer who will pay an attractive price, deliver certain funds in a timely fashion and, hopefully, empower your portfolio business to continue to grow and thrive in the future.

Every private equity investment needs a profitable exit; and every story—including that of *The Private Equity Toolkit*—needs a good ending. I hope that your transactions will do well and you will enjoy the enriching world of private equity investing. I wish you much success in your investment career.

References

Chapter 1

Teten, D. and Farmer, C. (2010). "Where are the deals? Private equity and venture capital funds' best practices in sourcing new investments," *The Journal of Private Equity*, 14(1), pp. 32–53.

Bruner, R. F. (2004). *Applied Mergers and Acquisitions*. Hoboken, NJ: John Wiley & Sons.

Chapter 2

Narayanan, V. K. and Fahey, L. (2001). "Macroenvironmental Analysis: Understanding the Environment Outside the Industry" in Fahey, L. and Randall, R. M. (eds). *The Portable MBA in Strategy*. New York: Wiley.

Porter, M. E. (1985). *Competitive Advantage: Creating and Sustaining Superior Performance*. New York: Free Press.

Grant, R. M. (2002). *Contemporary Strategy Analysis: Concepts, Techniques, Applications*. Cambridge, MA: Blackwell Publishers Inc.

Valentine, J. J. (2011). *Best Practices for Equity Research Analysts: Essentials for Buy-Side and Sell-Side Analysts*. New York: McGraw-Hill Education.

Teten, D. and Farmer, C. (2010). "Where are the deals? Private equity and venture capital funds' best practices in sourcing new investments," *The Journal of Private Equity*, 14(1), pp. 32–53.

PEI Staff. (2013). "Cold Call Captain", *Private Debt Investor Online.* January 12, 2013.

Holmes, C. (2007). *The Ultimate Sales Machine: Turbocharge Your Business with Relentless Focus on 12 Key Strategies.* New York: Portfolio.

Chapter 3

Bruner, R. F. (2004). *Applied Mergers and Acquisitions.* Hoboken, NJ: John Wiley & Sons.

Fuchs, F., Fuss, R., Jenkinson, T. and Morkoetter, S. (2017). "Winning a deal in private equity: Do educational ties matter?" *University of St. Gallen, School of Finance Research Paper No. 2017/15.*

BackBay Communications (2017). *Private Equity Brand Equity III.* Accessed March 22, 2019. http://www.backbaycommunications. com/wp-content/uploads/2019/12/PrivateEquityBrandEquity III-FINAL.pdf

Chapter 4

Gompers, P., Kaplan, S. N. and Mukharlyamov, V. (2016). "What do private equity firms say they do?" *Journal of Financial Economics,* 121(3), pp. 449–476.

Schwarzman, S. A. (2019). *What It Takes: Lessons in the Pursuit of Excellence.* London: Simon & Schuster UK Ltd.

Bazerman, M. H. and Moore, D. A. (2009). *Judgement in Managerial Decision Making.* Hoboken, NJ: Wiley.

Kahneman, D. (2015). *Thinking, Fast and Slow.* New York: Farrar, Straus and Giroux.

Rickertsen, R. and Gunther, R. E. (2001). *Buyout: The Insider's Guide to Buying Your Own Company.* New York: Amacom.

Finkel, R. A. and Greising, D. (2010). *The Masters of Private Equity and Venture Capital: Management Lessons from the Pioneers of Private Investing.* New York: McGraw-Hill.

Walton, E. J. and Roberts, M. J. (1992). "Purchasing a Business: The Search Process" in Sahlman, William A. and Stevenson, H. H. (eds). *The Entrepreneurial Venture*. Boston, MA: Harvard Business School Publications.

Chapter 5

Finkel, R. A. and Greising, D. (2010). *The Masters of Private Equity and Venture Capital: Management Lessons from the Pioneers of Private Investing*. New York: McGraw-Hill.

Kahneman, D. (2015). *Thinking, Fast and Slow*. New York: Farrar, Straus and Giroux.

Gompers, P., Kaplan, S. N. and Mukharlyamov, V. (2016). "What do private equity firms say they do?" *Journal of Financial Economics*, 121(3), pp. 449–476.

Shearn, M. (2012). *The Investment Checklist: The Art of in-Depth Research*. Hoboken, NJ: Wiley.

Grant, L. "Striking out at Wall Street," *US News and World Report*, June 12, 1994.

BeyondProxy LLC Staff. (2014). "Exclusive interview: Pat Dorsey, Chief Investment Officer, Dorsey Asset Management," *The Manual of Ideas*. VII (VII), pp. 13–33.

Dorsey Asset Management. (2017). *Competitive Advantage and Asset Allocation*. Accessed May 3, 2020. https://dorseyasset.com/wp-content/uploads/2016/07/mit-sloan-investment-conference_competitive-advantage-and-capital-allocation_dorsey-asset-management_march-2017.pdf

Mullins, J. W. (2003). *The New Business Road Test: What Entrepreneurs and Executives Should Do Before Writing a Business Plan*. London: Pearson Higher Education.

WWF and Doughty Hanson & Co. (2011). *Private Equity and Responsible Investment: An Opportunity for Value Creation*. Accessed April 30, 2020. http://assets.wwf.org.uk/downloads/private_equity_aw_lores_2.pdf

Seuss, Dr. (2017). *How the Grinch Stole Christmas*. London: HarperCollins Children's Books.

Chapter 6

Bloom, N., Sadun, R. and Van Reenen, J. (2015). "Do private equity owned firms have better management practices?" *American Economic Review*, 105(5), pp. 442–446.

Yeboah, H. J. N., Tomenendal, M. and Dörrenbächer, C. (2014). "The effect of private equity ownership on management practices: A research agenda," *Competition & Change*, 18(2), pp. 164–179.

Baker, G. P., and Smith, G. D. (1998). *The New Financial Capitalists: Kohlberg Kravis Roberts and the Creation of Corporate Value*. Cambridge and New York: Cambridge University Press.

Kerr, S. (1995). "An Academy Classic: On the folly of rewarding A, while hoping for B," *Academy of Management Perspectives*, 9(1), pp. 7–14.

Cornelli, F. and Karakas, O. (2013). "CEO turnover in LBOs: the role of boards," *SSRN Electronic Journal*. Accessed June 27, 2020. https://ssrn.com/abstract=2269124

Alix Partners. (2017). *Annual Private Equity Survey: Replacing a Portfolio Company CEO Comes at a High Cost*. Accessed June 27, 2020. https://www.alixpartners.com/insights-impact/insights/annual-private-equity-survey-replacing-a-portfolio-company-ceo-comes-at-a-high-cost/

Botelho, E., Powell, K. R., Kincaid, S. and Wang, D. (2017). "What sets successful CEOs apart," *Harvard Business Review*. May–June 2017, pp. 70-77.

Botelho, E. L., Powell, K. R. and Raz, T. (2018). *The CEO Next Door: The 4 Behaviors That Transform Ordinary People into World-Class Leaders*. New York: Currency.

Damon, B. (2016). "Three rookie mistakes experienced CEOs make in managing a private equity–backed company," *The Journal of Private Equity*, 20(1), pp. 35–37

Prince, C. J. (2018). "So you want to be a private equity CEO? Four questions to ask yourself," *Chief Executive,* July 25, 2018.

Ralph, O. (2019). "Dave North: Managing serial marriages with private equity," *The Financial Times,* March 24, 2019.

Carroll, L., and Haughton, H. (1998). *Alice's Adventures in Wonderland and Through the Looking Glass: The Centenary Edition.* London: Penguin Books.

Gehring, F. (2015). "How I did it. . . Tommy Hilfiger's Chairman on going private to spark a turnaround," *Harvard Business Review,* July–August 2015, pp. 33–36.

Harvard Business Review Editorial Team (2016). "How private equity firms hire CEOs," *Harvard Business Review,* June 2016.

Lorelli, M. K. (2014). "Private equity versus traditional CEO," *NACD Directorship Boardroom Intelligence,* July–August 2014, pp. 65–66.

Partnoy, F. (2018). "An SAT for CEOs," *The Atlantic,* June 2018. Accessed June 30, 2020. https://www.theatlantic.com/magazine/archive/2018/06/vista-ceo-testing/559148/

Vardi, N. (2018). "Richer than Oprah: how the nation's wealthiest African-American conquered tech and Wall Street," *Forbes,* March 2018. Accessed June 30, 2020. https://www.forbes.com/sites/nathanvardi/2018/03/06/richer-than-oprah-how-the-nations-wealthiest-african-american-conquered-tech-and-wall-street/#1fef871c3584

Dweck, C. S. (2007). *Mindset: The New Psychology of Success.* New York: Ballantine Books.

Spencer S. (2017). *How to Think About Assessing Leaders.* Accessed June 30, 2020. https://www.spencerstuart.com/-/media/pdf-files/research-and-insight-pdfs/pov2017-assessingleaders.pdf

Kaplan, S. N., Klebanov, M. M. and Sorensen, M. (2012). "Which CEO characteristics and abilities matter?" *The Journal of Finance,* 67(3), pp. 973–1007.

Ferriss, T., host. "Graham Duncan: talent is the best asset class," *The Tim Ferris Show,* Podcast, March 1, 2019. Accessed June 30, 2020. https://tim.blog/2019/03/01/the-tim-ferriss-show-transcripts-graham-duncan-362/

Chapter 7

Sahlman, W. (1997). "How to write a great business plan," *Harvard Business Review.* July–August 1997, pp. 98–108.

Finkel, R. A. and Greising, D. (2010). *The Masters of Private Equity and Venture Capital: Management Lessons from the Pioneers of Private Investing.* New York: McGraw-Hill.

Kawasaki, G. (2001). "The top ten lies of entrepreneurs," *Harvard Business Review.* January 2001, pp. 22–23.

Rose, K., host. "Building Wealthfront and Benchmark Capital—Andy Rachleff," *The Kevin Rose Show*, Podcast, October 13, 2020. Accessed February 14, 2021. https://podcast.kevinrose.com/building-wealthfront-and-benchmark-capital-andy-rachleff/

Kahneman, D. (2015). *Thinking, Fast and Slow.* New York: Farrar, Straus and Giroux.

Shearn, M. (2012). *The Investment Checklist: The Art of in-Depth Research.* Hoboken, NJ: Wiley.

Cahill, M. (2003). *Investor's Guide to Analyzing Companies and Valuing Shares: How to Make the Right Investment Decision.* Harlow: Prentice Hall/Financial Times.

Valentine, J. J. (2011). *Best Practices for Equity Research Analysts: Essentials for Buy-Side and Sell-Side Analysts.* New York: McGraw-Hill Education.

Osterwalder, A. and Pigneur, Y. (2010). *Business Model Generation: A Handbook for Visionaries, Game Changers, and Challengers.* Hoboken, NJ: Wiley.

Narayanan, V. K. and Fahey, L. (2001). "Macroenvironmental Analysis: Understanding the Environment Outside the Industry" in Fahey, L. and Randall, R. M. (eds). *The Portable MBA in Strategy.* New York: Wiley.

Fleisher, C. S. and Bensoussan, B. E. (2008). *Business and Competitive Analysis: Effective Application of New and Classic Methods.* Upper Saddle River, NJ: FT Press.

Porter, M. E. (1985). *Competitive Advantage: Creating and Sustaining Superior Performance.* New York: Free Press.

Grant, R. M. (2002). *Contemporary Strategy Analysis: Concepts, Techniques, Applications*. Cambridge, MA: Blackwell Publishers Inc.

de Kuijper, M. (2009). *Profit Power Economics: A New Competitive Strategy for Creating Sustainable Wealth*. New York: Oxford University Press.

Christensen, C. M. and Raynor, M. E. (2010). *The Innovator's Solution: Creating and Sustaining Successful Growth*. Boston, MA: Harvard Business School Press.

Seneca. (2004). *On the Shortness of Life*. London: Penguin Books.

Higgins, R. C. (2009). *Analysis for Financial Management*. Boston, MA: McGraw-Hill/ Irwin.

Walsh, C. (2008). *Key Management Ratios: The 100+ Ratios Every Manager Needs to Know*. Harlow; New York: Prentice Hall/Financial Times.

Gompers, P., Kaplan, S. N. and Mukharlyamov, V. (2016). "What do private equity firms say they do?" *Journal of Financial Economics,* 121(3), pp. 449–476.

Marks, D. H. (2011). *The Most Important Thing: Uncommon Sense for Thoughtful Investors*. New York: Columbia Business School Publishing.

Chapter 8

McKinsey & Company Inc. (2020). *Valuation: Measuring and Managing the Value of Companies*. Hoboken, NJ: Wiley.

Damodaran, A. (2012). *Investment Valuation: Tools and Techniques for Determining the Value of Any Asset*. Hoboken, NJ: Wiley.

Rosenbaum, J. and Pearl, J. (2009). *Investment Banking: Valuation, Leveraged Buyouts, and Mergers & Acquisitions*. Hoboken, NJ: Wiley.

Arzac, E. R. (2007). *Valuation: Mergers, Buyouts and Restructuring*. Hoboken, NJ: Wiley.

Bruner, R. F. (2004). *Applied Mergers and Acquisitions*. Hoboken, NJ: John Wiley & Sons.

Roberts, M. J. (1992). "Valuation Techniques" in Sahlman, W. A. and Stevenson, H. H. (eds). *The Entrepreneurial Venture*. Boston, MA: Harvard Business School Publications.

Fabozzi, F. J., Focardi, S. M. and Jonas, C. (2018). "*Equity valuation: science, art, or craft?*" *SSRN Electronic Journal*. Accessed August 14, 2021. https://doi.org/10.2139/ssrn.3254580.

Martin, R. L. (2016). "M&A: The one thing you need to get right," *Harvard Business Review*. June 2016, pp. 42–48.

Indap, S. (2017). "What happens in Vegas. . . the messy bankruptcy of Caesars Entertainment," *The Financial Times*, September 26, 2017. Accessed August 14, 2021. https://www.ft.com/content/a0ed27c6-a2d4-11e7-b797-b61809486fe2

Levine, M. "Largest leveraged buyout ever is finally bankrupt," *Bloomberg, April* 24, 2014. Accessed August 14, 2021. https://www.bloomberg.com/opinion/articles/2014-04-29/largest-leveraged-buyout-ever-is-finally-bankrupt

Gompers, P., Kaplan, S. N. and Mukharlyamov, V. (2016). "What do private equity firms say they do?" *Journal of Financial Economics,* 121(3), pp. 449–476.

Marks, D. H. (2011). *The Most Important Thing: Uncommon Sense for Thoughtful Investors*. New York: Columbia Business School Publishing.

Chapter 9

Arzac, E. R. (2007). *Valuation: Mergers, Buyouts and Restructuring*. Hoboken, NJ: Wiley.

Ippolito, R. (2020). *Private Capital Investing: The Handbook of Private Debt and Private Equity*. Chichester: Wiley.

Rosenbaum, J. and Pearl, J. (2009). *Investment Banking: Valuation, Leveraged Buyouts, and Mergers & Acquisitions*. Hoboken, NJ: Wiley.

Darley, M. (2009). "Debt" in Soundy, M., Spangler, T. and Hampton, A. (eds). *A Practitioner's Guide to Private Equity*. London: Sweet & Maxwell Ltd.

Weil, G. and Manges LLP. (2015). *A Comparison of Management Incentive Equity Arrangements in Private Equity Transactions Across the United States, Europe and Asia.* Accessed August 20, 2021. https://peblog. wpengine.com/wp-content/uploads/2016/02/95615261_1.pdf

Boston Consulting Group. (2015). *Private Equity Minority Investments: Can Less Be More?* Accessed August 20, 2021. https://www.bcg. com/publications/2015/private-equity-minority-investments-can-less-be-more

Chapter 10

Rosenbloom, A. H. (2002). *Due Diligence for Global Deal Making: The Definitive Guide to Cross-Border Mergers and Acquisitions, Joint Ventures, Financings, and Strategic Alliances.* Princeton, NJ: Bloomberg Press.

Gole, W. J. and Hilger, P. J. (2009). *Due Diligence: An M&A Value Creation Approach.* Hoboken, NJ: Wiley.

Howson, P. (2008). *Checklists for Due Diligence.* Aldershot: Gower.

Grove, A. S. (2002). *Only the Paranoid Survive: How to Exploit the Crisis Points That Challenge Every Company and Career.* London: Profile Books.

Michaels, D. and Gryta, T. (2020). "GE to pay $200 million to settle SEC accounting probe," *The Wall Street Journal, December 9, 2020.* Accessed October 13, 2021. https://www.wsj.com/articles/ge-to-pay-200-million-to-settle-sec-accounting-probe-11607553764

Kelly, J. (2020). "Wells Fargo forced to pay $3 billion for the bank's fake account scandal," *Forbes,* February 24, 2020. Accessed October 13, 2021. https://www.forbes.com/sites/jackkelly/2020/02/24/wells-fargo-forced-to-pay-3-billion-for-the-banks-fake-account-scandal/?sh=5f773e1842d2

Mulford, C. W. and Comiskey, E. E. (2005). *Creative Cash Flow Reporting: Uncovering Sustainable Financial Performance.* Hoboken, NJ: Wiley.

Schilit, H. M., Perler, J. and Engelhart, Y. (2018). *Financial Shenanigans: How to Detect Accounting Gimmicks and Fraud in Financial Reports.* New York: McGraw-Hill

Fisher, K. and Hoffmans, L. W. (2010). *How to Smell a Rat: The Five Signs of Financial Fraud.* Hoboken, NJ: John Wiley & Sons.

Chapter 11

Baker McKenzie. (2015). *Global LBO Guide.* Accessed October 13, 2021. https://www.bakermckenzie.com/-/media/files/insight/publications/global-lbo-guide/bk_global_lboguide_rebranded.pdf?la=en

Zeisberger, C., Prahl, M. and White, B. (2017). *Mastering Private Equity: Transformation via Venture Capital, Minority Investments & Buyouts.* Chichester: Wiley.

Ippolito, R. (2020). *Private Capital Investing: The Handbook of Private Debt and Private Equity.* Chichester: Wiley.

Buerkle, T. (1998). "BMW wrests Rolls-Royce name away from VW," *International Herald Tribune,* July 29, 1998. Accessed October 13, 2021. https://www.nytimes.com/1998/07/29/news/bmw-wrests-rollsroyce-name-away-from-vw.html

Nijs, L. (2014). *Mezzanine Financing: Tools, Applications and Total Performance.* Chichester: Wiley.

Bagaria, R. (2016). *High Yield Debt: An Insider's Guide to the Marketplace.* Chichester: Wiley.

Pignataro, P. (2014). *Leveraged Buyouts: A Practical Guide to Investment Banking and Private Equity.* Hoboken, NJ: John Wiley & Sons.

Nesbitt, S. L. (2019). *Private Debt: Opportunities in Corporate Direct Lending.* Hoboken, NJ: John Wiley & Sons.

Chapter 12

Goldman, Sachs & Co. (2017). *Talks at GS: Henry Kravis, 40 Years of Innovation in Finance.* Accessed October 19, 2021. https://www.goldmansachs.com/insights/talks-at-gs/henry-kravis.html

MacArthur, H., Elton, G., Haas, D. and Varma, S. (2017). "Rewriting the private equity playbook to combine cost and growth," *Forbes,* April 8, 2017. Accessed October 19, 2021. https://www.forbes.com/sites/baininsights/2017/04/08/rewriting-the-private-equity-playbook-to-combine-cost-and-growth/?sh=2f1d33224445

Boston Consulting Group. (2017). *Discovering How and Where to Add Digital to Your Private Equity Playbook.* Accessed October 17, 2021. https://www.bcg.com/en-gb/industries/principal-investors-private-equity/discovering-how-and-where-to-add-digital-to-your-private-equity-playbook

McKinsey & Company. (2019). *Pricing: The Next Frontier of Value Creation in Private Equity.* Accessed October 18, 2021. https://www.mckinsey.com/business-functions/marketing-and-sales/our-insights/pricing-the-next-frontier-of-value-creation-in-private-equity

Friede, G., Busch, T. and Bassen, A. (2015). "ESG and financial performance: aggregated evidence from more than 2,000 empirical studies," *Journal of Sustainable Finance & Investment,* 5(4), pp. 210–233.

McKinsey & Company. (2020). *The ESG Premium: New Perspectives on Value and Performance.* Accessed October 17, 2021. https://www.mckinsey.com/business-functions/sustainability/our-insights/the-esg-premium-new-perspectives-on-value-and-performance

WWF and Doughty Hanson & Co. (2011). *Private Equity and Responsible Investment: An Opportunity for Value Creation.* Accessed April 30, 2020. http://assets.wwf.org.uk/downloads/private_equity_aw_lores_2.pdf

Kaplan, R. S. and Norton, D. P. (1992). "The balanced scorecard – measures that drive performance," *Harvard Business Review.* January–February 1992, pp. 71–79.

Slatter, S. and Lovett, D. (1999). *Corporate Turnaround.* London: Penguin.

Schwarzman, S. A. (2019). *What It Takes: Lessons in the Pursuit of Excellence.* London: Simon & Schuster UK Ltd.

Baker, G. P. and Smith, G. D. (1998). *The New Financial Capitalists: Kohlberg Kravis Roberts and the Creation of Corporate Value.* Cambridge and New York: Cambridge University Press.

Diviney, R. (2021). *The Attributes: 25 Hidden Drivers of Optimal Performance.* New York: Random House.

Sands, J. (2020). *Corporate Turnaround Artistry: Fix Any Business in 100 Days.* Hoboken, NJ: Wiley.

Chapter 13

Finkel, R. A. and Greising, D. (2010). *The Masters of Private Equity and Venture Capital: Management Lessons from the Pioneers of Private Investing.* New York: McGraw-Hill.

McKinsey & Company. (2019). *Private Equity Exit Excellence: Getting the Story Right.* Accessed October 18, 2021. https://www.mckinsey.com/industries/private-equity-and-principal-investors/our-insights/private-equity-exit-excellence-getting-the-story-right

Achleitner, A. K., Braun, R. and Engel, N. (2011). "Value creation and pricing in buyouts: Empirical evidence from Europe and North America," *Review of Financial Economics,* 20(4), pp. 146–161.

Bain & Company. (2021). *Global Private Equity Report 2021.* Accessed November 1, 2021. https://www.bain.com/globalassets/noindex/2021/bain_report_2021-global-private-equity-report.pdf

Zeisberger, C., Prahl, M., and White, B. (2017). *Mastering Private Equity: Transformation via Venture Capital, Minority Investments & Buyouts.* Chichester: Wiley.

Bain & Company. (2020). *Global Private Equity Report 2020.* Accessed November 1, 2021. https://psik.org.pl/images/publikacje-i-raporty---publikacje/bain_report_private_equity_report_2020.pdf

Pérez Navarro, P. (2018). "Private equity strategies: IPOs, trade sales and secondary buyouts," *Colegio Universitario de Estudios Financieros.*

June 2018. Accessed November 1, 2021. https://biblioteca.cunef.
edu/files/documentos/TFG_GADE_2018-24.pdf

Chinchwadkar, R. and Seth, R. (2012). "Private equity exits: effect of
syndicate size, foreign certification and buyout entry on type of exit,"
SSRN Electronic Journal. August 2012. Accessed November 1, 2021.
https://www.researchgate.net/publication/256030307_Private
_Equity_Exits_Effect_of_Syndicate_Size_Foreign_Certification
_and_Buyout_Entry_on_Type_of_Exit

Reuters Staff. (2018). "CVC seeks to buy back Sweden's Ahlsell, valuing firm at $2.7 billion," *Reuters*, December 11, 2018. Accessed
October 10, 2021. https://www.reuters.com/article/us-ahlsell-m-
a-cvc-capital-partners-idUSKBN1OA0I9

Wiggins, K. (2020). "How selling to yourself became private equity's go-to deal," *The Financial Times*, December 28, 2020. Accessed
October 10, 2021. https://www.ft.com/content/ee914ea4-4ad9-
4eec-97c3-95af841122bf

Mendonça, E. (2020). "EQT funds and TA Associates partner to
acquire software developer IFS for €3bn," *Private Equity News*, July
14, 2020. Accessed October 10, 2021. https://www.penews.com/
articles/eqt-funds-and-ta-associates-partner-to-acquire-software-
developer-ifs-for-e3bn-20200714

Campbell, K. (2020). "Why Blackstone investors backed its $14.6bn
life science recap," *PERE*, October 22, 2020. Accessed October
10, 2021. https://www.perenews.com/why-blackstone-investors-
backed-its-14-6bn-life-science-recap/

Wiggins, K., Storbeck, O. and Nilsson, P. (2020). "BC Partners
seeks to sell Springer Nature stake to itself," *The Financial Times*,
December 4, 2020. Accessed October 10, 2021. https://www
.ft.com/content/537ee5cc-2a74-4397-bdfb-4d846e6b8200

James, R. (2021). "The largest 20 continuation funds mapped," *Secondaries Investor*, June 9, 2021. Accessed October 10, 2021. https://
www.secondariesinvestor.com/the-20-largest-continuation-
funds-mapped/

Index